FINAL RESTING PLACE

The Lives & Deaths of Famous St. Louisans

by Kevin Amsler

PRINTED IN THE UNITED STATES OF AMERICA.

SECOND EDITION.
ISBN 1-891442-35-X
LIBRARY OF CONGRESS NUMBER 2006920813

PLEASE CHECK OUT OUR WEBSITE FOR OTHER BOOKS ON ST. LOUIS HISTORY
WWW.STL-BOOKS.COM

VIRGINIA PUBLISHING CO.
P.O. BOX 4538
ST. LOUIS, MO 63108
(314) 367-6612

TABLE OF CONTENTS

AUTHOR'S NOTE

PART I: BELLEFONTAINE CEMETERY 1

PART II: BLOODY ISLAND 81

PART III: CALVARY CEMETERY 91

PART IV: A DISASTROUS YEAR: 1849 129

PART V: OTHER PROMINENT ST. LOUIS CEMETERIES 137

PART VI: OTHER NOTABLES BURIED IN ST. LOUIS 161

PART VII: NOTABLE ST. LOUISANS BURIED ELSEWHERE 177

APPENDIX: 6 DEGREES OF HISTORICAL SEPARATION

BIBLIOGRAPHY

INDEX

DEDICATED TO

JANE CATHERINE AMSLER

SHE TOLD ME NEAR THE END,
"DON'T CRY WHEN I'M GONE."

THAT WAS AN IMPOSSIBLE REQUEST.

Thomas Jefferson once called death "that great adventure, untried by the living, unreported by the dead." We have always been fascinated by famous people, whether they are political figures of 200 years ago, like Jefferson, or popular entertainers of modern times. We grew up reading of their accomplishments in school or watched them on television.

History gives us a link to the people of the past. I first felt this link in the 1980's by visiting Graceland Cemetery in Chicago. Much like Bellefontaine and Calvary, Graceland is an impressive historical cemetery on Chicago's Near North Side. Those buried there are exemplars of influential personalities: retailer Marshall Field, architectural giant Louis Sullivan, piano and organ manufacturer William Kimball, famed detective Allan Pinkerton, and meatpacker Philip Armour, to name just a very few. I spent hours roaming the grounds; and, after arriving home, began to research notable St. Louisans and where they were laid to rest. Although I didn't realize it at the time, the Graceland visit was the genesis for this book.

Final Resting Place is about the people who walked the streets of St. Louis before us and among us. Most of these people came from different times and different backgrounds, but all called St. Louis home, perhaps for the same reasons we live here. They are connected to us still; many provided a foundation for us, a building block on which to launch our own lives and experiences. Employees of Anheuser-Busch and Monsanto can thank their founders profiled in this book. When departing or arriving at Lambert Field, you can applaud the efforts of St. Louis aviation pioneer Albert Bond Lambert and his passion for turning a cornfield into an airfield. Visitors to Union Station can appreciate architect Theodore Link and his Romanesque masterpiece. And anyone who sat on their porch in the 1960's during a hot July evening listening to Harry Caray and Jack Buck call Cardinals baseball games enjoyed a special slice of St. Louis history.

I hope that the book is not only read, but experienced. Most people visit cemeteries only following the death of a loved one or friend. They don't appreciate these burial grounds as earthly museums that are free to visit every day of the year. In researching this book, I made several visits to Bellefontaine, Calvary, and the other burial grounds. Visiting these places can be an enjoyable and humbling experience. They evoke memories of achievements, of real people who were giants in their day. For some, the name recognition is there; many have streets, schools or even towns named after them. Some have statues erected in their honor around the city. Others, however, are not household names but are renowned in their particular field of endeavor. More than 20 people in the book have stars on the St. Louis Walk of Fame.

Taking a leisurely walk through these hallowed grounds is to find some of the most outstanding and unique monumental architecture of the time. Finding a specific grave is a thrill of discovery, whether it's a simple stone pressed flat to the ground or a grand mausoleum honoring the entombed. Reading the names and dates give you a sense of time and place. Were they a witness to the Civil War? Could they have visited the St. Louis World's Fair? You can imagine what it may have been like to see them or talk to them; to listen to William Clark describe the western expedition with Meriwether Lewis, to see Dred Scott's trial at the Old Courthouse as he sued for his freedom from bondage, or to ask George Sisler what it was like to play against Babe Ruth and Ty Cobb. Most importantly, it affords an opportunity to get close to a person in death as would have been impossible in life. No modern-day person had the opportunity to meet St. Louis founder Auguste Chouteau, but in a way you can meet him now in Calvary Cemetery and envision him and his men constructing the first buildings in what is today skyscraper-filled downtown St. Louis.

A visitor can find plenty of prominent "first" persons of St. Louis: William Carr Lane was the first mayor of St. Louis, while Alexander McNair became the first governor of Missouri by defeating his friend William Clark. Susan Blow established the first kindergarten in America at the Des Peres School in Carondelet. John Mullanphy was the first millionaire and true philanthropist in St. Louis, and his son Bryan was the first bachelor mayor of the city. Joseph Charless published the first newspaper west of the Mississippi River when he was invited to St. Louis by Meriwether Lewis. And in 1872, Frederick Dent, the one-time owner of White Haven (Grant's Farm) was the first and only St. Louisan to die in the White House -- while spending time at the mansion during the presidency of his son-in-law, Ulysses S. Grant.

This book is not meant to list the thousands and thousands of people buried around St. Louis. It merely touches on a few, with the hope that the reader will explore these peaceful havens and find even more intriguing people and impressive memorial architecture. Determining which individuals to include was an interesting and difficult task. The challenge was to decide who should be included. The original list was changed and updated many times. The individuals profiled must have been either born in St. Louis or buried here, preferably both. Some individuals with connections to St. Louis, such as Charles A. Lindbergh,

Ulysses S. Grant, or Scott Joplin, do not fit the criteria; and for that reason, although they are mentioned, they are not profiled in the book.

I have received a great deal of help from many people in preparing this book. Cemetery personnel at Bellefontaine, Calvary, Resurrection, St. Lucas, Sunset Memorial Park, and Oak Grove were helpful in locating graves. Members of the library staff at the University of Missouri-St. Louis, Webster University, the Missouri Historical Society, and the St. Louis County Libraries aided in the research for reference materials. In addition, I want to thank Mary Pool, assistant executive director of New Mt. Sinai Cemetery, and Annette Costello, office manager of St. Peter's Cemetery, for providing information about their burial grounds. And special thanks to Shirley Wotawa, who helped me with her extensive research and writing about St. Peter's Cemetery.

I reorganized portions of this edition in an attempt to include more individuals. For example, I started the Bellefontaine and Calvary chapters by listing people not mentioned in the earlier edition in order to make the reader aware of their existence in those cemeteries. Also, a new chapter was added, profiling other prominent burial places, such as Jefferson Barracks National Cemetery, New Mt. Sinai Cemetery, St. Peter's Cemetery, and Resurrection Cemetery. And some individuals who were not deceased in 1996 when the first edition was published are included for the first time, such as broadcasters Harry Caray and Jack Buck, Blues player Doug Wickenheiser, and St. Louis Hawks owner Ben Kerner. Perhaps the most enjoyable addition to the book for me was the "Six Degrees" chart, which can be found in the Appendix. It is my way of showing the connections among several Bellefontaine and Calvary residents.

Working on the original book was a therapeutic exercise. My mother had been ill with cancer for some time. Several operations helped her to beat the odds, but during the summer of 1996 the cancer once again enforced its will in her body. She passed away in October, two days after I first met the publisher to discuss this book. As before, the book is dedicated to her memory.

I want to thank my publisher, Jeff Fister, for his continued support. And thank you to the family members of those profiled in the book who called with kind words. Thanks also go to the people who invited me to do television, radio, and newspaper interviews and book signings. I was especially pleased with the segments on *Show Me St. Louis* on Channel 5 and two segments done by Patrick Clark for KPLR Channel 11. Their excellent editing techniques made me look like I actually knew what I was talking about. And I fondly remember a June 1997 radio interview with Mary Phelan and Ed Goodman on KEZK. Mary was so alive, and she had a genuine interest in the book and its subject matter. Eighteen months later, I was pained to hear that Mary died in an automobile accident just a few weeks after getting married.

In the first edition, I mentioned my one-year-old nephew, Jerry. Well, now he's ten and has a little sister, Victoria. They keep me young, active, and modest. And special thanks go to my lovely wife, Vickie. We were friends when the first edition came out and now she's my best friend. She has supported me in so many ways, not the least of which was proof-reading this manuscript and walking miles of cemetery grounds to snap new photographs for this book.

To her I say: Tí Amo, Bella!

~ Kevin Amsler

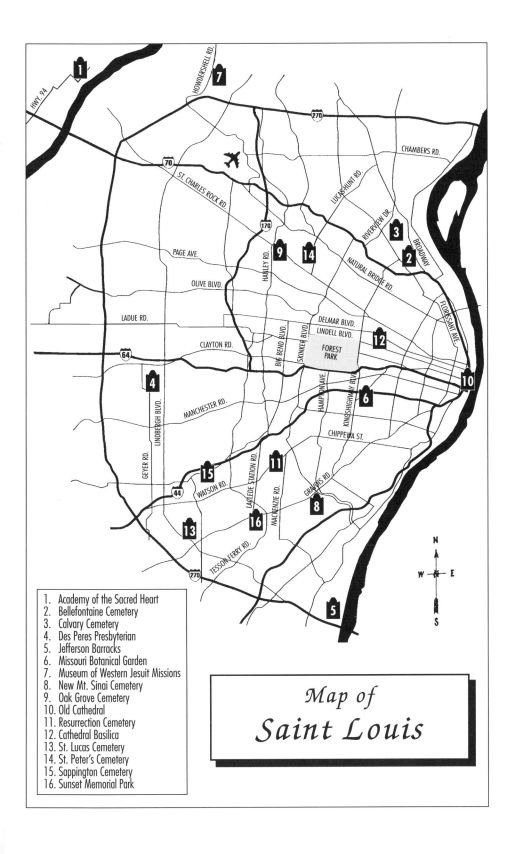

Map of
Saint Louis

1. Academy of the Sacred Heart
2. Bellefontaine Cemetery
3. Calvary Cemetery
4. Des Peres Presbyterian
5. Jefferson Barracks
6. Missouri Botanical Garden
7. Museum of Western Jesuit Missions
8. New Mt. Sinai Cemetery
9. Oak Grove Cemetery
10. Old Cathedral
11. Resurrection Cemetery
12. Cathedral Basilica
13. St. Lucas Cemetery
14. St. Peter's Cemetery
15. Sappington Cemetery
16. Sunset Memorial Park

I

Bellefontaine Cemetery

Bellefontaine Cemetery

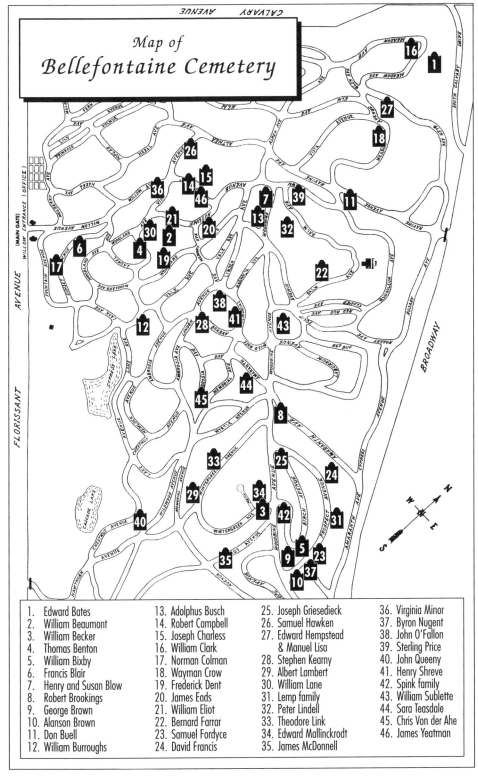

Map of Bellefontaine Cemetery

1. Edward Bates
2. William Beaumont
3. William Becker
4. Thomas Benton
5. William Bixby
6. Francis Blair
7. Henry and Susan Blow
8. Robert Brookings
9. George Brown
10. Alanson Brown
11. Don Buell
12. William Burroughs
13. Adolphus Busch
14. Robert Campbell
15. Joseph Charless
16. William Clark
17. Norman Colman
18. Wayman Crow
19. Frederick Dent
20. James Eads
21. William Eliot
22. Bernard Farrar
23. Samuel Fordyce
24. David Francis
25. Joseph Griesedieck
26. Samuel Hawken
27. Edward Hempstead & Manuel Lisa
28. Stephen Kearny
29. Albert Lambert
30. William Lane
31. Lemp family
32. Peter Lindell
33. Theodore Link
34. Edward Mallinckrodt
35. James McDonnell
36. Virginia Minor
37. Byron Nugent
38. John O'Fallon
39. Sterling Price
40. John Queeny
41. Henry Shreve
42. Spink family
43. William Sublette
44. Sara Teasdale
45. Chris Von der Ahe
46. James Yeatman

On March 7, 1849, a group organized by banker William McPherson and lawyer John Darby, Mayor of St. Louis, incorporated a new burial ground under the name "Rural Cemetery Association." The state of Missouri issued a charter for the 138 acres of land on Bellefontaine Road. A short time later, the name "Rural" was changed to "Bellefontaine" because the cemetery was to be located on the road leading to old Fort Bellefontaine. A portion of the grounds once was owned by John O'Fallon and the Hempstead family. Landscape architect Almerin Hotchkiss, the superintendent of Greenwood Cemetery in Brooklyn, was hired to develop the grounds. He was superintendent of Bellefontaine for 46 years and is buried on the grounds.

On July 23, 1849, the *Missouri Republican* commented:

> We look forward with confidence to the day, not
> distant, when the people of St. Louis will point
> to this cemetery with the same satisfaction that
> Boston does to Mount Auburn.

In January of the same year, the worst cholera epidemic in St. Louis history hit the city. At the height of the epidemic there were more than 30 funerals each day. Bellefontaine received interments from Christ Church Cemetery and other cemeteries when an 1849 public health law went into effect requiring burial grounds to be located outside the city limits.

Its original 138 acres have been expanded to more than 330 acres. Today, Bellefontaine is one of St. Louis' most renowned cemeteries. It has become the final resting place of governors, mayors, war heroes, business leaders, and some of the most prominent families in St. Louis history. Fourteen miles of road wind through the cemetery's beautiful environs; more than 100 varieties of trees mark the landscape. The rolling hills contain more than 82,000 gravesites.

Bellefontaine Cemetery is located in North St. Louis near the Broadway exit of I-70. The main entrance is located at 4947 West Florissant Avenue. The cemetery is open 8:00 a.m. to 5:00 p.m. daily, including Sundays and holidays. Office hours are 8:00 a.m. to 4:30 p.m., Monday through Friday, and on weekends and holidays by appointment only. Information is provided at the office, including a map of the grounds denoting many of the graves profiled in this book.

It is impossible to list all the notable people buried at Bellefontaine Cemetery, as it would number in the thousands. Biographies just on the former mayors of St. Louis and governors of Missouri resting at Bellefontaine could fill a book.

Besides the St. Louis mayors profiled in this chapter, there are no less than 17 others at Bellefontaine, including **Daniel Page** (1790-1869), a grocery store owner, banker, and the second mayor of St. Louis, for whom Page Boulevard is named. After serving one term in office, Mayor **John Wimer** (1810-1863) spent time in prison during the Civil War for being a southern sympathizer. He escaped and rejoined the Confederate forces, only to be killed leading a regiment in Hartsville, Missouri. And **Henry Overstolz** (1821–1887) was the first German-born mayor and first to serve under the Charter of 1876, which stipulated a four-year term and the separation of the city and county.

Among Missouri governors are: **John Miller** (1781–1846), the fourth governor of Missouri; **Trusten Polk** (1811–1876), who served only 53 days as governor, the shortest in Missouri history, after winning election to the U.S. Senate; **Hamilton Gamble** (1798–1864), a presiding judge in the Dred Scott case and governor during the Civil War; **Thomas Fletcher** (1827–1899), the first Republican governor; and **Frederick Gardner** (1869–1933), World War I governor who signed the Missouri suffrage bill, allowing women the right to vote. He died from a jaw infection after having a tooth removed.

Other prominent citizens include philanthropist **Robert Barnes** (1808-1892), benefactor of Barnes-Jewish Hospital; General **Daniel Bissell** (1769–1833), commander of Fort Bellefontaine; **Isaiah Sellers** (1802–1854), riverboat captain who first used the pseudonym "Mark Twain;" **John Gregg** (1867–1948), who devised the Gregg Shorthand System; **Herman Luyties** (1871–1921), owner of the first proprietary-drug store in St. Louis; **Albert Edwards** (1812–1892), brigadier general and founder of the firm, A.G. Edwards & Son; and **Dr. Joseph McDowell** (1805–1868) founder of the McDowell Medical College, a building that became the infamous Gratiot Street Prison during the Civil War. And restaurateur **Anthony Faust** (1836–1906) offered one of the best dining experiences in the country during the 1870's. His restaurant was known for its excellent service and superior cuisine, and it had the first electric lights ever used in St. Louis.

Some prominent women buried at Bellefontaine include **Irma Rombauer** (1877–1962), author of what is arguably the most famous cookbook in the world, *The Joy of Cooking*. The 54-year-old widow sold a mere 3,000 copies of her book when it debuted in 1931. But, as of 1997, the book and its later revised editions have sold more than 14 million copies. While a leader in the suffrage movement, **Edna Gellhorn** (1878–1970) gave speeches, led lobbying efforts and took part in demonstrations to empower women to push for what ultimately became the 19th Amendment. (She also was the mother of famous war correspondent and writer Martha

Gellhorn, third wife of Ernest Hemingway.) **Adaline Couzins** (1815–1892), married to the St. Louis chief of police during the Civil War, spent the war nursing wounded Union soldiers on the battlefield and on newly established hospital boats. After the war, she put her energies into the women's suffrage movement. Her daughter **Phoebe** (1839–1913) was the first female graduate of Washington University, in 1871, and the first woman appointed a U.S. Marshal. Once a supporter of women's suffrage, she later spoke out against it and alienated herself from everyone around her. She died destitute in an abandoned house. Perhaps the most notable example of cemetery architecture in St. Louis is the Wainwright Tomb. Designed by famed architect Louis Sullivan, this solid, cube-shaped monument with a center dome was commissioned by brewer **Ellis Wainwright** (1850–1924) in 1892. The tomb was listed on the National Register of Historic Places in 1970.

WILLIAM CLARK
(AUGUST 1, 1770-SEPTEMBER 1, 1838)

On September 23, 1806, Meriwether Lewis and William Clark cemented their names in history when they arrived in St. Louis from their two-year expedition across the Upper Louisiana Territory to the Pacific coast. Their detailed journals and maps were the first documented information about the untamed west.

William Clark was a native of Caroline County, Virginia. He grew up with nine brothers and sisters on a large estate on the eastern slopes of the Alleghenies. Five of his brothers fought in the Revolutionary War; one died of tuberculosis as a British prisoner. His older brother, George Rogers Clark, became a hero and was awarded a gold medal by General George Washington.

When Clark was 13, his family moved to Kentucky and settled in the wilderness south of Louisville. He signed on with the army in 1789 and was involved in military campaigns to thwart the continuing threat of the Indians. It was during this time that Clark met the man who would help him make his mark on history, Meriwether Lewis.

In 1803, when Thomas Jefferson chose Lewis, his private secretary, to lead an exploration of the far western territories, Lewis selected his old friend Clark to share leadership of the expedition. On May 14, 1804, Lewis and Clark and 45 men started on their journey into history. The 8,000-mile trip lasted two years, four months, and nine days. They explored the uncharted wilderness in a journey that took them up the Missouri River, across the Continental Divide and down the Columbia River to the sea. They kept detailed journals on the rivers, mountain ranges, animals, plants, and -- most importantly -- the western Indians.

Lewis and Clark officially presented their findings to Thomas Jefferson. They each received $1,228 and sixteen hundred acres of land and were appointed to positions: Lewis became the governor of the Louisiana Territory and Clark was named superintendent of Indian affairs and brigadier general of militia for the Louisiana Territory.

In October 1809, Meriwether Lewis was on his way to Washington, D.C., along the Natchez Trace in Tennessee when he was found shot to death. He was 35. Although many historians believe he committed suicide, the exact circumstances of his death are unknown. Clark was devastated when he received the news of his friend's death. He would never speak of it to anyone.

Clark made his home in St. Louis and became one of the most accomplished citizens in town. He and his wife, Julia, rented a house before later building one at Main and Vine. He accumulated vast real estate holdings in Missouri and Kentucky. Because of his position in Indian affairs, he developed close relationships with the Indians and often welcomed them to his home. Clark was also involved in the political and business environment of St. Louis. He was a founding member of the St. Louis Missouri Fur Company, along with Auguste and Pierre Chouteau and Manuel Lisa, and served as chairman for the St. Louis Schools board of trustees. Other members included Thomas Hart Benton, Alexander McNair, and the Chouteaus. And in June 1813, President James Madison appointed Clark governor of the Missouri Territory.

Despite such success, Clark experienced his share of tragedy. Julia, his wife of 12 years, died in June 1820 after an illness induced by childbirth. Two of their children also died: seven-year-old Mary in 1821 and John, a teenager, 10 years later. A year after his wife's death, Clark married Harriet Radford; the couple's infant son passed away in 1827. On the political side, he lost the Missouri gubernatorial election of 1820 to his close friend Alexander McNair.

William Clark was staying at the home of his eldest son, Meriwether Lewis Clark, when he died on Saturday evening, September 1, 1838. The September 3 issue of the *Missouri Republican* said of Clark:

Through a long, eventful and useful life, he has filled the various stations of a citizen and officer with such strict integrity and in so affable and mild a manner, that, at that day of his death, malice nor detraction had not a blot to fix upon the fair scroll which the history of his well-spent life leaves as a rich and inestimable legacy to his children, and the numerous friends who now mourn his death.

Clark was buried with full military honors. The ceremonies began at eleven o'clock at his son's home at Fifth and Olive. His funeral procession, which stretched more than a mile, was the largest in St. Louis history to that time. The hearse was pulled by four white horses, preceded by a company of soldiers. Clark's horse followed, with boots reversed in the stirrups to symbolize the explorer's death.

Thousands lined the streets leading to the farm of Clark's nephew, Colonel John O'Fallon. (The farm is now O'Fallon Park). As the procession approached the burial ground, minute guns were fired until Clark's remains arrived at the site. When Bellefontaine Cemetery was opened 11 years later, Clark's body and the remains of several family members were moved to a roadside family lot in the northern corner of the cemetery. When his youngest son, Jefferson, died in 1900, he willed $25,000 to construct a monument. The impressive granite obelisk and bust of William Clark centered in the lot were dedicated in October 1904 during the World's Fair.

William Clark faces the confluence of the Mississippi and Missouri Rivers where he and Meriwether Lewis set out to discover the west. The inscription beneath the bust reads in part: "Soldier, explorer, statesman and patriot, his life is written in the history of his country."

JOSEPH CHARLESS
(JULY 16, 1772-JULY 28, 1834)

Joseph Charless was an entrepreneur before the word had meaning. He was editor and publisher of his own newspaper, a bookseller, pharmacy owner, and hosteller. He was born Joseph Charles in Westmeath, Ireland on the 132-acre family farm. In 1794, he became a printer in Dublin before coming to America and establishing a bookstore and printing press in Lewistown, Pennsylvania. His dream was to publish a newspaper. His first issue, published just months after arriving in the States, appeared under the name *Mifflin Gazette*. It was also during this time that he changed the spelling of his last name by adding an "s." The change preserved the Irish pronunciation but differentiated him from others with the "Charles" name.

Charless left Lewistown for Philadelphia where he married a widow, Sarah Jordan McCloud. The couple would have five children -- three sons and two daughters. While in Philadelphia, Joseph worked on *The Aurora*, an influential newspaper run by Benjamin Franklin Bache.

In 1808, Meriwether Lewis, the territorial governor of Missouri, contacted Charless with an offer to come west and start a paper in news-starved St. Louis. Charless agreed and arrived in St. Louis to edit and publish the first issue of the *Missouri Gazette* on July 12 of that year. It was the first newspaper printed west of the Mississippi. This first publication was four pages long and 8-1/4 x 12-1/2 inches in size. Charless set high journalistic standards with the *Gazette* but made enemies in the process. He was physically assaulted on a few occasions and once was shot while working in his garden.

For a short time, Charless explored other business opportunities outside of publishing. In 1812, he and Dr. Barnard Farrar opened an apothecary shop (pharmacy) where they sold a variety of medicines and drugs. In less than a year, the two men discontinued the partnership and opened their own shops. Charless quit the pharmaceutical business entirely before the year was out. He invested in real estate and amassed a large amount of property. In 1819, he had a two-story brick house built on his property at Fifth and Main streets.

During his years in St. Louis, he became friends with the prominent Lucas family. When Thomas Hart Benton and Charles Lucas dueled on Bloody Island, Charless vented his bitter feelings toward Benton in his newspaper. He continued to attack Benton during the next year. In 1818, when Benton became the editor of the *St. Louis Enquirer*, an opposing newspaper, the two men traded words until Benton left St. Louis to serve in the U.S. Senate.

Charless sold the *Gazette* in 1820 and retired from publishing. He sent his regards to the people of St. Louis in his final issue:

Fellow Citizens and Patrons, my interests, although I leave this establishment, is still connected with yours. For 12 years I have lived among you. My family has been educated and brought up among you. My little property is in this state. Here are the tombs of my children, and here I expect to rest myself, when the cares and vexations of life are over. You must therefore believe me, when I say that nothing is, nothing can be so dear to me as your prosperity, and your welfare.

His first-born son, Edward, took over the newspaper in 1822. He renamed it the *Missouri Republican* and ran it successfully for 15 years.

Charless had a strong presence in St. Louis. He served as president of the Board of Aldermen in 1825 and 1826 and involved himself in several business pursuits, including a revival of the pharmaceutical business he had once enjoyed. After his son Joseph joined him, the company was renamed "Jos. Charless & Son." In one of his final ventures, Charless opened a boardinghouse on one of his properties to lodge traveling guests. His charge for one night's lodging was 25 cents, which he later reduced to 12-1/2 cents.

Joseph Charless died in his home on July 28, 1834; he was 62 years old. He was praised for his kind Irish manner and was labeled "the father of St. Louis journalism." He was buried at Bellefontaine Cemetery near Joseph, Jr., across Lawn Avenue from Robert Campbell and James Yeatman.

In November 1859, Joseph, Jr., was murdered on the streets of St. Louis by Joseph Thornton, against whom he had testified in court. At the time of his death, he was married to Charlotte Blow, daughter of Peter Blow. His Bellefontaine headstone reads, "Here Rest Beloved Till Christ Shall Bid Thee Rise."

Members of the Blow family also are buried in the Charless lot. They include Peter Blow, the original owner of Dred Scott, and his son Taylor, who gave Scott his freedom in 1857.

Manuel Lisa
(September 8, 1772-August 12, 1820)

Fur trader and explorer Manuel Lisa was born in New Orleans. Upon his arrival in St. Louis, he immediately became active in the fur-trading business. The Chouteaus dominated the market at the time, but Lisa was determined to break their monopoly. He led expeditions into Indian territory, where he served as an explorer and fighter. In 1807, he established a trading post at the Bighorn River in Montana, and one year later built a fort there -- the first located in the upper Missouri River region. He also built Fort Lisa at what is now Omaha, Nebraska. Lisa was among a group, which included the Chouteaus, that established the Bank of St. Louis in 1813.

His spirit and enthusiasm brought him to the attention of the Chouteaus, who along with William Clark and others formed the Missouri Fur Company in 1808. In September of that year, Lisa and his employee, George Drouillard, were on trial for the murder of Antoine Bissonette.

(Drouillard had been a member of the Lewis and Clark Expedition.) In May 1807, after signing a contract to work for Lisa, Bissonette deserted during a fur-trading expedition. Bissonette was captured by Drouillard but sustained a bullet wound and died while returning to St. Charles for medical treatment. Edward Hempstead, Lisa's attorney, argued the case to Judge John B.C. Lucas. The jury returned a verdict of "not guilty" because Bissonette had planned his desertion and broken his contract.

Lisa married three times. His first wife, Mitain, an Omaha Indian woman, bore him two children. His second wife, Polly, had three children, all of whom died before adulthood. In 1818, six months after Polly died, he married Mary Hempstead Keeney, widowed sister of Edward Hempstead. William Clark and Pierre Chouteau were among the wedding guests. The couple lived on Main Street between Market and Chestnut.

In the fall of 1820, Lisa returned to St. Louis from an expedition in ill health. Feeling weak and fatigued, he went to a sulphur spring near St. Louis in the hope that the waters would ease his pains. He stayed at the home of his sister-in-law, Susan Hempstead. Dr. Bernard Farrar attended to his patient day and night but could do nothing. Lisa made his last will and testament on Friday, August 11, and died the next day at 6:45 p.m. Lisa had dominated the fur trading industry for 20 years. His death left a notable absence.

After the funeral Mass at the Old Cathedral, Lisa was laid to rest in the churchyard at Walnut and Second Streets. His remains were later moved to the Hempstead Farm near the grave of his confidant, Edward Hempstead.

Lisa's obelisk monument was erected by his wife, Mary, in the Hempstead family lot in Bellefontaine. Weather has taken its toll on the stone and granite marker.

EDWARD HEMPSTEAD
(JUNE 3, 1780-AUGUST 10, 1817)

Edward Hempstead developed one of the most successful law practices in St. Louis and was the first delegate to Congress from the Missouri Territory. In August 1817, he was returning to St. Louis from St. Charles when he was thrown from his horse and injured his head. Although he was dazed, he thought the injury was minor and continued his journey to St.

Louis. On the morning of August 8, Hempstead was back in court arguing a case for a client. During the proceedings he suffered a brain hemorrhage and collapsed to the floor. Upon hearing of the incident, Stephen Hempstead, a Presbyterian minister, went to his son.

"Went into St. Louis this afternoon and found my son Edward in a fit of apoplexy and not able to speak," he wrote in his diary later that day. "Every medical aid was used to restore his system again, but to no purpose. He continued until 12:30 o'clock, and expired in the bloom of life, at the age of thirty-seven years and three months."

Edward Hempstead was a native of New London, Connecticut. His father had fought in the Revolutionary War, beginning with the battle of Lexington. Edward studied law under prominent Connecticut lawyers and became licensed in 1801. He practiced law for two years in Newport, Rhode Island, before coming west. He arrived in St. Louis a few months after the United States officially took possession of the Louisiana Territory. He was accompanied on his journey by William Henry Harrison, governor of the Indiana Territory and future ninth President of the United States.

He spent a year living in St. Charles practicing law before moving to St. Louis in the fall of 1805. Over the next several years, he built a reputation as a fair and honest man and a lawyer of high moral standards. Because of the respect he inspired among St. Louisans, he was elected in November 1812 as the first delegate to Congress from the Missouri Territory. Hempstead was a benefactor for the city and its children by founding the Board of Education and helping the St. Louis public schools obtain property and revenue to survive their growing pains.

The city mourned when news spread that Hempstead had died at half-past midnight. The citizens were shocked that a man of such promise and youth was taken from them. He was survived by his wife, Eliza, and son, Edward, Jr. The funeral and burial were held the next day at his father's farm, now part of Bellefontaine Cemetery. Reverend Giddings recited a prayer at the grave and committed the young lawyer to the earth. The Hempstead family now rests off of Meadow Avenue in the oldest section of Bellefontaine Cemetery.

Edward Hempstead's obituary appeared in the August 16th issue of the *Missouri Gazette*:

> Died on Sunday night last, after a short illness, Edward Hempstead, Esq., counselor and attorney-at-law, and formerly a delegate from this Territory to Congress. In the dear relation of husband, son, and brother, the deceased is believed to have fully acted up to his duty. The sorrow of his widow and relations offered the most eloquent expression of his worth.

*On Monday the corpse of the deceased was attended to the place of in-
terment by a greater number of respectable citizens than we have ever
witnessed here on a similar occasion.*

Thomas Hart Benton, longtime friend of Hempstead, wrote, "The
lives of useful and eminent man should be written, not for the dead, but
for the living. They should display not a vain panegyric, but a detail of
circumstance which would lead the living to the same line of conduct and
the same honorable result."

THOMAS HART BENTON
(MARCH 14, 1782-APRIL 10, 1858)

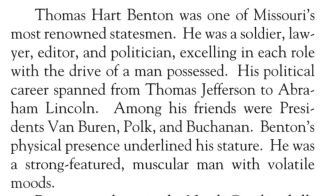

Thomas Hart Benton was one of Missouri's
most renowned statesmen. He was a soldier, lawyer, editor, and politician, excelling in each role
with the drive of a man possessed. His political
career spanned from Thomas Jefferson to Abraham Lincoln. Among his friends were Presidents Van Buren, Polk, and Buchanan. Benton's
physical presence underlined his stature. He was
a strong-featured, muscular man with volatile
moods.

Benton was born in the North Carolina hills
near Hillsborough in March 1782. In 1798, he left home to attend the
University of North Carolina at Chapel Hill, but in less than a year he
was expelled from the university for petty theft. The family later moved to
Tennessee, where he was admitted to the bar. In the War of 1812, Benton
served as a colonel of volunteers under General Andrew Jackson.

It was during this period, in 1813, when Benton made antagonistic
remarks concerning Andrew Jackson's integrity and judgment. The criti-
cism rose from a duel in which his brother, Jesse, was seriously wounded by
a friend of Jackson. On September 4, while Benton and his brother were
in Nashville on business, the dispute exploded into violence. Jackson appeared at Benton's hotel and, upon seeing Benton in the hallway, drew his
pistol. Jesse fired at Jackson from across the room before Benton fired on
the general. Jackson hit the floor with a wound in the left arm. Benton was
only grazed by Jackson's shot. Others joined in a vicious fight with guns
and daggers. Benton sustained five knife wounds, and his brother likewise
was stabbed several times. Jackson, although bleeding profusely, was saved

by the quick response of physicians.

After the war, Benton moved to St. Louis, a village inhabited by only 2,000 people. He started a law practice and later became editor of the *Missouri Enquirer*, which competed directly with Joseph Charless' *Missouri Gazette*. One of Benton's first friends, Edward Hempstead, the most prominent lawyer in St. Louis, played an important role in shaping Benton's interest in politics. The governor of the Missouri Territory, William Clark, appointed Benton to his first public position as a member of the Board of Trustees for Schools.

August 1817 was to be a bitter month for Benton. First, his sister Mary died. She was the last of his sisters, three others having died previously. Then, Edward Hempstead, Benton's good friend and mentor, died of a head injury a week after he was thrown from his horse. And on August 12, the day after Hempstead's funeral, Benton fought Charles Lucas in their famous duel on Bloody Island.

In 1820, Benton was elected as one of the first senators from Missouri. The election took place at the famous Missouri Hotel. Among others, he beat out Judge John B.C. Lucas, the father of his dueling opponent, Charles Lucas. Three years later, Senator Benton and Senator Andrew Jackson made peace and became friends. During his 30 years in the Senate, Benton opposed the annexation of Texas and was against rechartering the Bank of the United States. The latter stand earned him the nickname "Old Bullion."

In 1824, Benton spent Christmas Eve in Charlottesville, Virginia, with Thomas Jefferson. He was moved by the conversations with the sage of Monticello. In a speech later delivered to the U.S. Senate, Benton said, "the individual must manage badly who can find himself in the presence of that great man and retire from it without bringing off some fact or some maxim of eminent utility to the human race."

Benton's final session in Congress was a difficult one. In 1848, his son-in-law, Lieutenant Colonel John Fremont, was found guilty of insubordination and faced court-martial. His chief accuser was General Stephen Watts Kearny. Benton was relentless in his verbal persecution of Kearny. In the end, President Polk upheld the verdict but allowed Fremont to return to duty. One month later, former president John Quincy Adams, Benton's good friend, collapsed in the House chamber while listening to a debate. Adams died at the Capitol two days later. Benton gave a eulogy in the Senate and was a pallbearer at the funeral.

Benton retired from the Senate in 1850. At the time, cholera was still a threat to the population, and in 1852 his son Randolph succumbed to the disease. Benton and his wife Elizabeth were overcome by the death of their only remaining son; their boy McDowell had died years earlier. In a speech relating to the reinterment of family members in new Bellefontaine Cemetery, Benton said, "What is my occupation? Ask the undertaker, that good Mr. Lynch, whose face, present on so many mournful occasions, has become pleasant to me. He knew what occupies my thoughts and cares; gathering the bones of the dead -- a mother, sister, two sons, a grandchild -- planting the cypress over assembled graves, and marking the spot where I and those who are dear to me are soon to be laid." A short two years later, in September 1854, Elizabeth died suddenly in Washington, D.C. Benton was in St. Louis at the time and was distressed at not being with her at the end, "That I should have been absent at that moment! I who had always been with her, and striving to keep every sorrow from her heart!"

In retirement, he stayed in Washington, D.C., and wrote his autobiography, entitled *Thirty Years' View*. He also wrote an extensive examination of the Dred Scott decision. He ran for governor of Missouri in 1856 but lost the election. One year later, in May 1857, he was injured in a railroad accident and was confined to home for three weeks. That September, he took ill while working on the Scott manuscript. His physician diagnosed cancer of the bowel, a disease that caused painful seizures and spasms. Within two months, however, he improved enough to resume working.

The illness returned in March 1858, and by April his condition declined quickly. Frank Blair, a longtime personal and political friend, visited, but Benton was nearly incapable of any movement in his limbs and could speak only at a whisper. The great senator was fading fast. He told his son-in-law, John Fremont, of his remorse over the dueling incident with Charles Lucas in 1817, and asked Senator Sam Houston that no notice of his death be recognized in Congress. When President James Buchanan visited him, Benton spoke only three words to the president, "Preserve the Union!" Later that evening Benton told his daughters, "I am comfortable and content." They were his last words. Thomas Hart Benton died at 7:30 a.m. the next morning. Two days later, McDowell Jones, one of Benton's favorite grandsons, also died in the house.

The Monday, April 12, funeral was conducted in his Washington, D.C., home. Benton rested in a black coffin in the parlor. A smaller casket with his grandson McDowell rested beside him. President Buchanan, his cabinet, foreign ministers, and members of Congress attended the ceremony. Afterward, the coffins were taken to the train station in a driving rain.

The train arrived on the east side of the Mississippi River on April 14. The coffins were taken by ferry across to St. Louis. (Eads Bridge, the first bridge to span the river, wouldn't be built for another 16 years.) The next morning, Benton's body was taken to the Mercantile Library Hall at Locust and Fifth Streets, where he lay in state. Thousands paid their respects to the senator.

Homes and buildings around the city were draped in black, and flags were at half-mast the day of the funeral. On Friday afternoon, Benton's body was carried from the Mercantile Library to the Second Presbyterian Church at Walnut and Fifth. A large crowd gathered outside the church. When the service ended at 2:30 p.m., the procession marched toward Bellefontaine. Family, friends, military personnel, members of the bar, and city dignitaries made up a two-mile cortege. An estimated 40,000 people clogged the sidewalks, windows, and rooftops to watch the procession.

A short prayer service was held at the gravesite on Laurel Avenue. Thomas Hart Benton was then placed into the earth next to his wife Elizabeth; he was 76 years old. A red granite obelisk recognizes his service to the state of Missouri. A public school, a park, and three streets in St. Louis are named in his honor.

BERNARD FARRAR
(JULY 4, 1785-JULY 1, 1849)

Dr. Farrar was born in Goochland County, Virginia, and later settled with his family near Lexington, Kentucky. He began studying medicine at the age of 15, first with a doctor in Cincinnati, then with a physician in Lexington, before graduating from medical school at Transylvania University. His first wife, Sarah Christy, bore him a daughter and two sons who both died in infancy. After Sarah died in 1817, Farrar married Ann Thruston, niece of Governor William Clark. He arrived in St. Louis in 1807 and became the first American physician to practice west of the Mississippi. His medical practice was listed in the May 24, 1809 issue of the *Missouri Gazette*:

> *Dr. Farrar will practice medicine and surgery in St. Louis and its vicinity. He keeps his shop in Mr. Robidoux's house, Second Street.*

Farrar's first surgery took place the year he arrived in St. Louis. A man by the name of George Shannon, who had accompanied Lewis and Clark on their expedition, was shot in the knee by hostile Indians during another expedition. The wound was infected by the time he was brought back to St. Louis, and Dr. Farrar successfully amputated the leg. (Shannon

went on to become a judge in Kentucky.)

In 1810, Farrar was a participant in a duel on Bloody Island. He challenged a lawyer named James Graham after an insult had been exchanged. Farrar suffered only a minor injury, but Graham would ultimately die from his wound. Farrar was back on the island in August 1817, serving as the surgeon for Thomas Hart Benton in his duel against Charles Lucas.

Farrar entered the U.S. Army during the War of 1812 and served as a surgeon. He built a large practice after the war and often was called in to assist other physicians to treat extremely ill patients. He was well respected among his peers and fellow citizens for his impeccable professionalism and personal charm.

In 1849, the city was gripped by the cholera epidemic. By mid-June, Dr. Farrar himself was infected with the disease. He fought the illness for 10 days with all his strength. He welcomed friends into his home on Church, now Second Street, and tried to conduct himself in his usual manner. At about ten o'clock on the evening of June 30, he complained of having the chills. His wife Ann summoned a doctor. Within a short time, in the early morning hours of July 1st, Dr. Bernard Farrar was dead. He passed away just three days short of his 64th birthday. Farrar Street in north St. Louis is named for him. The Farrar family burial lot is located on Balm Avenue and centered by a yellow, eight-columned monument resembling a small Greek Temple.

HENRY MILLER SHREVE
(OCTOBER 21, 1785-MARCH 6, 1851)

Many historians have called Henry Miller Shreve the "Master of the Mississippi;" others refer to him as the "Father of the Mississippi Steamboat." Shreve was born in Burlington County, New Jersey, and grew up in Fayette County, Pennsylvania. From an early age he loved the river, with its rippling waters offering the most natural, smooth form of transport. Henry began work on keelboats in the Ohio and Mississippi valleys; by

his mid-20's, he was captaining his own vessel, transporting goods between New Orleans and various Midwestern cities.

When Shreve made his first trip to St. Louis in 1807, the town was still a small hamlet on the river. He unloaded his goods at a warehouse and was impressed by its operator, Auguste Chouteau, who was well known throughout the Midwestern territories. When Shreve ended his visit, he knew that he would return to St. Louis. For the next three years, he ran a St. Louis-to-Pittsburgh fur-trading business.

During the War of 1812, he carried military supplies in support of Andrew Jackson's forces. With its shallow hull and deck-mounted engine, which allowed for easier navigation, his steamship *Washington* revolutionized transportation on inland rivers. Many predicted it would fail, but within a few years Shreve had a fleet of successful ships. And in 1838 he received a patent for his snagboat, a vessel used to clear fallen trees and other debris that often clogged the rivers. Shreve's success on the river led to his appointment by President John Quincy Adams as superintendent of western river improvements. He held that position for 14 years, through both the Jackson and Van Buren administrations. His biggest accomplishment during this period was the removal of driftwood blocking 160 miles of the Red River in Louisiana.

In 1835, he helped to establish a port in Louisiana, and four years later the town adopted the name "Shreveport." The following year, he purchased 300 acres of land four miles northwest of St. Louis, between what is now Euclid and Taylor Avenues, near Bellefontaine Cemetery. He retired there to his new home, called "Gallatin Place." The rest of the acreage was developed into farmland. He spent his time supervising the farm and often visited the riverfront to greet old acquaintances.

On February 25, 1845, Shreve's wife Mary died, five days after her 54th birthday. Although Shreve was devastated by the loss, a housekeeper by the name of Lydia Rodgers, 30 years his junior, brought a youthful vigor into the household and lifted his spirits. The two were married within a year. They had a daughter, Mary, named after his first wife.

With a new-found purpose in life, Captain Shreve became more involved with the civic leadership of the city, along with his friend, John O'Fallon. He was the leading authority on the steamship business, and his expertise was often called on to settle problems. He later took part in the expansion of railroads into Missouri. In 1847, St. Louis became the first city west of the Mississippi to be directly connected to eastern cities by the telegraph. Shreve was chosen to send the first message in the ceremony to open the telegraph service; he wired a greeting from the people of St. Louis to President James Polk in Washington, D.C.

In May 1849, on the same day as the great St. Louis fire, Shreve's granddaughter Virginia died of cholera. That day marked the beginning of the decline in Shreve's physical and mental health. He had his second and last child with Lydia later that year, bringing him one of the final joys in his life. They named her Florence.

Another wave of cholera hit St. Louis in 1850 and killed two more of his grandchildren. The final blow to his well being came in January with the death of Florence. By March, weakened by the hardships that life had dealt him in the final years, he was ready to die. From his home, he could hear the faint sound of steamboat whistles on the river. He is said to have remarked, "When it reaches you from somewhere in the distance, a steamboat whistle is the sweetest music in the world." Henry Shreve died peacefully on March 6, 1851, and was buried the same day. The *Missouri Republican* paid tribute to him the next day:

> *He was for nearly forty years closely identified with the commerce of the West, either in flat-boat or steamboat navigation. His name has become historically connected with western river navigation, and will be cherished by his numerous friends throughout this valley.*

Shreve was buried at Bellefontaine Cemetery near his Gallatin Place estate. His first wife, Mary, was reinterred on his left. Lydia, who outlived him by 41 years, is buried on his right. Also beside him is a small monument inscribed "Our Little Florie," for his daughter. The monument of his friend John O'Fallon towers behind him.

WILLIAM BEAUMONT
(NOVEMBER 21, 1785-APRIL 25, 1853)

In 1822, Dr. William Beaumont was a military physician stationed at Fort Mackinac, Michigan. One day he was called in to treat a French Canadian by the name of Alexis St. Martin who was accidentally shot in the stomach at close range. St. Martin recovered from his wound but had a permanent hole in his stomach. For the next three years, Dr. Beaumont cared for his patient and performed the first experiments to study the digestive process.

Beaumont was one of nine children born in Lebanon, Connecticut. In 1807, he joined his brother Samuel in Champlain, New York, where he worked as a schoolteacher and put in hours at Samuel's dry goods store. When he decided that medicine was his calling, Beaumont began to study under the direction of Dr. Benjamin Moore.

When the United States declared war on Great Britain in 1812, Beaumont enlisted in the army and was assigned to the Sixth Infantry Regiment as a medical officer. One year later, he received word that Samuel had died suddenly of pleurisy. He stayed in the army after the war and married Deborah Platt in August 1821. The couple had two daughters and two sons; his son William, Jr., died in 1825 at the age of one.

Beaumont's book, *Experiments and Observations on the Gastric Juice and the Physiology of Digestion*, was published in 1833. The book detailed his study of the digestive system on his patient Alexis St. Martin. (St. Martin died in 1880 with the hole still in his stomach.) His studies established that food was digested by the juices of the stomach. The book was praised by doctors around the country, and Beaumont became the leading expert on digestion.

He first came to St. Louis in July 1834 to serve as surgeon and medical officer at Jefferson Barracks. He considered the barracks hospital one of the best on the frontier. Two years later, he was notified by Reverend William Greenleaf Eliot, grandfather of poet T. S. Eliot, of his election as chairman of surgery for the new medical school at St. Louis University. The two men became close friends.

In 1837, the Beaumont family moved to a new home in Counsel Hall, a building owned by William Clark. They lived in the second-floor apartments and shared meals with the Clarks. Beaumont's book had gained him fame throughout St. Louis, affording him and his family the opportunity to associate with other prominent St. Louisans. They often entertained friends, including a young army lieutenant, Robert E. Lee. It was during this period that Beaumont was becoming increasingly deaf.

Beaumont resigned from the army to operate a private practice in St. Louis. The family purchased property on the outskirts of the city and moved into a large frame house set on 40 acres. They called it "Beaumont Place." In 1846, he was appointed as a consulting physician in the new St. Louis City Hospital, the first public hospital in the city. That same year he began work on a second edition to *Experiments and Observations*.

In 1849, Dr. Beaumont treated hundreds of patients plagued by cholera, many of whom ultimately died. To William's joy, none of his children was affected by the disease. A year later, however, his youngest daughter, Lucretia, died a month after giving birth; the baby died soon afterwards. In March 1853, Beaumont slipped on a step at a patient's home and hit his head. He was dazed for some time. He was thought to be recovering when his doctor diagnosed a carbuncle, an inflammation of the skin and tissues, at the back of the neck. The ailment caused him great discomfort. To make matters worse, he soon came down with a severe fever and was by this time nearly completely deaf. Wanting to get his affairs in order before he died, he told his concerned family, "Don't say a word about my health or strength; both will hold out as long as I shall need them. Now we must work, not bemoan."

William Greenleaf Eliot spent much of his time at his friend's bedside. He gave communion and helped write Beaumont's will, which named Eliot as executor. The good doctor died on the night of April 25. Eliot eulogized Beaumont as maintaining strength, faithfulness, and passion to the very end. He is buried across Laurel Avenue from Thomas Hart Benton. Beaumont High School is named for him.

WILLIAM CARR LANE
(DECEMBER 1, 1789-JANUARY 6, 1863)

On April 5, 1823, William Carr Lane was elected the first mayor of St. Louis by collecting 122 votes, against 70 votes for Auguste Chouteau; a third candidate received 28. His starting salary was $300 a year.

He had a commanding, handsome appearance; his temperament could be dark one moment and genial the next. Lane had come to St. Louis from Fayette County, Pennsylvania, where he was born. He studied medicine at Dickinson College in Pennsylvania before apprenticing under a doctor in Louisville, Kentucky. He volunteered for the War of 1812 and served as a surgeon's assistant at Fort Harrison, where he treated soldiers suffering from malaria. Later, he left the army and enrolled in the University of Pennsylvania to continue his medical training. He returned to the military in April 1816 when President James Madison appointed him post surgeon.

While on furlough in February 1818, Lane married Mary Ewing. One year later, he again left the army and moved to St. Louis, where he and Mary became the parents of four children. Lane formed a medical partnership with Dr. Samuel Merry and acquired a reputation as an excellent and popular practitioner. His recognition as a doctor gained him the appointment as aide-de-camp to Governor Alexander McNair. He later was named quartermaster-general of Missouri. After only four years in the city, he was elected mayor of St. Louis, an achievement that testified to his stature and appeal. He said of his adopted city, "The majestic rise of our city is morally certain." As mayor, he expanded the city government, enhanced the riverfront, and improved overall health conditions. The people reelected him five times to one-year terms. Ten years later, he returned as mayor to finish an unexpired term, and the voters elected him two more times.

Lane also gave religion to the city. He and U. S. Senator Thomas Hart Benton established the first Episcopal church in St. Louis. Lane finished his political career as governor of the New Mexico Territory, a position he was appointed to in 1852 by President Millard Fillmore.

According to Bellefontaine records, William Carr Lane died of "congestion of the brain." His funeral was celebrated in his home at Fourth and Walnut. He is buried near Laurel Avenue between his wife Mary and daughter Anne, a short distance away from Dr. Beaumont.

JOHN O'FALLON
(NOVEMBER 17, 1791-DECEMBER 17, 1865)

John O'Fallon's father, James, immigrated to America from Athlone in central Ireland. He was a physician who served in George Washington's army during the Revolutionary War. After the war, James moved to Louisville, Kentucky, and made the acquaintance of his future wife, Frances Clark, sister of William Clark.

John was born in Kentucky and raised by his mother after his father died. Uncle William played a large role in young John's life. O'Fallon followed in his father's footsteps and went into the military. He fought as an army captain in the War of 1812 and was severely wounded in the famous Battle of Tippecanoe. Near the end of the war, O'Fallon was appointed commandant of Fort Malden. He resigned from the army after the war and came to live in St. Louis. William Clark, having concluded the westward expedition in 1806, was an Indian agent at the time. O'Fallon joined his uncle as assistant Indian agent. Through his connections with the army, he started a business buying and selling supplies to the military and made a substantial fortune. Politically, O'Fallon served the state of Missouri as a member of both the Senate and House of Representatives.

O'Fallon was nearly killed in August 1817 during the election between John Scott and Rufus Easton for the position of territorial delegate to Congress. Violence broke out when supporters of the two candidates clashed. O'Fallon, a Scott supporter, stabbed one man and baited another, Dr. Robert Simpson. Two days later, he again  provoked Simpson, who pulled a pistol and fired into O'Fallon's chest. However, the gun misfired, and O'Fallon was unharmed.

O'Fallon was known for his keen business sense and had a knack of investing in profitable enterprises. Among the positions he held was president of the Branch Bank of the United States, and first president of the Missouri Pacific Railroad, the Baltimore & Ohio Railroad, and the Wabash Railroad. His real estate investments included numerous tracts of land in downtown St. Louis and more than 600 acres north of the city. At this site he built his country estate, a brick mansion called "Athlone," after his father's Irish hometown. The 40-room mansion was a massive structure, with huge columns supporting the portico. The house was partially destroyed by fire in 1875 and later demolished. The acreage is now O'Fallon Park.

O'Fallon's great wealth allowed him to give generously to charitable and educational institutions. Much of his philanthropy benefited Washington University, St. Louis University, and the O'Fallon Polytechnic Institute. He also contributed to the building of a Methodist Church at Fourth and Washington Avenues and donated the land for Fairgrounds Park.

When his health began to decline in December 1865, he moved into a house on Washington Avenue to reduce the amount of travel required to conduct his businesses in the city. Only occasionally did he visit Athlone.

O'Fallon died of lung congestion on Sunday, December 17, 1865. Citizens mourned the passing of the great soldier as news spread of his death. The following day's issue of the *Daily Missouri Democrat* said of O'Fallon:

No one has been more thoroughly identified with the growth and history of St. Louis than Col. O'Fallon, and so familiar is his countenance to all of our people, that its absence will be most painfully marked. In his departure, one of the landmarks of our community is gone.

St. George's Episcopal Church hosted the funeral where hundreds were turned away when the church filled to capacity. Mayor James Thomas and other city officials attended, as did the directors of the Polytechnic Institute. Robert Campbell and Henry Shaw were among the pallbearers. Reverend Bishop Hawks praised O'Fallon: "Of his childhood, we learn that he was never known to possess even one bad habit. He never made use of an oath in his life. He never went to bed with prayers, nor rose without them. Always a child pure in heart, he at last culminated in the upright, just, honorable, and trustful man."

John O'Fallon's will read in part:

I, John O'Fallon, of Athlone in the County of St. Louis, do make and declare this, my last will and testament in manner and form following. First, I resign my soul into the hands of Almighty God, and my body I commit to my vault or earth in my lot, in the Belle Fontaine Cemetery. This lot and its magnificent monument in the form of a tall pedestal surmounted by the figure of 'Hope', is one of the most beautiful in that cemetery.

His burial lot is the largest in Bellefontaine Cemetery, his monument the tallest. It reads, "In peace and in war he fulfilled every duty of a citizen and soldier and lived and died without a blemish on his name."

EDWARD BATES
(SEPTEMBER 4, 1793-MARCH 25, 1869)

In 1813, Edward Bates left his native Virginia and followed his brother Frederick to the Missouri Territory. (Frederick became governor of Missouri in 1824 but died after serving only one year in office.) Once in St. Louis, Bates studied law and started a practice. He was working as a circuit attorney when Governor William Clark appointed him attorney for the Northern District of Missouri. From there he became the state's attorney general, and he served one term in the state House of Representatives before moving on to the U. S. Congress. Bates was instrumental in the formation of the Whig party in Missouri and gained national attention as president of the River and Harbor Improvement Convention in Chicago in 1847.

Bates was very outspoken about his opposition to slavery. He freed his own slaves, pushed for emancipation, and opposed the admission of Kansas as a slave state. At the 1860 Republican Convention in Chicago,

Frank Blair nominated Bates for president. Bates received little support, and the nomination went instead to Springfield lawyer Abraham Lincoln. When Lincoln offered Bates a position in his cabinet, he chose attorney general and became the first cabinet member from west of the Mississippi.

One month after he took office, the Confederates bombarded Fort Sumter and the Civil War erupted. It was a frustrating four years for Bates. In a cabinet dominated by the likes of Edwin Stanton and William Seward, Bates struggled to be effective. Although he respected Lincoln, Bates opposed many of the president's military policies and was against West Virginia's admission to the Union. He resigned in 1864 and returned to St. Louis, where he wrote a column called "Letters to the People of Missouri" for the *Missouri Democrat*. Bates was deeply saddened by the assassination of Abraham Lincoln. He wrote of the president, "I appreciated that character, in beautiful simplicity of truth and kindness, and in its strength and goodness."

Bates and his family lived in the three-story house at 16th and Chestnut. His personal life dealt him many harsh blows. Not only did he lose his brother Frederick, but a second brother, Tarleton, was killed in a duel. Bates and his wife, Julia Coalter, had 17 children, but only five lived to an advanced age.

Bates had financial troubles near the end of his life and was forced to sell many of his real estate holdings around St. Louis to pay his debts. The family moved into a new house at Morgan Street (now Delmar) and Leffingwell Avenue. In July 1865, Bates became ill with a troubling lung condition. On the 28th, the family was summoned to his bedside. When the doctor arrived the next morning he found Bates to be seriously ill. Within a few days, however, his condition improved enough to allow him to sit up in bed. Weeks later, he was once again receiving visitors. In September, he planned a reception in honor of President Andrew Johnson, and welcomed the president and former cabinet colleagues William Seward and Gideon Welles to his home.

Edward Bates spent the remainder of his time visiting with his grandchildren and entertaining friends, including Father Peter De Smet, the famous Jesuit missionary to the Indians. He also served as a vice president for an organization he co-founded, the Missouri Historical Society.

In early December 1868, his health again declined. In March, he suffered from a severe pain in his chest and later slipped into unconsciousness. He rallied briefly but died peacefully on March 25, 1869 with friends and relatives at his bedside. He was 75.

A simple service was conducted at his home on Morgan Street before burial at Bellefontaine Cemetery. Edward Bates now rests with his in-laws in the Coalter family lot off Meadow Avenue. Today, a monument honoring him stands in Forest Park.

STEPHEN WATTS KEARNY
(AUGUST 30, 1794-OCTOBER 31, 1848)

Kearny was born the youngest of 14 children on his family's estate in Newark, New Jersey. He joined the military and rose through the ranks to become a major by 1825. The next year, he received orders to move his command to Fort Bellefontaine near St. Louis. His troops stayed for two months before moving a short distance down the Mississippi in July to begin construction on a new army post. Jefferson Barracks, named for Thomas Jefferson, was to become one of the most famous army posts in America. Its central location in the Mississippi valley made it ideal for the army's regional depot and infantry training school. Kearny brought the first troops to Jefferson Barracks and supervised the construction. He went on to build several forts and barracks in the Midwest and the west. He was said to be firm yet fair with his soldiers.

St. Louis was a growing and influential society in the early 19th century. The town was known for its hospitality and for having a close-knit community. During this period, Kearny made acquaintances with some of St. Louis' prominent citizens, such as William Clark and Senator Thomas Hart Benton, who would become his bitter enemy in later years.

In 1828, Kearny commanded Fort Crawford in Wisconsin. It was there that he met a new medical officer named William Beaumont. By 1830, Kearny was back at Jefferson Barracks; and in September, he wed William Clark's stepdaughter, Mary Radford, at Clark's country home. The couple had 11 children. In March 1833, he was appointed lieutenant colonel of the First Dragoons, the first cavalry unit of the United States Army. The position earned him the nickname, "Father of the U. S. Cavalry." Kearny, by this time a general, took part in the Mexican War and spent several years in California building military posts and training soldiers. One of his aides was a young lieutenant named William Tecumseh Sherman. Another lieutenant, Ulysses S. Grant, first met Kearny at Jefferson Barracks in the early 1840's and wrote of him:

...one of the ablest officers of the day... under him discipline was kept at a high standard but without vexatious rules or regulations. Every drill and roll call had to be attended but in the intervals officers were permitted to enjoy themselves.

When he was assigned to Vera Cruz in 1847, Kearny's health deteriorated from fever. Diseases were widespread throughout Mexico; hundreds of soldiers died of yellow fever and dysentery. He was made military governor of Mexico City before returning in ill health to Jefferson Barracks. His condition didn't improve, even though he had his family around him.

His spirits were raised by the news that President James Polk had nominated him to the rank of major general. On September 7, 1848, Kearny received his commission. By this time he was dangerously ill; doctors could do little to provide for him. He spent his remaining days at the home of Meriwether Lewis Clark, son of William Clark.

On October 15, his wife, Mary, gave birth to a boy at Jefferson Barracks. At six o'clock in the morning, October 31, Stephen Kearny peacefully passed away without having seen his child. On Thursday morning, two steamboats brought Kearny's body up the Mississippi to St. George's Episcopal Church on Locust Street. A large crowd was awaiting the general outside the church. It was one of the largest funerals the city had witnessed up to that time. Kearny was praised by Reverend Bishop Hawks for his distinguished military career and his warm, sensitive manner. After the service, the 7th and 8th Infantry Regiments and a regiment of First Dragoons from Jefferson Barracks led the procession. A full military band played the muffled sounds of mourning. Following the hearse was the general's favorite horse, with boots reversed in the stirrups to symbolize the soldier's death. Behind the family were military officers, civic leaders, and a long line of military volunteers.

The procession, which stretched for one mile, moved down Olive Street and turned on Broadway toward the private cemetery on the estate of Colonel John O'Fallon. Reverend Hawks performed a short service at the grave, after which an honor guard fired a military salute. Kearny's body was placed in O'Fallon's family vault.

On November 6, the War Department officially announced his death to the country. The order stated, "His character and bearing as an accomplished officer were unsurpassed, and challenge the admiration of his fellow citizens and the emulation of his professional brethren." It went on to order flags at half-mast and the firing of 13-minute guns at noon.

In 1861, the remains were reinterred in Bellefontaine Cemetery. Kearny and his family are buried in a circular lot across the road from the magnificent monument of his friend John O'Fallon.

ROBERT CAMPBELL & WILLIAM SUBLETTE

Robert Campbell was one of St. Louis' wealthiest citizens when he died in 1879. The October 20 *St. Louis Globe-Democrat* wrote:

> *No man, who has been twenty years a citizen of St. Louis, need be told to-day who and what Robt. Campbell was. The man wrote his name with his deeds while he was yet alive.*

Campbell, a man known for his hospitable and congenial manner, was born in Tyrone, Ireland, on February 12, 1804. He came to St. Louis when he was 20 years old. In 1825, one year after arriving in St. Louis, Robert set out for the Rocky Mountains at the suggestion of his doctor, Bernard Farrar, to treat a bronchial affliction. During this sojourn, he met General William Ashley, a renowned fur trader in the west. Ashley took Campbell on expeditions and taught him the business. When Ashley retired in 1830, Campbell formed a partnership with one of Ashley's associates, William Sublette. The two became friends and business partners in the Rocky Mountain Fur Company. Both were wealthy when they retired from the fur trading business and returned to St. Louis in 1835. They opened Sublette & Campbell, a store selling army and Indian goods. The store burned to the ground in the Great Fire of 1849.

He met Virginia Kyle during a trip to North Carolina and married her in 1841. They had 13 children, 10 of whom would not live beyond the age of seven. In 1854, the couple moved to a Victorian mansion at 1508 Lucas Place and had a summer house built next door. Campbell made substantial money in the financial markets and invested large sums of money in St. Louis real estate, including ownership of the Southern Hotel in the 1860's. He also was president of the Missouri State Bank and the Merchants' National Bank, and a director with the Pacific Railroad, in which he had a large financial stake. And President Ulysses S. Grant appointed him a commissioner to help negotiate with the Indians. Campbell often entertained distinguished guests in his home, including William Sherman, Kit Carson, Washington Irving, and President Grant himself.

William Sublette was a native of Lincoln County, Kentucky. His family settled in St. Charles in 1818 before coming to St. Louis. As a young man, he headed west with his brothers, Milton and Andrew, to enter the fur-trading business. He was a frontiersman with a tough and courageous exterior and an engaging personality, all of which helped him in dealing with unpredictable Indians. He became an associate of General Ashley and through that relationship met Robert Campbell. He set up trading posts at the upper Missouri River and helped open the Oregon Trail by finding a shortcut called "Sublette's Cutoff."

After returning to St. Louis, he married Frances Hereford, a woman 23 years his junior. The couple lived on the large Sublette farm, called "Sulphur Springs," on the River Des Peres. The property was bounded by what are today Manchester Avenue on the north, Kingshighway on the east, Southwest Avenue on the south, and Tamm Avenue on the west.

In July 1845, Campbell asked Sublette to join him on an eastern buying trip. On July 14, Sublette and his wife, along with her sister Mary Hereford and Robert Campbell, left St. Louis by steamboat. Sublette became seriously ill as they left Cincinnati and, upon reaching Pittsburgh, was taken to the Exchange Hotel to recover. A consulting doctor attributed the illness to consumption, now known as tuberculosis. Sublette passed away on Wednesday, July 23. The next day, Campbell purchased a coffin for his friend and placed the family on a steamboat to return to St. Louis. Clouds and rain accompanied the August 8 funeral; Sublette was buried near his house on the Sublette farm. Frances later married William's brother, Solomon, and they had children before dying one month apart in 1857; Frances was only 35 years old, Solomon was 42.

In October 1868, after the Sublette farm was sold, Mary Hereford had 17 members of the Sublette family reinterred at Bellefontaine Cemetery. Sublette Park and Sublette Avenue are named for William and his brother, Solomon.

Campbell continued running the store after Sublette died. His childhood bronchial illness returned in the late 1870's; and, in an attempt to improve his health, he went to Sarasota Springs in New York, America's premier resort spa. He returned to his home on Lucas Place in September in a weaker state and was confined to bed. In October, he began to decline rapidly. His physician could give him only temporary relief. His wife Virginia and their three surviving sons, Hugh, James, and Hazlett, were present when Robert Campbell took his last breath. Family friend James Yeatman was also present. Robert passed at 10:50 p.m. on Thursday, October 16, 1879. He was 76.

The funeral took place at his home on Sunday, October 19. Campbell lay in a rosewood coffin with flowers collected around it. The mansion was crowded with mourners from all walks of life, including businessman Wayman Crow. Crow and Yeatman were named as pallbearers. Reverend Dr. Samuel Niccolis and Reverend Brooks led the prayers. Reverend Niccolis gave a half-hour eulogy in which he praised the memory of Campbell, saying, "A prince and a true man among his followers has fallen." The pallbearers removed the casket from the home to a hearse waiting outside. More than 60 carriages escorted Campbell to Bellefontaine where he was laid to rest beside his 10 children who preceded him in death. None of Campbell's surviving sons married or had children; so, with Hazlett's death in 1938, the family line came to an end.

Robert Campbell's house at 1508 Lucas Place is now a museum, which was opened in 1943 with the efforts of the William Clark Society, a local preservation group.

WAYMAN CROW
(MARCH 7, 1808-MAY 10, 1885)

When he was 12, Wayman Crow quit working the family farm in his native Kentucky and began an apprenticeship as a storekeeper for a dry goods business. Years later, when the company expanded, he was given control and financial interest in a new branch store in Cadiz, Kentucky. He built a respectable reputation in the community and was appointed postmaster of Cadiz when he was only 19 years old.

In November 1829, he married Isabella Conn and fathered nine children, although four died in childhood. In 1835, Crow was in St. Louis when he fell ill. As he recovered his health, he witnessed the apparent prosperity of the business owners in the city. By November he opened his first St. Louis business, Crow & Tevis, with his cousin, Joshua Tevis. The business later was known as Crow, Hargadine & Company. The wholesale dry goods business proved quite profitable for its owners.

In 1840, he served the city and state, first as president of the St. Louis Chamber of Commerce and then as state senator as a member of the Whig Party. While in the Senate, he helped to organize the Hannibal, St. Joseph and Missouri Pacific Railroads. He was a member of William Greenleaf Eliot's Church of the Messiah and contributed to the construction of two other churches of that denomination. His biggest accomplishment, however, was his 1853 drafting of the charter to establish Washington University. He appointed the board members and conducted the first meeting of university business in his home. William Eliot was named president of the board of trustees.

On November 1, 1855, Crow nearly lost his life on an ill-fated inaugural train ride across the new Gasconade Bridge. The bridge opened railroad traffic for the first time between St. Louis and Jefferson City. Aboard the Missouri Pacific Railroad for that first ride were many dignitaries, including Mayor Washington King and the city counsel. Shortly after the locomotive began crossing the span, the new bridge collapsed, hurling the train 30 feet into the river below. Thirty-one people were killed. Crow was injured but alive; Mayor Washington also survived the crash.

Crow was 77 years old when the effects of paralysis confined him to bed in his home at 603 Garrison Avenue. For three weeks, his health sank, although his spirits were strong. Wayman Crow died among family and friends on May 10, 1885, at 3:30 p.m. William Greenleaf Eliot said of his good friend, "For all these years, from early manhood to a ripe of age, he was one of my dearest and closest friends... His death is to me like the loss of a right hand -- nay, more than that, for a part of the directing power by which the hands work is also taken away."

Two days later, the body was taken from the front parlor of his home and removed to the Church of the Messiah for the two o'clock funeral Mass. He rested in a mahogany coffin covered with flowers. Six of Crow's employees served as pallbearers. In honor of Crow, operators of dry goods establishments throughout the city closed their businesses during his funeral. Mayor David Francis closed City Hall and was in attendance as were a large number of faculty and students from Washington University also were present. William Greenleaf Eliot eulogized his departed friend. Honorary pallbearers included General William Tecumseh Sherman, James Yeatman, and Henry Shaw.

Wayman Crow's grave on Meadow Avenue is marked by a tall granite obelisk with his name in large letters near the base.

STERLING PRICE
(SEPTEMBER 20, 1809-SEPTEMBER 29, 1867)

When Sterling Price was born, his family lived in Prince Edward County, Virginia, where they raised tobacco on a sizable piece of property. Price went to college at Hampden-Sydney and later studied law. In 1831,

he moved to Missouri and purchased a farm in Chariton County, near Columbia. He worked the land and practiced law for a time before serving three terms in the state legislature. Two years later, he married Martha Head; they had six children. In 1844, he was elected as a Democrat to the U. S. Congress, but left his congressional seat during the Mexican War to join the Second Missouri Infantry under the command of General Stephen Watts Kearny. President Polk appointed him brigadier general of the forces in New Mexico at the end of the war.

Price returned to Missouri and in 1852 was elected governor. He was widely respected for his diligence in making tough decisions and improving the standards of the people. Public schools were improved and railroad construction increased dramatically during his term. At the brink of the Civil War, he trained soldiers to fight for the Confederacy, and by doing so became an outcast in a state that would pledge its allegiance to the Union. Price contributed to the defeat of the Union army at Wilson's Creek, Missouri, in August 1861. As the war was coming to a close and Confederate defeat was certain, he relocated to Mexico, where his health suffered. He lost weight because of a stomach disorder and looked older than his 58 years. In April 1866, his family boarded a ship in New York to join him in Vera Cruz, Mexico, but a short time into the voyage the ship ran aground and sank. Although the family was returned safely to New York, they lost all their possessions. Price's health improved when his family finally arrived in May. They took up temporary residence in Cordoba while a new home was under construction in Carlota. It was during this time that both Price and his son came down with typhoid fever.

In January 1867, when his health was improved, he returned with his family back to Missouri, although he still had bitter feelings about his homeland and the war. They arrived in St. Louis and stayed at the Southern Hotel. He recovered by March and opened a tobacco business, "Sterling Price & Company," located at the corner of Commercial and Chestnut Streets. Meanwhile, his supporters collected money to help the family purchase a house on 16th Street.

Illness was again attacking his body by the summer of 1867. He now suffered from severe attacks of diarrhea and in September was diagnosed with having early signs of cholera. He once called out for "a prompt flank movement" while lapsing into delirium. An Episcopal minister was called in to baptize the general on his final evening. At 2:12 in the morning of September 29, his doctor checked his pulse and pronounced, "He is gone." Price's wife, children, and several friends were with him at the end.

On October 3 his body lay in state in the First Methodist Episcopal Church at Eighth and Washington. He rested in a silver-trimmed mahogany casket, the plate of which was inscribed, "Major General Sterling Price, died Sept. 29, 1867, aged 58 years. After life's fitful fever, he sleeps well." Hundreds viewed the general before the two o'clock funeral, which was attended by a great number of soldiers who had served under him. The procession to Bellefontaine Cemetery was the largest in the city to that time. The hearse was pulled by six black horses and driven by Jesse Arnot, the same man who led the funeral hearse for Abraham Lincoln. (Arnot is buried at Bellefontaine.) Six gray horses pulled a second hearse with the remains of his daughter-in-law, who died shortly before the general. Sixty to 70 carriages followed in procession.

A tall granite obelisk marks the Balm Avenue roadside grave of Sterling Price. The monument is inscribed:

Farmer, Legislator, Governor,
Brigadier General during the Mexican War,
Major General in the Confederate States Army,
His purity of character was equaled
only by his exalted patriotism.

WILLIAM GREENLEAF ELIOT
(AUGUST 5, 1811-JANUARY 23, 1887)

Born in New Bedford, Massachusetts, Eliot came from an ancestral line of highly educated people, including a president of Harvard. His father was a merchant and ship owner; his mother, Margaret Dawes, was a descendant of William Dawes, who made the famous midnight ride with Paul Revere. Eliot graduated from Georgetown in 1831 and three years later finished his education at Harvard University's Divinity School.

He came to St. Louis after graduation and established the First Congregational Church at Garrison and Locust, later called the "Church of the Messiah." He was ordained pastor of the church and held that post until 1871. He and his wife Abigail lived at 2660 Washington Avenue and

had 14 children, most of whom died before their parents, including a daughter who, in the winter of 1873, fell through a patch of ice and drowned while skating on a pond.

During the Civil War, Eliot was a member of the Western Sanitary Commission under its president, James Yeatman. The commission worked to aid civilians and soldiers by organizing medical facilities and distributing supplies. Eliot was a benefactor of educational institutions in the city. Along with Wayman Crow, he co-founded Eliot Seminary, which later became Washington Institute and finally, in 1857, Washington University. The institution was chartered on February 22, 1853 with the signature of Missouri Governor Sterling Price. Eliot was nominated president of the board of trustees and became chancellor in 1871. He would be associated with the university for the rest of his life. William also laid the groundwork for Mary Institute, named for his daughter, and was an incorporator of the Missouri Historical Society.

Eliot left St. Louis in 1887 for Pass Christian, Mississippi, hoping to recover from a pulmonary condition. Death came quickly on Sunday, January 23. Four days later, his body was brought back to St. Louis by train for a short service conducted in his home by two of his sons, Reverend Thomas Eliot and Reverend Christopher Eliot. Three other children survived their father. The body was taken to his Church of the Messiah for the funeral Mass. Alumni and directors of Washington University were present near the front of the church. The pallbearers were members of his family, with James Yeatman among the honorary pallbearers. The church had no decoration of mourning, as Eliot himself had requested.

A long procession followed the body to Bellefontaine. He now rests beside his wife Abby in the family lot, directly behind the grave of his friend, Dr. William Beaumont. His headstone reads, "Looking Unto Jesus."

HENRY AND SUSAN BLOW

Henry Taylor Blow and his daughter Susan played unique and distinctive roles that helped to bring about change in their respective fields. Henry was born in Southampton County, Virginia, on July 15, 1817. His sister Charlotte married Joseph Charless, Jr., son of the publisher of the *Missouri Gazette*.

Blow came to St. Louis when he was 13 and attended St. Louis University for two years. Several years later, he entered into a partnership with Joseph Charless to manufacture and sell drugs, oils, and paints. The partnership dissolved within a few years, but Blow kept the manufacturing business, which he expanded and incorporated as "The Collier White Lead and Oil Company." Blow also was president of the Iron Mountain Railroad, responsible for the construction of new rail lines. After the Civil War, he and his older brother Peter formed The Granby Mining and Smelting Company in southwestern Missouri to mine lead products. The business made the Blow family a vast fortune.

Blow was in good health his entire life, seldom experiencing a day of illness. He was said to be kind, sociable, and ambitious, but never arrogant. His manner helped him get elected to the state Senate in 1854 as a member of the Whig party. When the Whig party collapsed, he worked with the likes of Francis Blair and Edward Bates to establish the Republican Party in Missouri. He was a delegate to the Chicago Convention that elected Lincoln in 1860 and was propelled to the U. S. House of Representatives two years later. He served two terms, in which he wrestled with the politics of a country at war and its reconstruction afterwards. He returned to his mining business before finishing his political career by serving as Ulysses S. Grant's minister to Brazil. He returned to St. Louis in 1871, hoping to retire. Instead, he served his country one final time as a member of the Board of Commissioners for the District of Columbia.

Blow and his wife Minerva had four daughters and two sons. His most distinguished child was his daughter Susan, born in St. Louis on June 7, 1843. Susan and her brothers and sisters were given the best education St. Louis had to offer. This instilled in young Susan the importance of educating children at an early age. She studied with the best educators in New York and Germany and adopted many of their philosophies when she returned to St. Louis. In September 1873, with the support of the superintendent of schools, Dr. William Harris, she opened the first public kindergarten in America at the Des Peres School in Carondelet. One year later, she opened a training school for kindergarten teachers. She worked without financial gain and was never on the payroll of the St. Louis school system.

After Henry's wife died in June 1875, he went to Saratoga, New York, for rest and relaxation; but on September 11 he was stricken with a cerebral hemorrhage and died within the hour. The next day, the *St. Louis Globe-Democrat* said of him:

> *No death among the many whose names are intimately linked with the social and material history and progress of this community could occasion a more profound sorrow than that of Hon. Henry T. Blow, which occurred at Saratoga yesterday.*

The body was transported back to St. Louis for the funeral on Saturday, November 18. A train from the Iron Mountain Railroad offered free rides from the city to Carondelet for those attending the funeral. The service took place at 11:00 a.m. at his Carondelet home. The pallbearers were among the elite citizens of the city, including James Yeatman, James Eads, and Robert Campbell. His large, box-like monument at Bellefontaine stands just off the road on Woodbine Avenue near the grand mausoleum of Adolphus Busch. The inscription on his monument reads, "Be still and know that I am God."

In 1884, Susan Blow was forced to semi-retire because of illness. Ten years later, she resumed training teachers and often lectured on the importance of education. She moved to New York, where she published six books and worked at the New York Kindergarten Association. She died on Sunday evening, March 26, 1916, at The Berkeley on Fifth Avenue in New York. She had never married.

Susan's funeral was celebrated on Wednesday the 29th at the Christ Church Cathedral. More than 80 kindergarten teachers from around the country attended the 10:30 a.m. service. She was buried beside her father at Bellefontaine. Her headstone is as modest as her life.

DON CARLOS BUELL
(MARCH 23, 1818-NOVEMBER 19, 1898)

The Civil War general was born near Marietta, Ohio, and grew up in Indiana. He graduated 32nd in his class from West Point in 1841 and fought in the Mexican War under the command of Zachary Taylor. Buell later served as commander of Jefferson Barracks in St. Louis. He was promoted to brigadier general at the outbreak of the Civil War and assisted in organizing the Army of the Potomac. In November 1861, he was again promoted, this time to major general, and given command of the Army of

the Ohio. Buell's first major engagement took place in Tennessee on the second day of the Battle of Shiloh. His reinforcements helped General Ulysses S. Grant defeat the Confederates and take control of Tennessee.

In October 1862, Buell and his army fought the Confederates under General Braxton Bragg at Perryville, Kentucky. Neither army won a decisive victory; and, when Bragg's battered forces retreated, Buell did not pursue. This inactivity was viewed as a failure on Buell's part and he was removed from active duty. The general argued that he lacked the men and supplies to pursue Bragg. A military commission investigated his conduct and delivered a report in April 1863, but did not make a recommendation as to the future of Buell's command. It was later thought that Buell's allegiance to General George McClellan, who was running against Abraham Lincoln for president, precluded his receiving another command. Without an army or a command, he resigned from the military on June 1, 1864.

He returned to Kentucky and served as president of the Green River Iron Company from 1865 to 1870. He was working in the mining business when President Grover Cleveland appointed him pension agent for Kentucky, a position he held for four years before retiring to his country home in Rockport, Kentucky. During the warm weather months of 1898, Buell's health began to decline, and he died at 3:00 p.m. on Friday, November 19. Even though he had been ill for months, his death was unexpected. On the morning of November 22, accompanied by his niece and a local priest, Buell's body arrived in St. Louis from Louisville and was driven to the undertaking establishment of George Lynch. It then was transported to St. Francis Xavier Church at Grand and Lindell Boulevards to lie in state until the funeral. Six sergeants from the 12th Infantry served as pallbearers. Military men who had known Buell for a half-century were in attendance, as were soldiers from Jefferson Barracks.

A short prayer was recited at the grave before Buell was laid to rest beside his wife Margaret.

His wife had first been married to Brigadier General Richard Mason, who died of cholera in 1850 at Jefferson Barracks while serving as its commander. Mason was born in Stafford County, Virginia, and began his military career in 1817. He was at Jefferson Barracks in March 1833, where he served as a major under Stephen Watts Kearny in the First Dragoons, the first cavalry unit in the U.S. Army. Three years later, he became colonel of the regiment. During the Mexican War, Mason was appointed the first military governor of California.

Buell, Mason, and Margaret are all buried in the same wedge-shaped, roadside lot. Two large memorials mark the graves, one for Buell and Margaret, the other for Richard Mason. Mason's monument resembles a dismantled cannon.

JAMES YEATMAN
(AUGUST 27, 1818-JULY 7, 1901)

Thomas Yeatman was a prosperous banker and manufacturer. James, the second of his six children born in Tennessee, attended school at the New Haven Commercial School before becoming an apprentice in his father's business. In 1842, he came to St. Louis as his father's representative. His mild manner won him business and many friends. His house, called "the Belmont," was often a center of social entertainment.

Yeatman married Angelica Thompson in September 1838, but she lived only until 1849. He then married Cynthia Ann Pope in 1851, but she passed away three years later. He had five children from the two marriages.

On the business front, he was one of the founders of the Missouri Pacific Railroad and the Merchants' Bank. A decade after its founding, he became Merchants' president and reorganized it to the Merchants' National Bank, which he oversaw for the next 35 years. He was a busy civic leader in St. Louis, sitting on the board of several organizations, including Bellefontaine Cemetery. He was the first president of the Mercantile Library and an original trustee of Henry Shaw's Missouri Botanical Garden. His philanthropy supported charities and education, most notably the Missouri School for the Blind.

Yeatman was best known as president of the Western Sanitary Commission. Started in 1861, the commission did extensive work aiding military and civilian victims of the Civil War. They organized hospitals, recruited medical personnel, and distributed sanitary supplies. The commission also established one of the first railroad hospital cars and a hospital boat on the Mississippi. Soldiers affectionately referred to Yeatman as "Old Sanitary."

James Yeatman died of exhaustion in St. Louis (Mullanphy) Hospital at 1:25 a.m. on Sunday, July 7, 1901. The July 9 funeral took place at the home of his relative, Isaac Sturgeon, on East Grand Avenue. The home was crowded with friends and family; among them, former St. Louis mayor and Missouri governor, David Francis, and the surviving daughters of William Clark. Reverend Dr. Samuel Niccolis of the Second Presbyterian Church conducted the service. (The good reverend also had performed the ceremony at Robert Campbell's funeral 21 years earlier.) A choir from the church sang "Abide with Me" and "Asleep in Jesus." Yeatman's grandsons and nephews acted as pallbearers. The hearse was followed in procession by more than 100 carriages. The gates at Bellefontaine Cemetery were draped in black in honor of the former president of the cemetery. The Yeatman family lot is located next to that of his friend, Robert Campbell. The very detailed and ornate monument is adorned on each side with the likeness of an angel.

JAMES EADS
(MAY 23, 1820-MARCH 8, 1887)

On the morning that James Eads and his family stepped onto the levee in St. Louis in 1833, their steamboat became engulfed in flames. They lost all of their possessions and were left penniless. To support themselves, his mother opened a boardinghouse, while Eads worked for a dry goods store and sold apples and newspapers on the streets. At 18, Eads was working on the steamboat *Knickerbocker* when the ship wrecked on a snag. On that day, he came up with the idea of salvaging wrecks from the bottom of the Mississippi.

He developed a partnership with longtime friend Bill Nelson, and together they built a double-hulled ship with derricks, pumps, and a diving bell. In a short time, the *Submarine* proved to be a tremendous success. They salvaged wrecks from St. Louis to New Orleans; Eads personally made more than 500 trips to the bottom of the Mississippi in his diving bell. They were paid handsomely by insurance companies for the sunken cargo and were allowed to keep any salvage that had remained underwater more than five years. Soon Eads and his partner had a fleet of ships. By the age

of 25, Eads was a wealthy man, living on Compton Hill with his wife Martha.

James Buchanan Eads was born in Lawrenceburg, Indiana in 1820. He was named after his second cousin, who would later become the 15th president of the United States. At an early age he developed an interest in mechanics. He often experimented with machinery, and by age 13 had constructed a miniature steam engine.

Eads lost his wife to the cholera epidemic of 1852. Since he had often pushed his physical and mental capacity to near exhaustion, his own health was declining during this period. Hundreds of underwater trips in the diving bell had left him suffering from tuberculosis. He never understood the effects of decompression. When his doctor recommended retirement, Eads, who was 32 at the time, obliged for only a short while. He married again, to a woman named Eunice, with whom he had five daughters, and he went back to work.

In 1861, Edward Bates, Lincoln's attorney general, recommended that the government accept Eads' proposal to build a fleet of ironclad gunboats for the Union army. Lincoln agreed. Eads and Nelson employed 4,000 workers at the Union Marine Works in Carondelet. Because of the new invention of gaslights, the shipyard was able to run around the clock. His ships helped the Union army to capture Vicksburg and other Confederate strongholds.

After the war, his doctor again suggested retirement. Instead, Eads took on the ambitious project of building the first steel bridge to span the Mississippi River. He had never built a bridge before and had no formal education as an engineer. Construction began in August 1867; the newly invented cofferdams, or caissons, were employed to build underwater foundations. During construction, 14 workers died of what was then called "caisson disease" (the bends) because of improper decompression techniques. On July 4, 1874, thousands enjoyed the celebration as Eads Bridge was officially opened. General William Tecumseh Sherman hammered in the last spike, and a 100-gun salute was fired. A 14-mile parade with marching bands was followed by 14 locomotives that Eads sent across the bridge to proof its strength. Today, Eads Bridge is a historical landmark in St. Louis and one of the finest examples of innovative engineering and architecture that the city has to offer.

In the late 1870's, Eads designed and built jetties to remove sediment that had accumulated and formed sandbars where the Mississippi River joined the Gulf of Mexico in Louisiana. His ingenuity deepened the mouth of the river and provided a year-round shipping channel for large ocean vessels making their way to New Orleans. Eads became a hero in New Orleans for helping to revive commerce in the city.

His final project was an idea to build a canal across Panama. He proposed building a marine railway to move ships from the Gulf of Mexico to the Pacific Ocean, and he wanted the U.S. government to grant him exclusive rights to the project. Under doctor's orders, he went to Nassau in the Bahama Islands to rest his body and mind. One of his daughters escorted him on the trip. Regarding the railway project, he told his daughter, "I shall not die until I accomplish this work, and see with my own eyes great ships pass from ocean to ocean over the land." The government, however, declined his proposal for the Panama project.

He regained his strength but came down with a cold and congestion in the lungs. "I cannot die; I have not finished my work," he said to his daughter. But by Saturday, March 5, 1887, he was dangerously ill from pneumonia, and he died three days later. When the body arrived in St. Louis, it was taken to his daughter's residence. The funeral was held at Christ Church Cathedral. As Eads would have wanted, there was no drapery of mourning at the church, and only a small group of flowers rested on the steps in front of the casket. The church was filled to capacity; among the mourners were many of the Eads Bridge construction workers. Mayor David Francis and businessman James Yeatman also were in attendance.

A procession led to Bellefontaine, where a prayer was recited at the grave before the distinguished engineer was laid to rest.

FRANCIS BLAIR
(FEBRUARY 19, 1821-JULY 9, 1875)

Francis Blair was born in Lexington, Kentucky, and spent his elementary years in Washington, D.C., where his father was the editor of the *Washington Globe*. He attended Princeton and went to law school at Transylvania University in Kentucky before coming to St. Louis in 1842 to practice law with his brother Montgomery, who would later serve as one of Dred Scott's lawyers.

When the Mexican War broke out, Blair joined the army, and was appointed attorney general of the territory after the Americans captured New Mexico. During this time, he became embroiled in a controversy with Sterling Price, then the military governor of the territory. When Price had Blair arrested for insubordination, Blair resigned his position and made public his hatred for Price.

In 1847, Blair returned to the Midwest to marry Appoline Alexander, and once again resumed his practice of law. By this time, the slavery issue was beginning to divide the country. Blair expressed his anti-slavery views in his paper, called the *Barnburner*, and organized the Free Soil Party to further his opposition. He spent time in the Missouri legislature and the U. S. Congress, where he was well respected by his colleagues for his political brilliance and his honest, personal approach. His forthright and spontaneous style of speaking made him one of the best orators of his time.

In March 1849, Blair was involved in a duel, of sorts. Using the pseudonym "Radical," he was writing a series of articles in the *Missouri Republican* that were critical of political opponents such as Loring Pickering, the editor of the rival newspaper, *The Union*. The two traded blistering editorials, with Blair subsequently challenging Pickering to a duel, which the editor promptly declined. One morning, they accidentally met on Second Street, where they exchanged a few words before Blair attacked with his umbrella. Pickering pulled a knife but backed off when Blair threatened to shoot him. A week later, a Pickering accomplice fired three shots at Blair on the street. The assailant missed but was hit by shots from Blair's revolver. Blair pleaded guilty to challenging Pickering to the duel; he was sentenced to pay a fine of one dollar and to serve one minute in jail.

At the 1860 Chicago Republican Convention, Blair supported his friend and fellow Missourian Edward Bates for the presidency. When Bates' defeat looked inevitable, Blair placed his support behind Abraham Lincoln. Within a year, the Civil War erupted, and Blair returned to St. Louis to organize men to fight for the Union. His efforts helped to ensure that Missouri would not align itself with the Confederacy. Blair raised seven regiments of soldiers with his own finances and received an appointment as brigadier general. He was considered a "soldier's soldier" and was popular among his men. In May 1863, he fought in his first conflict, the Battle of Vicksburg. He was promoted to major general and was a member of General Sherman's "March to the Sea."

Blair was back on the political scene after the war. He received the 1868 Democratic nomination for vice president but lost the election by a wide margin to former Union commander Ulysses S. Grant. However, Blair didn't have time to relax, with his later election to the U. S. Senate.

His health began to decline in 1871 with an attack of paralysis, followed by a second, more severe attack. Blair's wife wrote home, "One arm the right one and leg are perfectly powerless. All we have to hope for is his grand constitution which may carry him thro without another attack." Treatments at the sanitarium in Clifton Springs, New York, improved his mobility, but he still required the assistance of a crutch or cane. On July 9, 1875, while walking about his bedroom, Blair fell and struck his head. He never regained consciousness. By 9:00 p.m., his pulse had slowed considerably. Francis Blair died soon after with his family by his side. He was 54.

With his passing, the country lost a great statesman and strong defender of a united government. William Tecumseh Sherman said of him, "Frank Blair was a noble, honorable, and magnanimous man. He was brave, open, and unselfish. His virtues will always be recognized and never forgotten, while his faults will be buried with him, as they hurt no one but himself." The city was draped in mourning on the day of his funeral. Hundreds viewed Blair as he lay in state at his home on Chestnut Street before a procession, which included his old regiment, the First Missouri, made its way to the First Congregational Church at Tenth and Locust.

Blair's grave sits atop a hill near the entrance of Bellefontaine. A granite cross with the inscription "Blair-Graham" marks the spot. In May 1885, several thousand people joined General Sherman and Blair's family at Forest Park for the unveiling of a statue of Blair posing as if giving his final speech to the crowd. The monument stands in the northeast corner of Forest Park.

NORMAN COLMAN
(MAY 16, 1827-NOVEMBER 3, 1911)

Norman Jay Colman was born in Richfield Springs, New York. He graduated from Louisville Law University in 1849 and married Clara Porter two years later. Colman practiced law in Albany, Indiana, for 12 years before coming to St. Louis. His wife Clara died in 1863; three years later he married Catherine Wright of St. Louis. They lived at 5499 Delmar Boulevard in a home they would own for the next 50 years.

Colman had a lifelong passion for agriculture. Upon relocating to St. Louis he established an agricultural journal called *Colman's Rural World*. Politically, he served on the Board of Aldermen for two years and spent another two years in the Missouri Legislature. In 1873, he was elected lieutenant governor. President Grover Cleveland was looking for a commissioner of agriculture in 1885 and selected Colman for the job. Four years later, when the position became a cabinet post, Cleveland officially appointed Colman as the first Secretary of Agriculture.

Colman continued to serve the city and the state by holding positions on the board of curators at the University of Missouri, the State Board of Agriculture, and the St. Louis World's Fair, and he was the first president of the Missouri State Fair. He also founded the Missouri State Horticultural Society.

In early November 1911, Colman was in Lexington, Missouri, en route by train to Plattsburg, Missouri, to purchase a horse for his farm near Creve Coeur Lake, when he suffered a severe stroke from a blood clot in his brain. He was still alive but unconscious when his son-in-law, Dr. C. M. Nicholson, went to Lexington to bring him back to St. Louis. Secretary Colman died at 2:00 a.m. the next morning, when the train was in Moberly. He was survived by three children.

When the train arrived at the Delmar station, Colman's body was taken to his home. On Monday, November 6, Reverend Dr. James Lee of St. John's Methodist Episcopal Church presided over the ten o'clock service. Reverend Lee eulogized Colman: "He was an idealist, but unlike artists, who worked their visions out on canvas, or in music, he sought to convert his ideals into better homes for the people's shelter and into better food for the people's hunger." Among those in attendance were Missouri Governor Herbert Hadley and members of the numerous organizations associated with Colman. The pallbearers were members of the St. Rose Hill Lodge, of which Colman was a member. A huge list of honorary pallbearers included David Francis (then Secretary of the Interior), William Marion Reedy, and Charles Lemp. Norman Colman is buried in a roadside grave on Fountain Avenue, the first road to the right of the main gate.

ADOLPHUS BUSCH
(JULY 10, 1839-OCTOBER 10, 1913)

German-born Eberhard Anheuser came to America in 1843 and located in St. Louis two years later. He was the wealthy owner of a soap factory at the time he purchased the Bavarian Brewery in 1860.

Adolphus Busch was born in German wine country near the city of Bad Schwalbach. His father, Ulrich, was a wealthy merchant and landowner who had 22 children. Adolphus came to St. Louis in 1857 and, at the age of 18, began work as a shipping clerk in a malt and hops storage house. It was his first taste of the brewing business. Two years later, he established a brewery supply business. In 1861, Busch married Anheuser's daughter Lilly in a double wedding; his brother Ulrich married Anheuser's other daughter, Anna.

He served in the Union Army during the Civil War and then rejoined his father-in-law at Eberhard Anheuser and Company. In 1876, the brewery introduced its trademark brand, *Budweiser*. Three years later, the brewery was renamed Anheuser-Busch. They employed 5,000 at the main brewery and at various branches around the country. Busch was named president after 74-year-old Eberhard Anheuser died on May 2, 1880, in his home at Tenth and Pestalozzi. He was laid to rest at Bellefontaine.

Busch started satellite businesses to benefit the brewery, including the Manufacturers' Railroad and the Adolphus Busch Glass Manufacturing Company, which became the largest bottle manufacturer in the world. He was also president of Busch-Sulzer Brothers Diesel Engine Company and Geyser Ice Company.

He enjoyed traveling often on his private rail car, *Adolphus*, in his leisure time. He and his wife had 13 children. Three of their daughters died at birth, and the oldest son, Edward, died at the age of 15 while attending Kemper Military School in Boonville, Missouri. Another son, Adolphus Jr., 30, a vice-president at the brewery, died in August 1898 of a perforated appendix. Busch's second son, August Busch, would eventually become his successor.

His philanthropy was well known and widespread. He donated large sums to Washington University, Harvard University, and the University of Missouri-Columbia. He was an active promoter of the St. Louis World's Fair and supported victims displaced by floods and earthquakes.

On Christmas Eve, 1907, Busch suffered a severe attack of pneumonia, which developed into dropsy. By May 1913, his physical health was deteriorating from heart disease and dropsy. He often used a wheelchair and installed an elevator in his Victorian residence at Number One Busch Place to help him get to the second floor. On June 9, he traveled with the family back to Germany. It would be his last trip to his beloved Villa Lilly, his German estate near the Rhine. He relaxed by entertaining guests and hunting deer in his private forest. By October, he was seriously ill, but he rallied temporarily when doctors removed fluid from his lungs. By the 10th, he was relaxed and smoked a cigar, but his son August later recalled, "Just after noon he became weak but was in no pain whatever. He spoke to all of us and was quite clear of mind on all subjects. I don't think father thought he was dying." At 8:15 that evening, Adolphus Busch died peacefully at the age of 74, the same age as his father-in-law, Eberhard Anheuser. His wife Lilly, son August, and three daughters were at his bedside. His good friend Carl Conrad, who developed the Budweiser brand, also was present. His estimated worth at the time of his death was $40 to $50 million.

According to the October 11 *St. Louis Post Dispatch*:

> *The news of Busch's death was received over the private telegraph wires at the brewery at 5 p.m. Friday, just as 5000 employees were being dismissed for the day. It was flashed from department to department, but many of the employees did not hear of it until they were on the streets and saw the flags from the buildings dropped to half-mast.*

The town of Bad Schwalbach mourned their native son. The body was transported to Bremen on a private rail car and transferred to the steamer *Kronprinz Wilhelm* for the trip back to America. When the ship pulled into New York harbor on October 21, son-in-law Edward Faust and longtime family friend Charles Nagel received the body, which was placed in the rail car *Adolphus* on a private train. Several members of the Busch family escorted the patriarch back to St. Louis.

The train pulled into St. Louis in a heavy rainstorm, and the casket was taken into Number One Busch Place as hundreds of people looked on. Busch was finally home, resting in the house where he had entertained the likes of Teddy Roosevelt and William Taft. The day before the funeral, brewery employees viewed their leader in the main drawing room of the mansion. He rested in a casket covered in orchids. The employees sent a wreath of roses that said, "Our Beloved President." The house was later opened to the public where as many as 30,000 people came to pay their respects to the beer baron.

Members of the St. Louis Symphony Orchestra played at the mansion on the morning of the funeral. When the funeral began at two o'clock, all business in St. Louis came to a stop for five minutes. In attendance were U. S. Congressman Richard Bartholdt and the presidents of Harvard and the University of Missouri. Also among the honored guests was Baron von Lesner, a representative of German Kaiser Wilhelm II. Charles Nagel gave the funeral oratory, calling Busch, "a giant among men. Like a descendant of one of the great and vigorous and ancient gods, he rested among us and with his optimism, his far seeing vision, his undaunted courage and his energy shaped the affairs of men." After the service, the casket was carried to a truck for the procession to Bellefontaine. A 250-piece band led the cortege through an estimated 100,000 people lining the route. A final prayer was recited before Busch was placed into the vault.

The current mausoleum for Adolphus and Lilly Busch is a pink granite, Gothic chapel, elegant in its ornamentation and detailing. Above the door are the Latin words of Julius Caesar, "Veni, Vidi, Vici," which translate to "I came, I saw, I conquered." Eberhard Anheuser is buried just behind the mausoleum.

SAMUEL FORDYCE
(FEBRUARY 7, 1840-AUGUST 3, 1919)

The multimillionaire capitalist was a native of Guernsey, Ohio. He was educated in Guernsey public schools and attended Madison College in Pennsylvania and North Illinois University. His first significant job was as a station agent for the Central Ohio Railway. Lieutenant Fordyce fought for General Grant during the Civil War, and at the Battle of Shiloh assisted Grant when the general's horse threw him. After serving in the First Ohio Cavalry in the Civil War, he established Fordyce & Rison, a banking institution in Huntsville, Alabama. It was there that he met Susan Chadwick, his future wife. The couple was married in 1866 and had three sons and a daughter.

A decade later, they moved to Arkansas, where he became interested in railroads. He helped to reorganize the St. Louis Southwestern Railway Company in 1885 and was named its president. He is credited with constructing more than 24,000 miles of railroad tracks throughout Missouri and Arkansas. He quickly built a reputation as a straightforward and fearless businessman. His philosophy of life was, "Reward your friends and punish your enemies." He was serving as vice president or director of numerous other railway lines and corporations when he moved his headquarters to St. Louis. He later became director of the St. Louis Union Trust Company and founded one of the largest American health resorts in Hot Springs, Arkansas.

His corporate position afforded him the opportunity to make friends of Presidents McKinley and Grant. He wrote about his first visit to the White House after Grant was elected:

Grant reached out his hand and shook hands with me. I said: 'General, you don't know me.' Whereupon he said, "I don't know your name, but you were one of my old soldiers." I said, 'General, where did you ever see me.' He said, "You were the young officer who caught my horse when he fell with me at Pittsburg Landing." The event happened nearly 15 years before this.

Fordyce spent most of his final days at his country home in Garland County, Arkansas. On July 19, 1919, he went to Atlantic City for an extended vacation to improve his health. By August 1, his health had declined quickly and his doctors summoned the family. His wife Susan, sons J.R. and Samuel, Jr., and his daughter Jane were by his side when he died of pneumonia at 12:30 in the afternoon on Sunday, August 3. His body was returned to St. Louis for a funeral in his home at 21 Washington Terrace. On August 6, friends and family gathered to say goodbye to the railroad magnate. Many of St. Louis' most prominent citizens turned out for the service. The casket was draped in an American flag denoting his military service. He is buried on Prospect Avenue near the Lemp mausoleum and across from the Bixby mausoleum.

EDWARD MALLINCKRODT
(JANUARY 21, 1845-FEBRUARY 1, 1928)

Edward Mallinckrodt was one of the wealthiest men in St. Louis at the time of his death in 1928. He grew up working on the family farm in north St. Louis. When he was 18, he became interested in agricultural chemistry after reading a book on the subject. His father agreed to send him and his brother Otto to Germany to study chemistry. They studied for the next three years at the Fresenius laboratory in Wiesbaden and the De Haen Chemical Works near Hanover. The brothers sailed back to the United States in 1867 and, with their elder brother Gustav, they began to manufacture chemicals under the name "G. Mallinckrodt & Company." Their first office was in a small building located on the family farm.

The first decade of the business saw much hardship. In 1876 and 1877, Otto and Gustav, respectively, died within six months of each other. Later that year, Edward Mallinckrodt was the victim of an explosion in the laboratory. He temporarily lost his eyesight but quickly made a full recovery. The one bright moment during this time was his marriage in June 1876 to Jennie Anderson of St. Louis.

He became president when the business was incorporated in 1882 as the "Mallinckrodt Chemical Works." The company prospered for the next 40 years, producing 1,500 chemical products and establishing offices in New York, New Jersey, Toronto, and Montreal. He also established the National Ammonia Company in 1889 and became its president. In addition, he held positions as director of the Missouri Botanical Garden, president of the Mercantile Library, and a board member of Washington University. The plant at 3600 North Second Street was located on a portion of the farm where Mallinckrodt was born.

Mallinckrodt accumulated vast real estate holdings in St. Louis, including the Arcade Building. His substantial wealth enabled him to benefit educational institutions, such as Harvard University, Washington University, and the St. Louis College of Pharmacy. He gave an endowment to St. Louis Children's Hospital to establish the Jennie Mallinckrodt Ward in memory of his wife, who died in 1913. He also gave generously to St. Luke's Hospital, where he was head of the board of trustees.

In 1928, days after his 83rd birthday, Mallinckrodt suffered a heart attack in his home at 16 Westmoreland Place. When a bout of pneumonia followed the attack, he was too weak to fight the illness and died at four o'clock in the morning on Wednesday, February 1. Two days later, on the same day that St. Louis Mayor Victor Miller laid the cornerstone for the new city courthouse, mourners filled Christ Church Cathedral to pay their respects. The *Globe-Democrat* reported, "The casket was covered with a large cross of white on a blanket of green. The chancel contained masses of flowers and greenery."

After the service, Edward Mallinckrodt was buried at Bellefontaine. He rests in a magnificent, white granite mausoleum on Wintergreen Avenue. Above the gated door are his name and the biblical quote,

*Yea though I walk through the valley
of the shadow of death I will fear no evil.*

ROBERT BROOKINGS
(JANUARY 22, 1850-NOVEMBER 15, 1932)

Robert Brookings attended school at West Nottingham Academy in Cecil County, Maryland, but withdrew at the age of 16. He came to St. Louis, where his older brother worked as a "drummer," or traveling salesman, for Cupples & Marston, a manufacturer of wood products. With the help of his brother, Brookings started as a receiving clerk at $25 a month before becoming a traveling salesman like his brother. In 1871, when he was only 21 years old, he was offered a partnership in the business because of his hard work and persistence. Brookings spent the next 25 years building Cupples into a leader in its field. He expanded the company's product line and accumulated a personal fortune before retiring at the age of 46.

In retirement, Brookings turned his attention to Washington University. He was made president of the Washington University Corporation in 1897 and was a contributing factor in making the school one of the most prestigious institutions in the country. He was involved in purchasing property and constructing new buildings for the university, and convinced the board of directors to establish a medical school, the development of which he financed himself. Even his home on Ellenwood Avenue was given to the university as a residence for the chancellor. In 1929, the philanthropist was awarded the honorary degrees, Doctor of Laws and Doctor of Medicine. He previously had received honorary degrees from Harvard, Yale, and the University of Missouri.

In 1917, President Woodrow Wilson appointed Brookings chairman of the Price Fixing Committee of the War Industries Board. His primary responsibility was setting prices on commodities. After World War I, he moved permanently to Washington, D.C., where he was commissioned by President William Taft to do a study of the president's budget plan. In 1923, he established the Robert Brookings Graduate School in Economics and Government, later called the "Brookings Institute." He also was the author of several books on economic theory and government. In June 1927, at the age of 77, he married his longtime friend, Isabel Valle January. She was 26 years his junior.

Brookings had problems with his eyesight in his later years. When he completely lost sight in one eye, he underwent a series of operations at the Wilmer Eye Institute of the Johns Hopkins Hospital in Baltimore. Needing a therapeutic rest to gain back his physical strength, he spent the summer of 1932 at Gloucester, Massachusetts, and Saratoga Springs, New York. By October, he returned to Washington, D. C., but within a short time he came down with chills and a fever that developed into an acute inflammation of the kidneys. He fought the illness for two weeks before his body gave out on November 15.

Senator Harry Hawes, an alumnus of Washington University, said of Brookings, "He had been my friend for thirty years, and, through personal contact and correspondence, I had grown to greatly admire him for his sturdy qualities. He was a very patriotic man, a man of unusual intelligence and stamina and a benefactor to the nation."

A funeral service was held on November 17 at Washington Cathedral. Trustees of the Brookings Institute were the honorary pallbearers. Afterward, the body was cremated and brought to St. Louis by his wife, Isabel, and his nephew, Harry Wallace. On Saturday, November 19, another funeral service took place at Graham Chapel on the campus of Washington University. Classes at the university were canceled for the day. The chapel was filled with civic and business leaders as well as the faculty and students of the university. Brookings' cremated remains rested in a casket covered with a blanket of roses. His six grandnephews served as pallbearers. His ashes were buried in a roadside grave on Amaranth Avenue.

THEODORE LINK
(MARCH 17, 1850-NOVEMBER 12, 1923)

Theodore Link was born near Heidelberg, Germany; he studied architecture and engineering at the École Centrale in Paris. He came to the United States in 1870 and practiced architecture in New York and Philadelphia before coming to St. Louis as a technical representative of the Atlantic & Pacific Railroad Company. In September 1875, he married Annie Fuller; they had four sons and a daughter. The family resided at 628 North Spring Avenue.

He left his railroad position to become assistant chief engineer at Forest Park and, later, the superintendent of public parks for St. Louis. Link went back to the East Coast for a time before returning to St. Louis in 1883 to open his own office in the Chemical Building, where he designed numerous churches, libraries, and other public facilities. He designed the buildings for the Washington University Medical School, including Barnes Hospital, and constructed his share of residences, many in the Clayton and Central West End areas. He served as one of the architects for the 1904 World's Fair, where he designed the Mississippi State House and Metallurgy buildings.

Link was a fellow of the American Institute of Architects and a member of the Missouri State Society of Architects. At one time, he served as president of the St. Louis Artists' Guild.

Link was one of 10 architects from around the country invited to submit designs for a train station in St. Louis. He won the commission in 1891 and set about building the grandest structure in the city. Union Station was comprised of a 750-foot-long main building, a 10-acre train shed and 19 miles of track. The main building is Romanesque in style and built with a limestone and brick façade and red tile roof. Twenty thousand people attended the grand opening on September 1, 1894. In its heyday, more than 100,000 passengers a day passed through the Union Station terminal.

In November 1923, the 73-year-old architect came down with a severe cold while in Baton Rouge, Louisiana, supervising the construction of Louisiana State University and the Greater Agricultural College. His wife, Annie, and son, Clarence, were by his side during his final hours. Theodore Link passed away on November 12. His body was returned to St. Louis two days later for the funeral in the chapel at Wagner Undertaking on Olive Street. He was laid to rest in a roadside grave on Wintergreen Avenue in front of his parents.

DAVID FRANCIS
(OCTOBER 1, 1850-JANUARY 15, 1927)

The *St. Louis Globe-Democrat* announced the passing of one of Missouri's most distinguished citizens on the morning of January 16, 1927:

David Rowland Francis, 76, former Mayor of St. Louis, former Governor of Missouri, former Ambassador to Russia and former Secretary of the Interior in the Cabinet of President Cleveland, died at 6:10 o'clock last night of infirmities of age.

Francis moved to St. Louis from Richmond, Kentucky, and was one of the first graduates of Washington University. After college, he worked with his uncle at Shryock & Rowland, a wholesale grocery house. He established his own commission business in 1884, D. R. Francis & Brother, handling the exportation of grain. During this time, he became vice-president of the St. Louis Merchant's Exchange.

He had a meteoric rise in politics. Francis, a lifelong Democrat, won the election for mayor of St. Louis in 1885, when he was only 35. He was popular during his term and worked hard to improve the city's economic base. Three years later, he became governor of Missouri. As governor, Francis was a strong proponent of public education at both the elementary and university level. He would be a powerful figure in Missouri politics for the rest of his life. For one year, 1896 to 1897, Francis served as Secretary of the Interior for the final year of President Grover Cleveland's term.

When his one term in Jefferson City ended, Francis built a large home on Newstead Avenue. It was there that he and his wife Jane raised six sons. The house was often the center of social activities in the St. Louis area. While in St. Louis for dedication ceremonies of the World's Fair, President Theodore Roosevelt and former President Grover Cleveland were guests at the home. In 1920, Francis leased the house to the Junior Chamber of Commence and the Boy Scouts, and he donated the acreage on Eichelberger Street that is now Francis Park.

Francis returned to private business after his governorship. He owned the *St. Louis Republic* newspaper, which later merged with the *Globe-Democrat*. In October 1919, the Republic published its final issue. Perhaps his greatest achievement for St. Louis was his work on the St. Louis World's Fair. Francis was chairman of the executive committee and president of the exposition company responsible for putting on the fair. On April 30, 1904, Francis conducted the opening ceremonies. Secretary of War William Howard Taft attended for President Roosevelt. Francis Field at Washington University, built during the fair and used as an Olympic site, was named in his honor.

In 1916, Francis served as ambassador to Russia under President Wilson. He left his post at the outbreak of the Russian Revolution. He later wrote of his experiences in his book, *Russia from the American Embassy*, published in 1921. He continued to give his time in support of the Democratic Party.

In 1922, Francis had a mild stroke that left him unable to form some words. His speech continued to deteriorate for the rest of his life. By January 1927, he had been ill and bedridden for much of the past year. According to his granddaughter, "He had nurses around him 24 hours a day." He spent most of his time at his Ellenwood Avenue home, which he had purchased after his wife's death. Five of his six sons were at his bedside, along with his personal physician, when David Francis took his last breath at 6:10 p.m., Saturday, January 15.

On January 18, his body was removed from his house and taken to his former residence on Newstead Avenue. He lay in a casket covered with lilies in the front parlor. Mourners were allowed to view the body before the service. The ceremony was conducted by two Presbyterian ministers and attended by dignitaries from the city, state, and the nation. Ten surviving directors of the World's Fair, as well as former St. Louis mayors Edward Noonon, Rolla Wells, and Henry Kiel, were among those present.

Following the service, the six sons of David Francis carried their father's remains to the hearse. A 35-car procession moved to Bellefontaine Cemetery. David was laid to rest beside his wife, Jane, on Prospect Avenue. In 1924, after the death of his wife, Francis had commissioned a memorial statue for her. The dark, shrouded angel with its head bowed in mourning now watches over Francis and his family.

CHRIS VON DER AHE
(OCTOBER 7, 1851-JUNE 5, 1913)

Chris Von der Ahe was the flamboyant, hard-drinking owner of the St. Louis Browns baseball club. He knew little about the game, once boasting that he had the largest baseball diamond in the game until his manager told him that all baseball diamonds are the same size. He viewed the sport more as a show than a game. He was once referred to as "the P. T. Barnum of baseball" for his tireless showmanship; he even erected a life-sized statue of himself at the front gate of his ballpark. With his thick German accent, he called himself "der poss bresident." And he wasn't without his absurd quirks. After games, the gate receipts were thrown into a wheelbarrow and gallantly pushed down the street to his office. He walked alongside with an armed guard and a smug air of satisfaction.

Von der Ahe was born in Hille, Germany. He came to America and settled in St. Louis in 1870. He opened a grocery with a small saloon at Sullivan and Spring Avenues on the city's north side. When Grand Avenue Grounds was erected across the street, Von der Ahe made his fortune when spectators purchased his grocery products and filled his saloon to capacity before and after games. In 1880, after the collapse of a team called the "Brown Stockings," he and other local businessmen, including Al Spink, later the founder of the *Sporting News*, organized the Sportsman's Park Club and Association. The group took over the lease on the stadium, which they renamed Sportsman's Park, and refurbished the park with a grandstand and bleachers. The group sponsored a professional team also called the Brown Stockings (later shortened to simply the Browns) and helped to establish the American Association, consisting of six teams. That first season of 1882 saw the Browns finish fifth of six teams in the league. Von der Ahe moved his grocery and saloon to a more prominent location at Grand and St. Louis Avenues and bought out his partners' share of the Browns to make himself sole owner of the team.

Von der Ahe's domestic life consisted of three marriages, producing one son, Edward. In 1882, after his Browns had been playing for a year, Von der Ahe organized the American Baseball Association and was named its first president. Under the leadership of manager Charles Comiskey, his St. Louis Browns won pennants from 1885 to 1888. In 1886, they won the baseball championship from the Chicago White Stockings. Von der Ahe was not known for his generosity, as he paid minimal salaries and often fined his players large amounts of money for insubordination. To his credit, he was a baseball innovator; he was the first owner to use a tarpaulin to cover the field on rainy days and the first to sell souvenirs of his team.

The Browns played poorly during the decade of the 1890's. In 1890, Von der Ahe lost several of his best players to a new league called the Player's League, which collapsed after one year. The departure of Charles Comiskey in 1892 brought the team to near collapse. Von der Ahe moved the Browns to a park at Natural Bridge and Vandeventer, the current site of Beaumont High School. When attendance declined, he attempted to draw crowds by staging Wild West shows, fireworks displays, and boxing matches, and even hired an all-female brass band to play between innings.

Von der Ahe was a free spender and faced financial problems that would ultimately liquidate both his fortune and his fame. In 1888, he purchased some apartment buildings in St. Louis; but when the buildings were not profitable, he was forced to sell some of his players to offset the loss.

The beginning of the end, however, happened on April 16, 1898, when a fire broke out in the grandstands during a game. About 100 spectators of the 6,000 in attendance were injured. Lawsuits showered down on Von der Ahe, who had already accumulated massive debts. In 1899, he was forced to sell his players and, finally, the team itself, for $33,000. He then was ousted by the other owners as president of the American Baseball Association.

After the collapse of his baseball empire, Von der Ahe opened a saloon on Market Street across from the Municipal Courts Building, but the saloon closed after a short time. The once wealthy, prominent baseball man was now in financial ruin and fell into obscurity. In the spring of 1908, the St. Louis Browns and St. Louis Cardinals played a preseason series at Sportsman's Park in which the $5,000 in gate receipts for the third game went to the bankrupt Von der Ahe. By January 1913, his health was declining. He was confined to his St. Louis Avenue home, suffering from dropsy and cirrhosis of the liver from his years of hard drinking. In February, he had an emotional visit with his old manager, Charles Comiskey. Von der Ahe told him, "I've got a lot and a nice monument already built for me in Bellefontaine Cemetery." Chris Von der Ahe died at 3:15 in the afternoon of June 6. His third wife, Anna, was by his side.

At two o'clock on Sunday, June 8, the funeral took place in the front parlor of his home. Hundreds of floral arrangements were placed around the casket. Reverend Frederick Craft of the German Evangelical Bethany Church used a baseball analogy for his eulogy: "First base is enlightenment, second base is repentance, third base, faith, and the home plate the heavenly goal! Don't fail to touch second base, for it leads you onward to third. All of us finally reach the home plate, though some may be called out when they slide home." The pallbearers consisted of baseball notables, including former Browns manager Charles Comiskey, then owner of the Chicago White Sox, and Ban Johnson, president of the American League. Al Spink and his brother Charles also were in attendance. After the service, the body was placed in a hearse and taken to the cemetery. Von der Ahe had built his monument at Bellefontaine when he was at the top of his financial game. His life-sized statue, which once stood at his ballpark, now caps his monument at Bellefontaine.

THE BROWN BROTHERS

George Warren Brown, born March 21, 1853, was chairman of the board of Brown Shoe Company, the pioneering shoe manufacturing company he founded in November 1878 and ran for the next 38 years. He had come to St. Louis in April 1873 to work as a shipping clerk at Hamilton-Brown Shoe Company, a wholesale shoe company in which his brother Alanson was president and partner. At the time, shoes were imported to St. Louis from the East Coast, and custom shoemaking was done only for the wealthy. George left the company five years later and established the first successful shoe manufacturing company in St. Louis.

George and Alanson were born and raised in Granville, New York.

Alanson was the older of the two, born March 21, 1847. He worked for a drug and grocery store before coming to St. Louis in 1872; here he met James Hamilton, and together they formed the Hamilton-Brown Shoe Company, with offices at 12th and Washington. Alanson married Ella Bills in 1877; they had six children. The family resided at 4616 Lindell Boulevard.

In 1878, along with two partners, George organized Bryan, Brown, and Company. The business started meagerly, with five shoemakers and little capital. But the company grew, and in 1893 the name was changed to the Brown Shoe Company, with offices at 17th and Washington. The company's *Buster Brown* label became a trademark for children's shoes. George married Betty Bofinger in 1885; the couple lived with their adopted son Wilbur at 40 Portland Place.

Near the end of April 1913, Alanson came down with leucaemia, a rare and incurable disease. He and his family went to San Antonio, Texas, in an attempt to improve his health. On May 10, a telegram from Alanson's son to the *St. Louis Globe-Democrat* read:

Alanson David Brown died here to-day at 11:40. Due notice of funeral will be given.

Besides his wife Ella, two of his four surviving daughters and his son were at his side. The body was returned to St. Louis for the May 14 funeral in his home. Directors of the 1904 World's Fair, of which he was a member, attended the services as a group. All the Hamilton-Brown Shoe factories were closed on the day of the funeral. Reverend Dr. William Williamson of the Third Presbyterian Church presided over the ceremony.

On December 1, 1921, George and his wife went to Tucson, Arizona in an attempt to improve his health, which had begun to fail him 18 months earlier. He had suffered from a bronchial infection for several years, and when it reoccurred his doctors suggested that a warmer climate might help his recovery. But to the surprise of many, he unexpectedly died at 9:00 a.m., Tuesday, December 13. His wife Betty telegraphed the news to St. Louis. Directors of the Brown Shoe Company met the train on Saturday morning and viewed the body of their chairman before it was taken to his home for the funeral.

On Monday, December 19, St. Louis employees of Brown Shoe Company were given the day off. The 2:30 funeral was attended by nearly 250 people and presided over by Reverend Dr. Benjamin Young, pastor of the Union Methodist Church, of which Brown was a member. Officers and directors of Brown Shoe served as pallbearers. At the time of his death, the company employed 6,000 workers in its office and factories.

George is now buried in a hexagonal mausoleum at the corner at Woodbine and Prospect avenues. Inscribed above the iron-gated doors are the words, "God Hath Given Us Eternal Life." His brother, Alanson, is laid to rest in a domed, colonnaded, circular mausoleum across Prospect Avenue.

WILLIAM BURROUGHS & HIS NAMESAKE GRANDSON

William Burroughs had a natural ability with mechanical devices and the inner workings of machines. Born in Auburn, New York, on January 28, 1855, he spent much of his childhood in his father's machine shop. While working as a clerk for a bank, he came up with the idea for a machine that could calculate numbers.

He moved to St. Louis with his idea in 1881. He worked in the factory at Hall & Brown Woodworking Company and spent his free time developing his invention at his machine shop at the Boyer Machine Company on Dickson Street. Finally, in 1885, when he was 35, he built a working model that could do simple mathematical calculations. He established the American Arithmometer Company with three partners and sold stock to finance his machine. Burroughs continued to tinker with his innovation until, in 1891, he built an adding machine that could print out calculations. Two years later, he received a patent for the revolutionary device and started production in conjunction with Boyer Machine Company. As word spread about the ease and usefulness of the adding machine, it sold out quickly to businesses throughout the country.

In 1896, a year before he retired, Burroughs received an honorary medal for his invention from the Franklin Institute in Pennsylvania. He died on Friday, September 15, 1898 in Citronelle, Alabama. He was only 43. He was survived by a wife and four children, ranging in age from 7 to 18. His funeral took place in Citronelle, after which his remains were transported back to St. Louis. His tall, granite obelisk faces the road near Cypress Lake and is inscribed, "Erected by his associates as a tribute to his genius." Seven years after his death, the American Arithmometer Company relocated to Detroit and, in his honor, was renamed the Burroughs Adding Machine Company.

Burroughs' grandson, also named William, was born at the family home on Pershing Avenue on February 5, 1914. He graduated from Harvard with a degree in English before moving to New York City, where he met poet Allen Ginsberg and writer Jack Kerouac. It was in New York that he began a long relationship with Beatnik writers and drug addiction. During his 15-year heroin addiction, he bounced around the globe, living in New Orleans, Mexico City, Paris, London, northern Africa, and South America. In 1951, he accidentally shot his wife in the head while "playing William Tell" during a party in Mexico. He fled Mexico to escape prosecution and was never tried for her death. The couple had a son who died of cirrhosis of the liver in 1981, from his own alcohol and drug problem.

Burroughs' first novel, *Junky*, was published in 1953 under the pen name "William Lee." In his most prominent work, *Naked Lunch*, published in 1959, he coined the phrases "Steely Dan" and "heavy metal." He often invoked themes of homosexuality, drugs, and science fiction in the story lines of his two dozen books. Many of his writings contained references to St. Louis landmarks, such as Forest Park and the Mississippi River. Burroughs is among the celebrities on the cover of the Beatles album, *Sgt. Pepper's Lonely Hearts Club Band*.

The "Beat Generation" author died on Saturday, August 2, 1997, in a Lawrence, Kansas hospital, one day after suffering a heart attack. He had been living in Kansas since 1981. Burroughs is buried in an unmarked grave in the family plot.

John Queeny
(August 17, 1859-March 19, 1933)

"John Francis Queeny, Philanthropist, Head of Monsanto Co., Dies," read the *St. Louis Globe-Democrat* headline.

Queeny was born in Chicago and was 11 years old in October 1871 when the Great Chicago Fire destroyed thousands of buildings and took hundreds of lives. His father, John, had lost property in the fire. Queeny's first job was with Tolman and King, a wholesale drug company. From there, he took a position in 1891 as buyer for Meyer Brothers Drug Company in St. Louis.

At the time, many chemical companies used saccharin as a sweetener. Saccharin had to be purchased from Germany because no company in the United States produced it. In 1901, Queeny established his own small chemical company to produce the much-needed saccharin and other products. He called his firm "Monsanto" after his wife, Olga Monsanto Queeny. The office was located at 1812 South Second Street and employed three people. The business expanded quickly, aided by the fact that Monsanto was the only company in America producing saccharin. The company went on to make vanilla and aspirin.

He became chairman of the board of Monsanto in 1927 when his son Edgar ascended to the presidency. At that time, the company employed more than 2,000 people and had branches in the U. S. and England. He once owned the old Southern Hotel and was a member of many city organizations, including the Missouri Historical Society, and was director of the Lafayette-South Side Bank and Trust Company. He also was known for his generous charitable donations and educational philanthropy.

By early 1933, Queeny's health was declining from a malignant tumor. On March 19, his wife and son Edgar were at his bedside when he died at the age of 74. His body was taken to the Arthur Donnelly Mortuary on Lindell, where visitation took place. On March 21, a private family funeral was held before burial on a steep hill at Bellefontaine.

ALBERT LAMBERT
(DECEMBER 6, 1875-NOVEMBER 12, 1946)

Aviation pioneer Albert Bond Lambert was born in St. Louis and started his career working in his father's drug business, Lambert Pharmaceutical Company, where he was an executive for many years. He began to cultivate his interest in air travel around 1906, when he met several international balloon pilots in Paris. He held balloon license No. 18, dated 1907. He formed the Aero Club of St. Louis to promote the sport of ballooning by staging races and air shows. His first airplane flight was with Orville Wright, and he so enjoyed it that he took flight instruction. He was given pilot license No. 61 in September 1911, the first St. Louisan to have a private pilot's license. With the advent of airplanes, Lambert envisioned the explosion of what he considered the best form of transportation. Lambert wrote, "There is something about being an early bird that makes one feel kind of proud, with a degree of satisfaction in looking back over our many trials and tribulations during the early progress and traditions of aviation – and then visualize it as it is today."

In 1910, Lambert helped to organize a 10-day aviation meet that included former president Theodore Roosevelt's first plane flight. Roosevelt thus became the first American president to fly in an airplane. Lambert flew at an exhibition at Fairgrounds Park in 1911 and established an air mail route within the city. During World War I, Major Lambert trained pilots. He was discharged in 1919, and one year later began working to transform his 550-acre cornfield in Bridgeton, called "Kinloch Field," into an airfield. Upon its completion, he maintained the new Lambert Field at his own expense. He was the first man to land a plane at the airfield. In 1923, Lambert Field hosted an international air race, which brought Charles A.

Lindbergh to St. Louis for the first time. Lindbergh stayed, and became a pilot for an air mail route between St. Louis and Chicago operated by the Robertson Aircraft Company. Lambert was one of the financial backers of Lindbergh's *Spirit of St. Louis* and his transatlantic flight in 1927. The next year, in accordance with an earlier agreement, Lambert sold his airfield to the city of St. Louis. Politically, he served the city with his election to the City Council in 1907, and later as president of the Police Board.

Lambert and his wife, Myrtle, were married in 1899 and lived at 2 Hortense Place. Tragedy struck the family in 1929 when one of their three sons was killed in a plane crash. On Monday, November 11, 1946, he worked on his expansion plans for Lambert Field at his North Kingshighway office. He was in good health when he went to bed that evening. Early the next morning, Lambert died in his sleep; family members found him around 9:00 a.m. A physician was summoned and pronounced him dead of heart disease. He was 70. Mayor Kaufmann said of the aviator, "In the passing of Major Albert Bond Lambert, St. Louis has lost a distinguished and valuable citizen. He was truly our leading pioneer in aviation. He believed in it, and seeing its great potential when most other men were scoffing, he lived to see many of his plans materialize."

Flags at Lambert Field were lowered to half-mast for one week. Reverend Rufus Putney of the Prince of Peace Church led the prayers at the funeral service in Lambert's home. Governor Lloyd Stark and Mayor Aloys P. Kaufmann were among those in attendance. Policemen on motorcycles escorted the body to Bellefontaine Cemetery. A large, white cross with the "Lambert" name adorns the hillside grave off of Woodbine Avenue.

WILLIAM DEE BECKER
(OCTOBER 23, 1876-AUGUST 1, 1943)

The August 2, 1943, issue of the *St. Louis Globe-Democrat* told the story:

> *Mayor William Dee Becker and five other city and county leaders were among 10 persons killed yesterday afternoon when a wing broke from an army glider in which they were riding at Lambert-St. Louis Field and the craft plummeted 2000 feet to the field as 5000 horrified spectators watched. It was the worst air disaster in the history of St. Louis.*

William Becker was born in East St. Louis, Illinois, but his family moved to the Missouri side of the river when he was three. He attended Harvard before returning home to study law at the St. Louis Law School, forerunner to Washington University School of Law. He was admitted to the bar and served as a judge on the St. Louis Court of Appeals from 1917 to 1940.

Becker married Margaret Louise McIntosh in 1902. The couple lived for a time on Lindell Boulevard before moving to an apartment on Delmar. In 1940, while still serving as a judge, Becker won the election for mayor of St. Louis. As mayor, he was a proponent of aviation and its benefits. He wanted St. Louis to be the center of flight in the coming decades, and pushed for the needed expansion of Lambert Field and development of a second airport. His other priorities were to clean up blighted neighborhoods in the city and develop the riverfront. Sadly, the aviation mayor didn't have the time to achieve his goals.

On Sunday, August 1, 1943, thousands of spectators gathered for an air show at Lambert Field. Around three o'clock in the afternoon, Mayor Becker and several city and county officials were interviewed over the public address system before their flight on an army glider. For most of the officials, it was their first ride in a glider. Mayor Becker's wife told the crowd, "I want to go up too. I'm pretty angry with the army because it won't let me." The men then boarded a glider designed and built by Robertson Aircraft Corporation. The glider, towed by a 150-foot cable from a C-47 airplane, had made a successful test flight earlier in the day. The plane took off and circled the airfield twice to gain altitude. On the third pass, directly in front of the main body of spectators, the airplane released the glider at about 3,000 feet. Almost immediately, the right wing of the glider buckled and separated from the fuselage. The glider was sent spinning toward the tarmac. The occupants were equipped with parachutes but could not save themselves in the twisting descent. Within seconds, the glider hit the ground in a horrific crash; its estimated speed at impact was 230 miles an hour. The time was 3:55 p.m.

Emergency crews rushed to the scene. When the dust cleared, wreckage could be seen strewn about the field. The spectators were stunned. One observer told the *Globe-Democrat*, "Women all around me were screaming and fainting. I saw men with their eyes staring straight ahead as if they were hypnotized... Many covered their eyes or turned their heads as the crash came, as if hoping to thus avert the catastrophe." All the bodies were recovered. Albert Bond Lambert had been scheduled to be aboard the glider but missed the flight while admiring the gliders on display in the hanger.

Aloys P. Kaufmann, president of the Board of Aldermen, was sworn in as mayor of St. Louis on August 2. He called for flags to fly at half-mast until after the funerals. William Becker was the second mayor to die

in office. (Arthur Barret had died within a few months of taking office in 1875.) Letters of condolence were received from the governor of Missouri and civic and business leaders throughout the bi-state area. Archbishop John Glennon paid tribute to the mayor and sympathized with the families.

Mrs. Becker was grief-stricken by the death of her husband and was unresponsive to the reporters that clamored outside her home. On August 2, Mayor Becker lay in state in the chapel at Lupton Funeral Home on Delmar Boulevard. Hundreds filed past his closed gray casket. In a bit of irony, William had paid his respects to a friend at Lupton on his way to the airport for the glider flight. In less than 24 hours, he himself was resting in the same chapel.

August 3 was proclaimed a day of mourning in the city of St. Louis. At two o'clock, as Mayor Becker's funeral began, all businesses in the city suspended operation for one minute. The funeral took place at the Scottish Rite Cathedral on Lindell Boulevard. Twenty-five hundred people were in attendance; another thousand waited outside. Dignitaries included Missouri Governor Forrest Donnell and the three current judges on the Court of Appeals, which Becker had once served. Reverend C. Oscar Johnson of the Third Baptist Church celebrated the service. He called Becker "one of God's noblemen, a great human being, a man who loved people, a man who sought to help the poor and the downtrodden."

After the service, a procession of a dozen cars made their way to Bellefontaine Cemetery for a private ceremony. Hundreds of onlookers were at the cemetery when the procession arrived. Reverend Johnson recited a short prayer, bringing the service to a close. Becker is buried along Wintergreen Avenue, across from Edward Mallinckrodt.

Besides Mayor Becker, the other men on the glider included:

CHARLES CUNNINGHAM, the deputy comptroller for the city of St. Louis. His funeral, at St. Rose's Catholic Church on Goodfellow, was attended by Mayor Kaufmann and members of the Board of Aldermen. His burial took place at Calvary Cemetery.

JACK DAVIS was a private in the 71st Troop Carrier Command. He was the mechanic for the glider. His remains were cremated, and his ashes were taken to Indianapolis for burial at Fort Benjamin Harrison Cemetery.

MAX DOYNE was the director of public utilities for the city of St. Louis. Mayor Kaufmann and other city officials attended the funeral at Herman Rindskopf Funeral Home on Delmar. Rabbi Julian Miller quoted Mayor Becker as saying of Doyne, "He is my right-hand man -- I never made a better appointment." Burial was at New Mt. Sinai Cemetery on Gravois Road.

THOMAS DYSART was president of the St. Louis Chamber of Commerce. The brief service at Christ Church Cathedral was filled to capacity. He was laid to rest at Bellefontaine.

PAUL HAZALTON was Lieutenant Colonel of the Army Air Force in St. Louis. A military chaplain performed the funeral in the chapel at Jefferson Barracks. His body was cremated and sent to National Cemetery in Arlington, Virginia.

MILTON KLUGH was the pilot of the ill-fated glider. He was a captain with the 71st Troop Carrier Command. He had eight years of experience flying gliders and was considered one of the best glider pilots in the country. His body was cremated and sent to New York for a funeral at the Church of Heavenly Rest.

HAROLD KRUEGER was vice-president and chief engineer at Robertson Aircraft Corporation. His funeral took place in his hometown of Glen Ellyn, Illinois.

HENRY MUELLER was the presiding judge of the County Court of St. Louis County. He was invited aboard the glider moments before takeoff. Funeral services were held at the George Pleitsch Funeral Home on Easton Avenue. He was buried in Lake Charles Cemetery.

WILLIAM ROBERTSON was president of Robertson Aircraft. He was an aviation pioneer who worked with Albert Lambert to select a site for the airport. Robertson employed Charles Lindbergh as an air mail pilot for his St. Louis-to-Chicago air service. The glider that took his life was manufactured of plywood at his Oleatha Avenue plant. Robertson's funeral was at St. Michael and St. George Episcopal Church on Wydown Boulevard. Employees of Robertson Aircraft were present, as were various military personnel. He was laid to rest at Bellefontaine.

SARA TEASDALE
(AUGUST 8, 1884-JANUARY 28, 1933)

Teasdale's life was cast in the same mold as Emily Dickinson and Elizabeth Barrett: she spent most of her life in a depressed and unhappy state and often lived as if impoverished. She was shy and spent much of her youth alone in her room, writing poetry. Her style was simple, straightforward, and classical, usually written in the form of sonnets and quatrains. The St. Louis-born poet, who attended Mary Institute and Washington University, grew up with an obsessive fear of illness and dying. In one of her sonnets, called *Fear*, she wrote:

> *The cold black fear is clutching me to-night*
> *As long ago when they would take the light*
> *And leave the little child who would have prayed,*
> *Frozen and sleepless at the thought of death.*

Her first book of poetry, *Sonnets to Duse and Other Poems*, was published in 1907 and established her as a major figure in poetry. The book was published by William Marion Reedy, the well-known editor of the *Mirror*. In 1918, her book entitled *Love Songs* won the Columbia University Poetry Society prize, forerunner of the Pulitzer Prize for poetry.

In 1914, she married Ernst Filsinger, owner of a St. Louis shoe manufacturing company, at her family's fashionable home at 38 Kingsbury Place. A few years later, she and her husband moved to New York City, where she had lived before the wedding. The marriage conflicted with her constantly hopeless and painful view of life, living within herself in silent desperation. The couple was incompatible and divorced, childless, in 1929. She went on to live her life as she was accustomed, as a semi-invalid.

Her feelings toward St. Louis were mixed, once calling it a "howling wilderness." Shortly after returning to St. Louis for her marriage, she claimed, "For the first time in years St. Louis seems really a good sort of place."

In 1932, while doing research work in London, she came down with pneumonia in both lungs. The illness exacerbated her depression, and her health declined steadily after she arrived back in New York in September. She was unable, and perhaps unwilling, to shake the effects of the pneumonia. The bedridden poet was cared for by her sister Mamie and friend Margaret Conklin. Teasdale spent her time reading her favorite authors and writing to friends. In one such letter to a poet friend, she wrote, "The illness seemed to me a becoming time to make my final exit. But apparently that is to be delayed, and I am not too glad."

Mamie knew her sister was becoming dangerously depressed. Teasdale was taking sleeping pills at an alarming rate, so Mamie hired Rita Brown, a nurse, to be with her constantly. By December, Teasdale convinced herself that her blood vessels were ready to rupture and a stroke was immediate. Her doctor made no such claim. It was another example of her hysterical obsession with illness and dying. Before the year was out, she went to Winter Park, Florida, to stay with a friend. For two weeks she lay alone in a darkened room waiting for death to take her.

By mid-January she was back in New York. On the 27th, a blood vessel broke in her hand. She was convinced that her long-predicted stroke would now occur and gave Mamie the power of attorney for her estate in case she was debilitated. The doctor agreed with the family that a psychiatrist should be called in. Margaret Conklin spent the evening of January 28 with Teasdale listening to Beethoven's Fifth Symphony.

In the early morning hours of Sunday the 29th, Teasdale drew a bath, lay in the warm water, and closed her eyes. She had taken a heavy dose of sleeping pills while Rita Brown was sleeping. At 9:00 a.m., the nurse checked Teasdale's room but didn't find the poet in bed. Brown searched the apartment and discovered the body in the bathroom.

Reporters were already at the door by the time Mamie arrived. The coroner's preliminary report suggested that it was an accidental death caused by "chronic pneumonia" and "submersion in tub." The newspaper quickly reported the death as accidental and not suicide. On January 30, the same day that Adolf Hitler became Chancellor of Germany, the *St. Louis Post-Dispatch* ran the headline, "Accidental Death, Autopsy Report on Sara Teasdale." The final coroner's report, however, showed signs of morphine and phenobarbital in her system. This report was never made public.

On Wednesday, February 1, funeral services were conducted at Grace Episcopal Church in New York City. Her body was cremated, and the ashes buried in Bellefontaine Cemetery. A small, simple monument marks her final resting place. Mamie did not honor her sister's wishes that her ashes be scattered at sea, "that there may remain neither trace nor remembrance."

Margaret Conklin edited the final version of Teasdale's last book, *Strange Victory*. The volume was published in October 1933.

JAMES MCDONNELL
(APRIL 9, 1899-AUGUST 22, 1980)

James McDonnell, Jr., built his dream into an aviation empire that employed more St. Louisans than any other local company. The Denver native attended school in Little Rock, Arkansas, after his family moved to the Midwest. After high school, he attended Princeton University, and it was as a freshman there that he took his first airplane ride. Years later,

he said, "It was the first time I went up in an airplane, and I liked it. It confirmed the interest I felt I had in aviation."

World War I broke out while he was still an undergraduate, so he postponed his studies to join the army. After the war, he finished his education at Princeton before receiving a master's degree from M.I.T., where he studied the physical mechanics of airplanes and flight. He then joined the U.S. Army Air Corps Flying School in San Antonio. It was there that he became one of the first soldiers to make a parachute jump.

McDonnell concluded his military service and began a career working for several aircraft companies. In 1928, he suffered a serious back injury when he crash landed a plane he was piloting. In 1939, after working as an aeronautical engineer in Baltimore, he moved to St. Louis to lay the foundation for his own aircraft manufacturing company. St. Louis offered everything he needed to launch a successful business: an established airfield and experienced aircraft workers. In July, McDonnell Aircraft Corporation rented a second-floor office in a building near Lambert Field. McDonnell oversaw every aspect of his business, which consisted of an office staff of two men. His company had no sales or earnings during the first year.

He married Mary Finney in 1934; she passed away from cancer in 1949. They had two sons, James III and John, who would succeed their father at McDonnell-Douglas. He later married Priscilla Forney and adopted her son and two daughters.

When the United States entered World War II, the demand for military aircraft exploded, and McDonnell employed more than 5,000 people to produce aircraft components, mostly for Douglas Aircraft Company. McDonnell's first major government contract in 1942 was the building of the FH-1 Phantom, the first carrier-based jet fighter. He later built the Whirlaway, the first twin-engine helicopter. McDonnell was cementing his position at the forefront of aircraft manufacturers. With the advent of space flight, he won a NASA contract in 1959 to build the Mercury capsule, in which astronaut John Glenn orbited the earth. He later built the larger Gemini spacecraft. In 1967, when Douglas Aircraft Company merged with McDonnell Aircraft, McDonnell was named chairman and chief executive officer. One year later, the company began producing the DC-10 wide-body jet.

In 1972, his nephew, Sanford McDonnell, was named the chief executive officer, while McDonnell stayed on as chairman of the board. The philanthropic arm of the company, the McDonnell Foundation, made tremendous contributions to Washington University, St. Louis Country Day School, and the McDonnell Planetarium.

In August 1980, the 81-year-old McDonnell suffered a stroke, which dissipated his strength and led to his death on Friday the 22nd. Flags at McDonnell-Douglas were lowered to half-mast in honor of their leader. His company, which started with two workers, employed more than 83,000 St. Louisans at the time of his death.

Graham Chapel at Washington University hosted the August 30 funeral. Management officials at McDonnell-Douglas were joined by other business and political leaders, such as August Busch III and Senator John Danforth. Chancellor of Washington University William Danforth gave the eulogy. Music was performed by the St. Louis Symphony Brass Ensemble. The burial at Bellefontaine was private. The McDonnell family lot gently slopes toward the road, with a row of shrubs on either side of the garden bench monument.

THE LEMP FAMILY

The Lemp story is one of great success and affluence -- and terrible tragedy. Johann Adam Lemp was born in Germany and left the fatherland in 1838 to come to St. Louis, where he established A. Lemp & Company, a family grocery at the corner of Sixth and Morgan. He expanded the business to manufacturing vinegar and later, when the explosion of the German population in St. Louis led to large beer sales, to brewing beer. He soon quit the grocery business to concentrate all his resources in beer production. In 1840, the family business was born under the name "Western Brewery," located at 37 South Second Street at Walnut, near the current location of the Gateway Arch.

Lemp and his wife Justine had one child, William, who was born in Germany on February 21, 1836, two years before the Lemps came to St. Louis. William was educated at St. Louis University before joining his father at Western Brewery and, later, forming his own brewery with Wilhelm Stumpf. William enlisted in the army during the Civil War and soon after married Julia Feickert. The couple had nine children.

Adam Lemp died on August 23, 1862, and was buried at Bellefontaine near the Joseph Charless family lot. Upon his father's death, William returned to Western Brewery, where he developed an ability to foresee developing trends. In 1864, he undertook a major expansion of the brewery and built a new plant at what is now DeMenil Place and Cherokee. The plant was located directly over a maze of natural caves, which were used for refrigeration and aging of the beer. The Lemps' mansion stood nearby on South 13th Street. By 1875, William Lemp was the largest brewer in St. Louis, producing 42,000 barrels a year. He was popular among the citizens of St. Louis and was on the board of several organizations, including the St. Louis World's Fair Committee, but he would not live long enough to see the Fair.

On November 1, 1892, the business was incorporated under the name "William J. Lemp Brewing Company." William, Jr., was made vice-president, and another son, Louis, was given the title of superintendent. By the end of the century, the brewery employed more than one thousand people and was producing 500,000 barrels a year, with sales of $3,500,000. The Lemps' most popular brand was *Falstaff*.

William, Jr., was born in St. Louis on August 13, 1867. He attended Washington University and the United States Brewers Academy in New York. He was well known for his outgoing, flamboyant lifestyle. He married Lillian Handlan in 1899; they had one child, William III. The couple lived at 3343 South 13th Street. Louis was born on January 11, 1870. He learned the brewing trade from some of the best master brewers in Germany. He was active in political and civic organizations in St. Louis and was a successful breeder of horses. In 1906, he sold his interest in the brewery and moved to New York City to work full time with horses. He and his wife Agnes had one daughter, Louise. He died on October 7, 1931, in his New York apartment. Years later, Louise had her parents' ashes placed in the mausoleum at Bellefontaine.

The original heir apparent to the brewery was William's son, Frederick. He was born on November 20, 1873, and attended both Washington University and the U. S. Brewers Academy. He was the most ambitious and hard-working member of the Lemp children. In the summer of 1901, the 27-year-old was ill and left St. Louis to recover in Pasadena, California. His health improved steadily and he was planning to return to St. Louis when he suffered a relapse and died on December 12, 1901, with his wife and daughter by his side. The cause of death was heart failure. His parents were devastated by the loss of their young son. In 1902, William erected a magnificent mausoleum at a cost of $60,000 to honor his son. It is the largest mausoleum in Bellefontaine, located directly across Prospect Avenue from the Wainwright Tomb.

William was dealt another blow in January 1904, when another Frederick, his closest friend, Milwaukee brewer Frederick Pabst, died. One of William's three daughters was married to Pabst's son, Gustav. William's physical and mental health declined during the next month, and he paid little attention to the brewery. On February 13, 1904, his depression grew unbearable. When he awoke in the morning, he was not feeling well. After breakfast at 9:30 a.m., he returned to his bedroom at Lemp mansion and shot himself in the head with a revolver. When a servant found the bedroom door locked, she went to the brewery to find his sons, William, Jr., and Edwin. They broke the door down and found their father lying on the bed, the gun still in his right hand. He was still breathing but unconscious. The Lemp family doctor and three other doctors arrived to examine William, but they could do nothing. William died at 10:15 a.m., just as his wife Julia returned home. No suicide note was found. His estate and brewery were worth an estimated $16 million at the time of his death.

The funeral took place the next day in the mansion's south parlor. The brewery was closed for the day and employees came to pay their respects before the private service. Dr. Max Hemple of the German Ethical Society celebrated the service in German. Adolphus Busch, a longtime friend of Lemp, was an honorary pallbearer. At 2:30 in the afternoon, a procession of 40 carriages made for the cemetery. Lemp was laid to rest in the family mausoleum two months before the St. Louis World's Fair. His crypt was left unsealed so that two of his children, who were out of the country when their father died, could see him one final time. His wife Julia died of cancer in April 1906. In 1911, the Lemp mansion was converted into new offices for the brewery.

William, Jr., took over the brewery after the Fair closed in November 1904. He and his wife, Lillian, were involved in a very public divorce in February 1909. The trial took place at the Old Courthouse and was the talk of the town. A year later, William moved to Alswel, a country estate in Webster Groves overlooking the Meramec River. He married Ellie Limberg in May 1915.

Elsa Lemp, the youngest of William, Sr., and Julia's children, was born on February 8, 1883. In 1910, she married Thomas Wright, the president of a St. Louis metal company. They were divorced in 1919, but remarried the next year. The couple lived at 13 Hortense Place. Elsa often suffered from acute indigestion and nausea, which aroused bouts of depression. At 8:45 on the morning of March 19, 1920, Elsa Lemp Wright shot herself in the chest. Her husband heard the shot and came into the bedroom to find her lying on the bed with the revolver in her hand. Her eyes were open and she tried to speak but was unable to do so. She died moments later, leaving no explanation for the tragic suicide. Her brothers, William, Jr., and Edwin, came to the house, as did Samuel Fordyce, a family friend. Upon arriving,

William was quoted as saying, "This is the Lemp family for you." On March 23, a short service took place at the house before her burial in the Bellefontaine mausoleum.

The passing of the 18th Amendment in January 1920 had devastating effects on the Lemp family business.   Prohibition forced brewers around the country to produce new products in order to survive. Like many brewers, the Lemps produced a "near beer." However, the product was not profitable, and when the family became disinterested in developing new products, William decided to close the plant and liquidate the assets. He sold the *Falstaff* trademark to Joseph Griesedieck for $25,000. In June 1922, the Lemp Brewery was auctioned off to the highest bidder.

William was despondent over the closing of the brewery and felt responsible for the collapse of the business his grandfather Adam had started more than 80 years earlier. As with other members in the family, his mental health was unstable. On December 29, 1922, at nine in the morning, he sat in his office at the mansion. He told his secretary, Henry Vahlkamp, that he was not feeling well. A short time later, William pulled a revolver from his desk drawer and, like his sister, shot himself in the chest. Vahlkamp and other employees rushed in and found him on the floor by his desk. He was still alive. They summoned a doctor, but it was too late. William III fell to his knees beside his father and cried. His wife Ellie was notified at their apartment in the Chase Hotel.

The funeral took place at two o'clock on New Year's Eve in the offices at the mansion. William was placed in the mausoleum above his sister Elsa.

William's brother, Charles, also worked for the brewery but later went into banking and finance. He was a recluse who never married. In 1929, he moved back into the mansion, where he would live the remainder of his life. At age 77, with his health declining because of arthritis, he shot himself in his bedroom. It was eight o'clock in the morning, May 10, 1949, when a servant found Charles with a gunshot wound to his head. He was the fourth Lemp to commit suicide and third to die in the mansion. He was the only Lemp, however, to leave a suicide note. He wrote, "In case I am found dead blame it on no one but me." Edwin carried out Charles' funeral instructions for cremation and burial on his farm. No funeral ceremony was conducted, nor was the death announced. After Charles' death, the Lemp Mansion became a boarding house. In 1977, a restaurant opened in the mansion.

Edwin Lemp was the last surviving member of William's children. In 1911, he moved to Cragwold, his estate in Kirkwood. Two years later, he left the family business and retired at the age of 33. Edwin was 90 when he died on November 30, 1970. He never spoke of the family tragedies. He is buried in the Lemp family mausoleum.

William's son, William III, attempted to revive the brewery after Prohibition was repealed. He took over Central Brewers in East St. Louis, Illinois, and in 1939 changed the name to William J. Lemp Brewing Company. The brewery had financial troubles from the start and eventually declared bankruptcy. William III died on March 12, 1943; he was only 42. He also is buried in the mausoleum, above his brother Edwin.

The Spink Family

For more than 100 years, the *Sporting News* has been a publishing institution in St. Louis. It was the first paper to compile statistics on batting average and fielding percentage. The paper's roots began with Al Spink. The native of Quebec, Canada, was born on August 26, 1853. He started his journalism career as a reporter for the *New York Times* and the *New York Herald* before working for the *St. Louis Post-Dispatch* and the *St. Louis Chronicle*. In the early 1880's, he helped to establish the St. Louis Browns with Chris Von der Ahe and is credited with naming the ballpark, Sportsman's Park. Spink established the *Sporting News* on March 17, 1886, with an eight-page publication that sold for five cents. His brother Charles joined him as manager of the paper.

Spink lived at 3449 South Grand Avenue with his wife Bertha and their four children. He sold his shares in the paper to Charles in 1894 and left the paper five years later. He moved to Chicago and died in his Oak Park home on May 27, 1928. Baseball Commissioner Kenesaw Mountain Landis eulogized him at the May 29 funeral. "The last few months of his life were a period of torture and suffering, and yet throughout it all his first consideration was for others lest his condition add to the burden of those around him." He was 74 when he was buried in Chicago's Woodlawn Cemetery.

When Charles Spink bought out the publishing business from his brother, baseball was enjoying such great popularity that Charles devoted his entire publication to the game. The *Sporting News* became known as the "Baseball Bible." The paper's income was supplemented by trade publications such as the *Sporting Goods Dealer* and *Toys and Novelties*. His position afforded him the opportunity to develop friendships with the likes of Ban Johnson, president of the American League, and Charles Comiskey, former St. Louis Browns manager and owner of the Chicago White Sox.

Charles Spink was born in Quebec, Canada. He lived with his wife Marie, two daughters and a son at 5235 Lindell Boulevard. On April 20, 1914, he was taken to St. Luke's Hospital, suffering from acute indigestion. He had been battling the ailment for two years, and his newest attack was not thought to be life threatening. Two days later, however, he underwent surgery for acute intestinal trouble, but never regained consciousness. He died in the hospital at 2:00 a.m., April 22, at the age of 51. His brother Al was by his side. He left his wife and children an estate worth an estimated $1,000,000.

His son Taylor said of him, "My father was a self-made man. He fought for everything throughout his life, and with such men, of such brilliant character, seemingly the easiest thing is to die, realizing, like all of us, that our time must come at some time and God's will must be done." An Episcopal service was held on April 23 in Charles' home. Pallbearers included Charles Comiskey and William Dee Becker. Charles was buried in the Spink mausoleum on the north side of Woodbine Avenue.

Charles' son, John George Taylor Spink, born November 6, 1888, took over the paper after his father died. Twenty-six-year old Taylor had married a week before his father's death and was on his honeymoon in Chicago when his father became ill. He had joined the paper as an office boy at 18, and in the end ran the paper for 48 years, longer than his father and uncle combined. He was a driven man, often working 16 hours a day, 7 days a week. He continued to devote the paper exclusively to baseball, just as his father had done. He was the official scorekeeper for 11 World Series and, in 1919, helped to uncover the Black Sox scandal. He also published the *Official Baseball Guide* and the *Baseball Register*.

Taylor suffered from emphysema for many years. He spent time in Arizona in February 1962, and upon returning to St. Louis was confined to bed. He was stricken with a heart attack and died in his home at 631 East Polo Drive in Clayton on Friday, December 7, 1962. The official cause of death was heart disease. His was survived by his wife Blanche, one daughter and a son, C.C. Johnson Spink. The Saturday funeral was conducted by Reverend J. Francis Sant at Lupton Chapel on Delmar. August Busch, Jr., who was among the baseball executives in attendance said, "Baseball and Taylor Spink were and are inseparable." Taylor was buried in the family mausoleum. Two months before his death, in October 1962, the Baseball Writers' Association had established a writer's award in his name at the Hall of Fame.

Globe-Democrat columnist Bob Burnes wrote of him upon his death:

> *There is no particular category into which he fits. You could supply a dozen adjectives, some of them pleasant, some of them complimentary and some otherwise, and they wouldn't describe all the sides of this man who built his publication into a remarkably fine sounding board for baseball.*

The fourth member of the Spink family to serve as editor and publisher of the *Sporting News* was Taylor's son, C.C. Johnson Spink. He was born in St. Louis on October 31, 1916, and named after his grandfather Charles and Ban Johnson. He was schooled at St. Louis Country Day, Culver Military Academy, and Trinity College in Hartford, Connecticut, and served in the Coast Guard and as a war correspondent during World War II. In the 1960's, he moved the paper away from its sole coverage of baseball and converted the format to cover all sports. Johnson received numerous civic awards for his work in the community and was a physical fitness advocate who served on President Eisenhower's Council on Physical Fitness. He served as publisher of the *Sporting News* until January 1977, when he sold his interest to the Times-Mirror Corporation. He continued as a consultant until his retirement five years later.

Johnson died after a brief illness in 1992. He was survived by his wife Edith, the former mayor of Ladue. His funeral Mass was celebrated at the Church of St. Michael and St. George in Clayton. He joined his father and grandfather at rest in the Spink Mausoleum.

Other Notables at Bellefontaine

PETER LINDELL (MARCH 24, 1776-OCTOBER 26, 1861) was a native of Worcester County, Maryland. He was a successful merchant who came to St. Louis in December 1811 and was befriended by Manuel Lisa. His three brothers, Robert, Jesse, and John, followed him to St. Louis and assisted him at the family general store on Main Street. The extensive inventory of goods made the store a huge success. The brothers were wealthy when they left the merchant business in 1824.

Under Peter's leadership, they amassed an even larger fortune when they began to buy real estate in the heart of St. Louis. They accumulated 40 blocks, and another 1,200 acres outside the city limits. They also ran the Lindell Hotel on Washington Avenue. Lindell Boulevard, which once ran down the middle of his property, is named for him. Peter, a lifelong bachelor, died suddenly and unexpectedly in 1861; at the time, he was worth approximately $6,000,000. A large obelisk marks the final resting place of Peter and Jesse (died February 2, 1858) in the Lindell family lot.

FREDERICK DENT (OCTOBER 6, 1783-DECEMBER 15, 1873) was the father-in-law of Ulysses S. Grant and one-time owner of the Grant's Farm property. The Cumberland, Maryland, native was a soldier and fur trader who purchased the White Haven estate from Ann Lucas Hunt. Dent and his wife, Ellen, had eight children, the most prominent of whom was their daughter Julia. Although Dent was not pleased with his daughter's selection for a husband, Grant and Julia married in August 1848 at Dent's city home at Fourth and Cerre. James Longstreet, later a Confederate General, was a member of the wedding party.

When Grant was president, Dent spent a good amount of time at the White House and died there in December 1873 after slipping into a coma. According to Bellefontaine burial records, the cause of death was "old age." He was 89. The funeral was conducted in the Blue Room. President Grant accompanied the body back to St. Louis for burial. Dent's wife, Ellen, who died and was buried at White Haven in 1857, was reinterred beside her husband.

Julia Dent died December 14, 1902, and was buried with her husband in Grant's Tomb in New York City.

SAMUEL HAWKEN (OCTOBER 26, 1792-MAY 9, 1884) was the gunsmith who, with his brother **Jacob** (1786-1849), designed the Hawken rifle. Their shop was located on Washington Avenue. Their invention, the most advanced rifle of its time, was used from the Alleghenies to the Rocky Mountains by men like Kit Carson and Buffalo Bill Cody. Hawken also founded Union Fire Company No. 2 and became one of the best volunteer firemen in the city.

Hawken was born in Hagerstown, Maryland, and fought in the War of 1812 before coming to St. Louis in 1822. He died at his son-in-law's farm of "debility senile" at the age of 92. A large crowd attended his funeral on Sunday, May 11, at the First Presbyterian Church on 14th and Lucas. His roadside grave marker on Vine Avenue, which was erected by grandsons, depicts his famous rifle, etched in the granite.

VIRGINIA MINOR (MARCH 27, 1824-AUGUST 14, 1894) was a prominent leader in the women's suffrage movement in the mid- to late 19th century. She was born in Goochland County, Virginia, and received most of her education at home. She married her relative, attorney Francis Minor, in 1843, and moved to St. Louis a year later. During the Civil War, Minor volunteered at hospitals to care for the sick and wounded.

In 1866, their only child died at the age of 14. That same year, Minor thrust herself into the advancement of women by establishing the Woman Suffrage Association of Missouri and becoming its president. At the suffrage convention held in St. Louis in 1869, she made an emotional speech that brought her national attention and propelled the suffragist cause around the country.

On October 15, 1872, she attempted to register to vote but was turned away for not being a male citizen. She sued in St. Louis Circuit Court but lost the decision, which was later upheld on appeal at the Missouri Supreme Court. The case was presented to the United States Supreme Court by her husband, Francis; unfortunately, the judges agreed with the Missouri courts, denying her and other women the right to vote. She continued unsuccessfully to push for the equal rights of women, and in doing so laid the groundwork for the 20th Amendment.

Minor died of atrophy and abscess of the liver at 4:00 p.m., August

14, 1894, in Baptist Sanitarium. The funeral took place the next day at her residence, 8311 Lucas Avenue. A quartet played "Nearer, My God, to Thee" as the casket was removed from the house. Her will stated, "I give $1,000 (one thousand dollars) to Susan B. Anthony, of Rochester, N. Y., in gratitude for the many thousands she has expended for woman." She also left $500 to each of her two nieces on the condition that they remained unmarried. She is buried with her husband and child on the west side of Vine Avenue.

BYRON NUGENT (JULY 31, 1842- APRIL 4, 1908) founded a small company, B. Nugent & Bro. Dry Goods Company, and built it into one of the largest mercantile operations in the Midwest. He was born in Marysburgh, Ontario, Canada, and educated there before coming to the United States in 1865. After spend-  ing time working at Lord & Thomas (now Lord & Taylor) in New York, he went to Chicago, where he was employed by a wholesale store. In 1869, he established his own small store in Mount Vernon, Illinois. His brother Morgan joined him that first year and stayed until his death.

Nugent married Julia Lake in January 1873, and two months later moved his business to St. Louis. His first dry goods store, at Broadway and Franklin, was called B. Nugent. A short time later, three of his brothers joined the business. In 1878, the store was moved across the street to a larger facility at 815 North Broadway. Eleven years later, B. Nugent & Bro. Dry Goods Company moved again to Broadway and Washington.

Nugent, his wife, and two sons lived at 29 Westmoreland Place. He came down with Bright's disease in August 1907 while vacationing in Massachusetts. He recovered when he returned to St. Louis, but became ill again in October and was homebound from that day on. In March, he suffered another attack and was confined to bed. He died of myocarditis (inflammation of the heart) at 2:15 p.m., Saturday, April 4, 1908. The funeral was conducted in the main hall of his home on April 7. The dry goods store was closed, as it had been since his death. Fellow merchandiser Charles Stix, of Stix, Baer, and Fuller was in attendance. After a double quartet played "Abide with Me," the body was taken outside in a torrential rainstorm. The pallbearers were employees from the business. A procession stretching several blocks took the dry goods magnate to rest in the family mausoleum on Prospect Avenue. There he joined his son, Byron, Jr., who had died in July 1906.

WILLIAM BIXBY (JANUARY 2, 1857-OCTOBER 29, 1931) was a native of Adrian, Michigan. He attended Amherst for his master's studies, and at age 16 began working for a Texas railroad. When the railroad was taken over by the Missouri Pacific Railroad, he came to St. Louis to work as a purchasing agent for the company. From there, he took a position at the American Car and Foundry Company, where he made it to the top of the corporate ladder, serving as chairman of the board until he retired in 1905 at the age of 48. He later became president of the Laclede Gas Light Company.

Bixby was a member of many civic organizations and often donated both time and money. He was president of the Art Museum and the Missouri Historical Society, director of the Public Library, an original incorporator of the American Red Cross, and served on the board of St. Luke's Hospital. He made significant contributions to the Art Museum and also donated a large collection of rare books and manuscripts to the Historical Society.

Bixby was 74 when he died of a heart attack in his home at 26 Portland Place. He had been in ill health and declined further after the death of his wife on August 12, 1931. He was survived by his four sons and two daughters. A simple funeral service was held in the living room of his home on October 31, 1931. Nearly 500 family and friends congregated in the home to hear Reverend Dr. W. C. Timmons, pastor of the First Congregational Church, celebrate the memorial service. Bixby's four sons and two sons-in-law served as pallbearers. No eulogy was given, as he had requested. In mournful respect of their one-time leader, the Missouri Historical Society and the Art Museum were closed during the afternoon of the funeral. William Bixby joined his wife in the family mausoleum on Prospect Avenue.

JOSEPH GRIESEDIECK (JULY 11, 1863-JULY 14, 1938) was president of Falstaff Brewing Company. The native of Stromberg, Germany, came to the U. S. with his father, Anton, when he was 4. By the age of 15, he was working for a malt house. He went to Philadelphia for a time to work at a brewery before returning to St. Louis to operate the National Brewery at 18th and Gratiot. He later became vice president and general manager, and his brewery merged with Independent Breweries Company.

In 1912, he formed the Griesedieck Bros. Brewing Company with his brother. The brewery was located at 18th and Shenandoah. Five years later, he left the business to open the Griesedieck Beverage Company, a manufacturer of beer and soft drinks, and in 1921 became president of the Falstaff Brewing Company. He purchased the *Falstaff* trademark from William Lemp. During Prohibition, the company processed ham and bacon.

On July 11, 1938, Griesedieck was about to celebrate his 75th birthday at his home on Rott Road near Kirkwood when he fell in his bedroom and was taken to St. John's Hospital with a fractured hip. He died three days later from complications. He was survived by his wife Mathilda and son Alvin. He had been a brewer in St. Louis for nearly 50 years. On Saturday, a funeral service was held at the Arthur Donnelly Mortuary on Lindell before a funeral Mass at the New Cathedral. He is buried with his family on Woodbine in front of a tall, circular monument topped with the figure of an angel.

II

Bloody Island

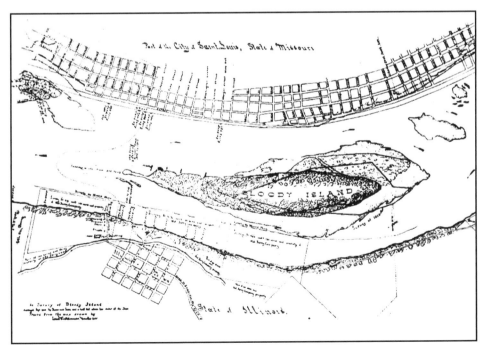

Bloody Island

The date was September 26, 1817. An early autumn morning sun lit the way for rowboats moving toward "Bloody Island," a sandbar island in the middle of the Mississippi River across from St. Louis. On this day, Thomas Hart Benton and Charles Lucas, two prominent St. Louis lawyers, were coming to the island for their second duel in as many months. Seven individuals were on the island this morning: supporting Benton were his second, Luke Lawless, and Dr. Bernard Farrar. Representing Lucas were his second, Joshua Barton, his physician, Pryor Quarles, and friend Eli Clemson.

Thomas Hart Benton, age 35, with strong, muscular features, challenged the boyish-looking, 25-year-old Charles Lucas to this duel. Both men were bachelors in the prime of their lives. As Lawless and Barton prepared the pistols, Benton removed his jacket and rolled up his sleeves to wash his arms and neck in a basin of water. Benton was perspiring heavily in the hot and humid conditions. Lucas stood quiet, not wanting his opponent to sense his nervousness.

"Gentlemen, are you ready?" called Eli Clemson.

"Don't see you I am not ready?" Benton angrily responded. He dried himself and accepted the pistol from Lawless. Barton handed Lucas his pistol and the men positioned themselves a mere 10 feet apart as their associates looked on with a sense of doom. At this distance, a fatality was certain. With the pistols pointing down against the sides of their legs, a sense of peace and stillness filled the air. The men stared each other down, neither saying a word.

"Gentlemen," said Colonel Clemson as he looked to each man. But instead of counting to three and then calling "Fire," Clemson mistakenly stopped after counting "one, two, three." Surprised by the change in procedure, there was a momentary pause before both men raised their pistols and fired.

Dueling was born during medieval times and flourished with the knight's propensity for violence. It became a sport of kings in the Renaissance period, with a code of rules to give it an air of legitimacy. In 1777, as dueling became more popular, an accepted set of rules was established. Europe's elite and those striving for higher status could partake in a game of combat reserved for gentlemen. Although the acts were barbarian in nature, they were fought with honor and respect. The tradition continued when dueling came to America, with society's upper class and military personnel challenging one another for honor and satisfaction. Dueling became an inauspicious part of civilized society, a way of settling disputes, many of which ended in the death of one or both of the participants.

Sandbar islands first appeared in the Mississippi River about 1800. Large deposits of sand built up to form several islands, which caused navigational problems in the river. Willows and cottonwood trees grew unimpeded on these islands. As the sandbars rose out of the water, the current formed a new channel on the Illinois side. The river was spreading, and by 1840 it would stretch to 1-1/2 miles wide in some places.

Duncan's Island, located on the Missouri side of the river, south of the city, was named for Bob Duncan, who raised a crop of corn on the island in 1830. The other significant sandbar, the larger of the two, would gain an infamous name: Bloody Island.

The number of duels that took place in Missouri in the early 19th century is impossible to enumerate. Bloody Island became a popular backdrop because it did not fall under the jurisdiction of either Missouri or Illinois laws. Although both states had laws against dueling, they hardly could be applied to an island to which neither had rights. And the island itself had no laws. In 1822, the Missouri Legislature passed a law to prohibit duels, and in 1835 passed another making it a felony to partake in a duel even if no one was harmed. These laws had little effect and were seldom enforced.

As to the procedures of dueling, each principle in a duel had a "second," or assistant, with the responsibility of issuing or accepting the challenge, deciding the terms, preparing the weapons, and stepping in if the principal was unable to perform his duty. The challenged party in a duel was allowed to choose the location and the weapons; Bloody Island and pistols were often the choice in St. Louis. After the choice of weapons was determined, the distance at which the duelists would stand was agreed upon. If a duelist fired a shot before the "fire" command was given, the second was permitted to shoot the man who had fired. Each man also was permitted to have a doctor or surgeon on hand.

One of the earliest duels on Bloody Island took place in 1810 and involved Dr. Bernard Farrar, the first American doctor to practice west of the Mississippi. Farrar, who was stationed at Fort Bellefontaine at the time, was asked to act as a second for his brother-in-law, Lieutenant John Campbell, a soldier accused by a young lawyer named James Graham of cheating in a card game. Campbell challenged Graham, and when Farrar delivered the message as Campbell's second, Graham claimed that his opponent didn't have the right to fight as a gentleman because of his cheating. Following the code of the duel, Farrar immediately challenged Graham to protect the family honor; in effect, the insult had now been transferred to him, even though Graham was a friend. With pistols in hand, the two men stepped off the distance and fired at one another. Although Graham was considered an excellent shot, Farrar's pistol delivered the damage. Farrar was slightly wounded, but Graham more seriously, receiving shots in the side, the leg, and the hand. Farrar attended to his opponent and friend and worked to stop the bleeding. Graham would ultimately die of his wounds, but not before writing that the affair was conducted in an honorable way.

Although most duels were fought with pistols, some participants engaged with other weapons. In 1845, two men named Kibbe and Heisterhagen resolved their dispute with swords. The duel was stopped when Heisterhagen wounded Kibbe in the face. Both parties were satisfied and the affair was settled. Another duel, which was to take place with sabers, involved the great emancipator Abraham Lincoln. In 1840, while still a Springfield lawyer, Lincoln was challenged to a duel by a man named James Shields. A very critical article was written about Shields, and he accused Lincoln of being the author. The two met with cavalry sabers, not on Bloody Island but on the Missouri shore of the Mississippi across from Alton, Illinois. Before they were to clash, Lincoln explained that he did not write the article, and Shields was satisfied. The duel was canceled and the two became friends.

Some of the most famous duels on the island took place between 1816 and 1831. Many of the principals were left dead or wounded. In August 1816, Joshua Barton, who served as Charles Lucas' second, came to Bloody Island to duel Thomas Hempstead, brother of Edward Hempstead. Barton was elected to the Missouri Legislature and later resigned that position to become Secretary of State and U. S. district attorney for Missouri. Edward Bates, his law partner, agreed to serve as Barton's second. Hempstead, born in 1791, was the U. S. military storekeeper for St. Louis and paymaster of the Missouri Militia. Ironically, his second was Thomas Hart Benton. The dispute grew out of political differences involving the 1816 election. To promote this as a high-class, gentlemanly affair, the seconds published the "Rules of the meeting between Mr. J. Barton demanding and Mr. T. Hempstead answering." This bitterly charged political duel ended when the duelists fired their first shot, each missing their opponent, and claimed themselves satisfied with the result.

In 1823, Barton was back on the island after writing an article in the *Missouri Republican* supporting his brother, U. S. Senator David Barton, in charges against General William Rector. Rector, the U. S. surveyor-general of Missouri, Illinois, and Arkansas, was accused of awarding a large number of contracts to family and friends. Thomas Rector, William's brother, challenged Barton on the charge. At 6:00 p.m., June 30, Barton faced Rector as a large group of citizens stood on the St. Louis shore awaiting news from the island. Details of the duel are not known except for the result: Joshua Barton was killed while Thomas Rector was unharmed. (Rector died violently in 1825, possibly attacked with a knife.) The Rector family is said to have had a victory party later in the evening. William Rector lost his appointment as surveyor general when President James Monroe reconsidered his selection.

According to Charles Dickens in his *American Notes*, the duel that gave the island its name was the 1831 duel between Thomas Biddle and Spencer Pettis.* Major Thomas Biddle first came to St. Louis in August 1820 to serve as paymaster at Jefferson Barracks. He later served as director of the St. Louis branch of the United States Bank. He married John Mullanphy's daughter, Ann, in September 1823. Spencer Pettis, a lawyer by profession, came to St. Louis in 1824 from Culpepper County, Virginia, and became Secretary of State under Missouri Governor John Miller one year later. He entered the U. S. House of Representatives in 1831.

In July 1831, as Pettis was running for reelection, he wrote an article in Thomas Hart Benton's *Missouri Enquirer* criticizing Biddle and his brother Nicholas, the president of the United States Bank. Pettis agreed with President Andrew Jackson not to recharter the bank, thus shutting it down. Biddle took offense at the public insult and wrote contemptuous and abusive articles of his own. In one article, he compared Pettis to "a dish of skimmed milk." Weeks before the congressional election, Biddle went to the City Hotel at Third and Vine Streets, where Pettis was staying, and instructed a servant to tell Pettis to show himself. When Pettis sent down word that he didn't wish to be disturbed, Biddle mounted the stairs and found him sleeping in the hall in an attempt to escape the heat and mosquitoes in the rooms. Pettis suddenly was roused by several blows from a horsewhip. Biddle was arrested for assault with intent to kill, but was later released. A beaten and bloodied Pettis told his friend Benton of his intention to duel Biddle, but Benton convinced him to wait until after Pettis won reelection. In the meantime, Pettis practiced firing a pistol with his second, Captain Martin Thomas.

* Pettis is spelled with an "i" in every source used, though it is spelled with a "u" in letters and newspapers of the time.

On August 2, Pettis won reelection to the House. After yet another incident with Biddle in the weeks following the election, and not forgetting or forgiving Biddle's cowardly act of abuse, Pettis challenged his opponent. Captain Martin Thomas delivered the challenge. A positive reply was given by Biddle's second, Major Benjamin O'Fallon, brother of John O'Fallon. At 5:30 p.m., Friday, August 27, they would settle their differences once and for all. A large crowd gathered on the Missouri shore. Others hung from windows and stood on rooftops to gain a better view. As the challenger, Biddle chose to stand only five feet apart because he was nearsighted. (In an ironic twist, the pistols had once been owned by Aaron Burr and were used in his duel with Alexander Hamilton.) At the command, each turned and fired, and both men collapsed to the ground, severely wounded. Biddle was shot in the stomach, while his ball went entirely through Pettis' body. The weapons were fired so simultaneously that the crowd on shore heard only one shot. Biddle and Pettis were standing so close that witnesses said the barrels of their guns overlapped. According to the August 30 *Missouri Republican*:

> *Major Biddle was shot thro' the abdomen, the ball lodging within. Mr. Pettus was shot through the side, just below the chest, the ball passing entirely through the body.*

Dr. Hardage Lane, Biddle's surgeon, went to his patient. "I feel very much hurt, Dr. Lane," Biddle told him. Lane examined the wound and stopped the bleeding but could do nothing more.

The crowd waited as both men were brought back to the Missouri shore by their seconds. When Pettis arrived, he asked Benton if he were foolish to take part in the duel. "No sir, you have shown yourself to be the bravest of the brave," Benton told him. Pettis was taken to Major Joshua Brant's house at Fourth and Washington, where he died Saturday afternoon, Thomas Hart Benton by his side. He was a bachelor, and only 29 years old. A large segment of the population paid respects at his Sunday afternoon funeral. He was buried in one of the city cemeteries with no monument to mark his grave. He later was reinterred in Calvary Cemetery. Thomas Biddle died on Monday morning, August 30. His funeral took place the next day during a torrential rainstorm, with burial in the Catholic Cemetery on Franklin Avenue. John Mullanphy gave the news to Thomas' brother Nicholas. "Oh my god what dreadful news I have to communicate to you," he wrote. "Your good your worthy And noble Brother is no more, he died about six o'clock this morning of a wound he recd. in a duel with Mr. Pettus on friday last." Biddle and his wife, Ann Mullanphy Biddle, are today buried in a large tomb in Calvary. Upon moving Biddle's remains to Calvary on September 18, 1858, the undertaker found among his bones the projectile that killed him.

Next to the famous Alexander Hamilton–Aaron Burr duel in July 1804, in which Hamilton was killed, the two 1817 duels between Thomas Hart Benton and Charles Lucas may be the most famous and documented duels in American history. Before concluding the Benton–Lucas affair that started this chapter, let's look at what prompted the incident.

In 1816, Thomas Hart Benton and Charles Lucas, son of John B.C. Lucas, were prominent lawyers in St. Louis. In St. Louis Circuit Court in October of that year, during the closing arguments of a case in which they faced each other, Lucas accused Benton of misstating evidence. In the end, the jury's verdict came down in favor of Lucas's client. Benton took personal offense at the attack and challenged Lucas to a duel, but Lucas refused, stating that he did not wish to settle professional differences in a personal manner.

Charles Lucas was born near Pittsburgh, Pennsylvania, on September 25, 1792. He was the second son of the prominent and wealthy judge, John Lucas. He came to St. Louis with the family when he was 13 and later fought in the War of 1812. He received the best education and opportunities of the time. He graduated law school and was highly regarded around the city as an excellent young lawyer. He was later appointed U. S. Attorney for the Missouri Territory.

On Monday, August 4, 1817, Lucas and Benton once again confronted each other, this time at a polling place on Election Day. Lucas told election officials that Benton had not paid his taxes and hence had no right to vote. Benton responded by saying, "Gentlemen, if you have any questions to ask, I am prepared to answer, but I do not propose to answer charges made by any puppy who may happen to run across my path." Lucas was enraged by Benton's tone and had his second, Joshua Barton, deliver a letter to settle the dispute. Benton had spent the previous night with the body of his friend Edward Hempstead, who had died of a hemorrhage after being thrown from his horse. He told Barton, "I accept but I must now go and bury a dead friend; that is my first duty. After that is discharged, I will fight, tonight, if possible; if not, tomorrow morning at daybreak. I accept your challenge, sir."

That evening, Lucas left a note for his father, who was an ardent opponent of dueling. "Embarked as I am in a hazardous enterprise, the issue of which you will know before you see this, I am under the necessity of bidding you, my brothers, sister, friends, adieu."

At 6:00 a.m. the next morning, August 12, 1817, the two parties arrived at the island. Along with Benton was his second, Colonel Luke Lawless, and Dr. Bernard Farrar, who had previously taken part in a duel himself. Accompanying Lucas were Joshua Barton and Dr. Pryor Quarles. Barton and Lawless had met the day before to decide the terms. Benton and Lucas took their positions, appearing calm and relaxed. They faced each other at 30 feet apart, pistols at their sides. When the "Fire" command was given, both men pulled the trigger. Lucas collapsed to the ground with a bloody wound to the neck, just to the left of his windpipe, while Benton stood uninjured; only later did he notice a slight contusion below the right knee. Lucas said he was satisfied, but Benton asked Lucas to stand and continue or to fight again another day. Dr. Quarles worked to stop the bleeding and placed Lucas in the boat, where he fainted before reaching the Missouri shore.

Lucas recovered from his wound within a few weeks and was again challenged by Benton. The seconds had failed to reach a reconciliation following the first duel, so the participants were once again rowing toward the island in the early morning hours of September 26. The conditions would remain the same as the first duel, except that the distance between the men was changed to 10 feet. The same men were present, with the addition of Colonel Eli Clemson in support of Lucas. It was Clemson who made the mistake of counting "one, two, three" without giving the firing command. After a momentary pause, both men raised their pistols and fired.

Lucas collapsed to the ground. His shot missed, but Benton's had found its mark. The bullet passed through Lucas' left arm and entered the left side of his chest. Benton approached his victim and offered a hand.

"Charles, it is an unfortunate affair! It is very unfortunate!" Benton told Lucas, and asked for forgiveness.

"Colonel Benton, you have persecuted me and murdered me. I cannot forgive you!" Lucas responded. He then had a quick change of heart and added, "I can forgive you -- I do forgive you!" Lucas held out his hand and Benton took hold.

"Your friends are with you," Benton said, and turned away to leave the island, having soaked its ground with more blood. Moments later, Charles Lucas died. He had celebrated his 25th birthday one day earlier.

Thomas Hart Benton regretted the incident for the rest of his life. He later wrote about the "pang which went through [his] heart when he saw the young man fall, and would have given the world to see him restored to life." He seldom spoke of the duel, except on few occasions to close friends.

Lucas' body was taken to his home. He is buried with the rest of his family at Calvary Cemetery.   Joseph Charless, a strong critic of dueling, wrote in his *Missouri Gazette*:

> *The infernal practice of duelling has taken off, this morning, one of the first characters in our country, CHARLES LUCAS, Esq., Attorney at Law. His death has left a blank in society not easily filled up. Tale bearers this is thy work! Innocent blood lies at thy doors!*

By the 1830's, city officials were interested in eliminating the island because of continued navigational problems. The combination of Bloody Island and Duncan's Island, just to the south, was making it difficult for ships to maneuver up and down the river, and too many were running aground in the shallow water. Since the river was a major component to the success of St. Louis, the problem needed correcting. Mayor John Darby sought help from the federal government; and, in 1835, General Charles Gratiot, Jr., who was commander of the Army Corps of Engineers, appointed Lieutenant Robert E. Lee and Second Lieutenant Montgomery Miegs to expand the harbor. (In 1864, it was Miegs who established the military cemetery in Arlington, Virginia, on the grounds of Arlington House, the estate owned by Robert E. Lee.) They first arrived in St. Louis in 1837 to examine the situation and develop a plan. Lee returned to Arlington House and came up with the idea of establishing a system of underwater dikes to push the water toward the Missouri side. The first dike, on the southern tip of Bloody Island, would direct water at Duncan's Island, while another dike was to extend from the northern point of Bloody Island to the Illinois shore. The plan was adopted from earlier proposals by Gratiot and the "Father of the Mississippi," Henry Shreve.

When he returned to St. Louis in May 1838, Lee and his family lived at Council Hall, owned by William Clark and inhabited by Dr. William Beaumont. The southern dike was constructed of rocks, stones and sand, and succeeded in increasing the depth of the river by eliminating a portion of Duncan's Island. In July 1839, Lee completed work on the second dike. By the following year, the depth of the river allowed even the largest ships to navigate the waters safely. By 1856, Bloody Island was merged into the Illinois shore and forever disappeared from the map.

Duels still occurred, even though the island had been eliminated. In order to stop the practice, delegates to the 1865 Missouri Constitutional Convention wrote a new section into the Constitution. It stated that "no person who shall hereafter fight a duel, act as a second, accept or carry a challenge or agree to go out of the state (for instance, to Bloody Island) to fight a duel, could hold any office in the state." Because most of the duelists tended to be office holders, dueling, in effect, disappeared.

III

Calvary Cemetery

Calvary Cemetery

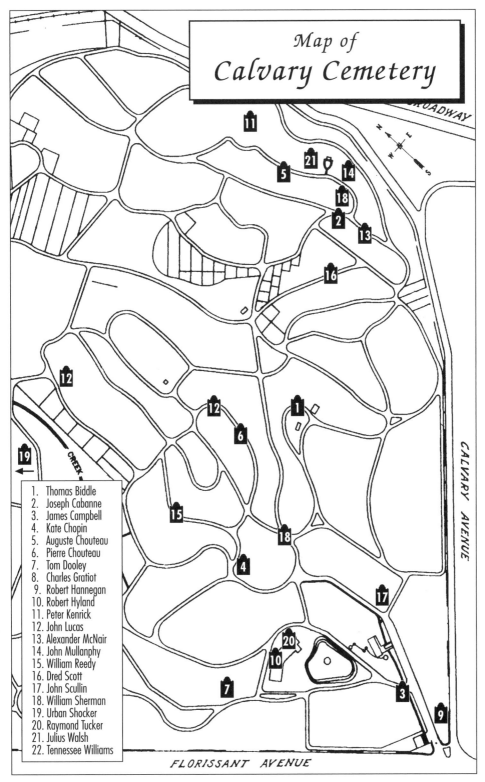

Map of
Calvary Cemetery

1. Thomas Biddle
2. Joseph Cabanne
3. James Campbell
4. Kate Chopin
5. Auguste Chouteau
6. Pierre Chouteau
7. Tom Dooley
8. Charles Gratiot
9. Robert Hannegan
10. Robert Hyland
11. Peter Kenrick
12. John Lucas
13. Alexander McNair
14. John Mullanphy
15. William Reedy
16. Dred Scott
17. John Scullin
18. William Sherman
19. Urban Shocker
20. Raymond Tucker
21. Julius Walsh
22. Tennessee Williams

BROADWAY

CALVARY AVENUE

CREEK

FLORISSANT AVENUE

After the 1849 outbreak of cholera in St. Louis, cemeteries were forbidden by law to be located within the city limits. The Catholic cemeteries in the city were filled to near-capacity levels because of the cholera epidemic. Archdiocese records showed that, on one day alone, June 25, 1849, 99 of 126 total burials were attributed to cholera. The Catholic establishment was in need of a new, larger burial ground.

In 1853, Archbishop Peter Richard Kenrick purchased 323-acre "Old Orchard Farm," northwest of the city, from Kentucky politician Henry Clay. Adjoining lots were added later. Part of the land had once been an ancient Indian burial ground. Soldiers from nearby Fort Bellefontaine also were interred there. After the purchase of the grounds, the bones were collected and buried in a mass grave, marked by a large crucifix. It is located at one of the highest points of the cemetery. Archbishop Kenrick is buried in the Priests' Lot directly in front of the crucifix.

Kenrick lived in the mansion on the grounds for many years. In 1857, he divided the farm in half, establishing Calvary on the eastern portion. The Calvary Cemetery Association was incorporated in March 1867, with Archbishop Kenrick as its first president. Bodies buried in many of the Catholic cemeteries in the city, such as Rock Springs and Holy Trinity, were reinterred in Calvary. The cemetery now contains more than 315,000 graves in its 477 acres. Like Bellefontaine, the cemetery takes advantage of its wooded environment, with spacious, tree-covered lawns. The roads within the gates gracefully conform to the contours of the rolling hills.

The mausoleum near the entrance was dedicated in June 1961. Calvary is located next to Bellefontaine Cemetery, at 5239 West Florissant Avenue at Union Avenue. The cemetery is open daily. The office is open Monday through Friday, 8:30 a.m. to 4:30 p.m., Saturday 8:30 a.m. to 12:30 p.m. A free map, along with information regarding some of the prominent citizens buried there, is provided at the office. Information also is available at the Catholic Cemeteries web site, www.stlcathcem.com.

Much like Bellefontaine Cemetery, Calvary is a treasure of cemetery architecture. And no less impressive are the prominent people buried there. Once again, St. Louis mayors are in abundance, including **John Darby** (1803–1882), an original trustee of Bellefontaine Cemetery; **James Barry** (1800–1880), mayor in 1849 during the cholera epidemic and Great Fire; **Arthur Barrett** (1836–1875), who died at the age of 39, one week after his inauguration; and **A. J. Cervantes** (1920–1983), mayor during the revitalization of downtown, during which Busch Stadium and the Gateway Arch were completed. Missouri governors include **Thomas Reynolds** (1821–1887), who took his own life at the age of 48. Even a member of Jefferson Davis' Confederate Congress, **William Cooke** (1823–1863) is buried at Calvary.

Representing the other side of the law are gangsters such as **William "Dinky" Colbeck** (1891–1943), a Mafia leader who once shared a federal penitentiary cell with Al Capone. After his release, he again pursued criminal activities until being machine gunned by a rival gang. **John Vitale** (1909–1982) was another gangster leader, constantly in trouble with St. Louis police for everything from drugs and gambling to murder. A more recent organized crime figure was **James Michaels, Sr.** (1906–1980), who was involved in the power struggle over Laborers Union, Local 42, dubbed "the Syrian-Lebanese war." Michaels was killed by a faction led by the Leisure family when a bomb detonated in his car as he drove down Interstate 55 near Reavis Barracks. One year later, Michaels' nephew, **George "Sonny" Feheen** (1937–1981), was killed by the Leisures when his car exploded in the parking garage of the Mansion House Center.

Other people of interest are **Antoine Soulard**, surveyor general for Upper Louisiana; prominent businessman **Henry von Puhl** (1784–1874); banker and real estate investor **Louis Benoist** (1803–1869); and **Frederick Switzer, Sr.** (1865–1949), founder of the Switzer Candy Company.

THE CHOUTEAUS AND PIERRE LACLÈDE

In December 1763, Pierre Laclède and Auguste Chouteau stood atop a bluff overlooking the Mississippi River. Laclède described to the boy the benefits the site had to offer: trees for lumber, stone outcroppings for foundations and clean water, and the bluffs, which provided a natural wall against the threat of flooding. It was the ideal location to build a fur-trading post. They marked their spot at approximately the same location that the Old Courthouse stands today.

The Chouteaus, the founding family of St. Louis, were involved in virtually every aspect of the small French village. They developed the land, constructed homes and warehouses, brought commerce to the village, and served the people by representing St. Louis' political interests. They would become the most powerful family in the region.

Pierre Laclède Liguest was baptized in 1729 into a prominent family in Bedous, France. He dropped the name "Liguest" when he settled in New Orleans in 1755. He helped to establish Maxent, Laclède, and Company, a fur-trading company, and by 1762 was trading exclusively with the Indians in the Missouri valley. Laclède made hundreds of trips up and down the Mississippi trading his products.

Auguste Chouteau was born in New Orleans to René Auguste Chouteau and Marie Thérèse Bourgeois. The exact date of birth is conjecture,

although most historians accept it to be either September 7, 1749 or September 26, 1750. His father abandoned the family and returned to France a few years after his birth. A short time later, his mother met Pierre Laclède. The couple had four children; the oldest, Jean Pierre, was born October 10, 1758 in New Orleans. Since the Catholic Church did not allow divorce and remarriage, the children were born with the name Chouteau rather than Laclède.

Pierre Laclède became a father figure for young Auguste, who worked as a clerk in his stepfather's business and quickly learned the fur-trading industry. In August 1763, Laclède took him along on the fur-trading expedition up the Mississippi River. In early November, they arrived at Ste. Genevieve, the first village established west of the Mississippi. They lodged and stored their merchandise at nearby Fort Chartres at the invitation of the commander, M. Neyon de Viliers. In December, Laclède and Chouteau headed north up the Mississippi to explore possible sites for a new settlement and headquarters for Laclède's business. They went as far north as the mouth of the Missouri River before deciding on a location just south of its confluence with the Mississipppi. Laclède marked the spot and returned to the fort to tell the commander, "I have found a situation where I am going to form a settlement which might become hereafter one of the finest cities in America."

Laclède spent the cold winter months developing a design for his village. The streets were to be laid out in a grid pattern, much like New Orleans. He decided to name the new settlement after Louis IX, who was the patron saint of the current French monarch, Louis XV. (It was Louis XV's grandson, Louis XVI, who, with his wife Marie Antoinette was guillotined in 1793 after the fall of the Bastille.)

On February 14, 1764, as winter was losing its grip on the region, Laclède, Chouteau, and a group of workmen landed at the designated site. The next day, Laclède departed and the workers began cutting down trees and clearing the land. By early April, when Laclède returned, Chouteau and his men had constructed several cabins. Laclède's large residence was located on Main Street between Market and Walnut. As the village grew, Indians from surrounding regions began coming to trade furs.

Pierre Laclède appointed his stepson a partner in his business. Chouteau spent most of his time among the Osage Indians with whom the Chouteaus were given exclusive trading rights. The Indians knew him as an ambitious yet fair man. He developed a relationship with them that continued for years and earned him a significant fortune. Laclède's son Pierre, Chouteau's half-brother, worked for the family business as well. The two brothers became close, and Auguste taught young Pierre about fur trading, including the art of negotiating with the Indians.

The brothers were of very different character. Auguste was calm and reserved in his manner, often keeping his feelings to himself. Outwardly, he was courteous and communicative, even though he spoke only French. Pierre was more outgoing, emotional, and tough, although he was well respected for his fair judgment.

In June 1778, Pierre Laclède was returning to St. Louis from a two-year trading expedition in New Orleans with a huge inventory of merchandise. He became ill as he made his way up the Mississippi River and died on June 20th at a village called "Post of Arkansas" on the Arkansas River. The fur trader was buried in an unmarked grave along the river. An expedition was sent later to recover his body, but the burial site could not be found. Today, the exact location of his remains is unknown.

Auguste took over the business in St. Louis, while Pierre remained as the business agent with the Indians. With the help of favorable government treatment and grants, the Chouteaus virtually monopolized the fur-trading business in St. Louis. They prospered further as the population grew and word spread of their success. Looking beyond the business of fur trading, Auguste invested in new ventures, including real estate, dry goods stores, and banking.

In July 1783, when Pierre was 25, he married Pelagie Kiersereau. The couple had three sons and a daughter before Pelagie's unexpected death in 1793 at the age of 26. Less than a year later, Pierre married 15-year-old Brigitte Saucier. His wife cared for his four children and later had five sons of her own.

Auguste married for the first time in 1786. By this time, he was the wealthiest man in the village. His wife, Marie Thérèse Cerre, was the daughter of a wealthy St. Louis merchant. She was 17; Auguste was in his mid-30's. They had nine children, but the first two daughters died before the age of eight. In 1789, Auguste purchased Laclède's old home on Main Street and added a second story, turning the home into a stately mansion. It was the most lavish house in St. Louis and became the gathering place for the village elite. Pierre and his wife lived in a mansion farther down Main Street that was destroyed by fire in 1805.

In the early 1800's, St. Louis was a village with narrow, unpaved streets; the population of about 1,400 spoke French exclusively. The Chouteaus continued to have an immense influence in the St. Louis community. During this time, Auguste was suffering from a chronic case of arthritis, which made even the simplest task painful to perform. He was appointed colonel of the militia in 1808, and both he and Pierre were elected to the board of trustees for the city a year later, with Auguste as chairman. In 1813, President James Madison appointed Auguste as a member of the Territorial Legislative Council, which was established to govern the Missouri territory. Pierre was made an Indian agent because of his influence with the native Americans.

On November 23, 1816, Auguste informed the *Missouri Gazette* of his intention to retire from the fur-trading business. Pierre also retired, allowing the next generation of Chouteaus to run the business. Auguste and Pierre, however, continued to work on their real estate and banking interests. Auguste laid the groundwork for the Bank of St. Louis and established the Bank of Missouri in 1816. Prominent men such as John O'Fallon, Alexander McNair, and John B.C. Lucas placed their influence behind the new Missouri Bank. Both Auguste and Pierre ran for mayor of St. Louis in the 1820's, but both lost their respective elections.

A great celebration took place in 1825 when French Revolutionary War hero the Marquis de Lafayette visited St. Louis. Auguste and Mayor William Carr Lane were among the delegation welcoming the general. A public reception was held at Pierre Chouteau's mansion.

Auguste Chouteau produced his will on February 13, 1829, writing, "I, Auguste Chouteau…knowing that there is nothing more certain than death, and nothing more uncertain than the hour of it…." He left his wife their home, another nearby house, and possession of a dozen slaves. The remaining land, buildings, and slaves were to be divided evenly among his seven children.

He died on the morning of February 24, 1829. That day's *Missouri Republican* announced the event:

DIED, in this city, this morning, the venerable Col. AUGUSTE CHOUTEAU, the Patriarch of St. Louis. At the advanced age of eighty years, he closed a life of singular usefulness, possessing, in every vicissitude, the esteem of his fellow citizens. His eulogy is written in the hearts of the numerous circle of friends whom he had attached to him by his philanthropy, his unpretending benevolence, and the amenity of his manners.

His funeral was 9:00 a.m. the next day, with burial in the cemetery next to the unfinished cathedral on Walnut Street. The epitaph on Auguste Chouteau's tombstone read:

Auguste Chouteau born in New Orleans September 26, 1750 sent by M. L. de Laclede he was the first to arrive in this savage land and founded the town of St. Louis February 13, 1764. His life has been a model of civic and social virtues. He died February 24, 1829, and rests in this tomb.

When Calvary Cemetery opened its gates, his remains were moved. His new grave marker read, "His life was a model without a stain." In 1921, Auguste's great-great grandson, Henri Chouteau, had a new tombstone made. He removed the reference to Laclède and changed the year of Auguste's birth to 1740. There is no evidence that the year is accurate.

Auguste's personal effects were appraised at more than $17,000, with another $82,000 owed to him in mortgages and promissory notes. At the time of his death, he also owned 21,482 acres of land in Illinois and several Missouri counties, including most of St. Louis.

Pierre continued his work for the city, but later relinquished his duties as he slowed with age. In February 1847, when St. Louis held its first anniversary celebration, Pierre, the last surviving link to the origins of the village, rode in the parade and took part in a banquet, at which he toasted the first inhabitants of St. Louis. He made his will that same year and died a year and a half later, on July 9, 1849, during the cholera epidemic. Although not as wealthy as his brother, Pierre left an estate worth $70,000 plus various real estate holdings.

Both Chouteaus are buried in Calvary with their families. Auguste's tablet monument is located near the Priests' Lot in Section 7. The inscription still inaccurately lists 1740 as the year of his birth. His son Henry is on one side, daughter Gabriel on the other. (Henry was killed in the train crash during the Gasconade Bridge opening ceremonies.) The Pierre Chouteau family lot sits high atop a hill, Section 13. The circular lot is centered with a large cross. His mother, Madame Marie Thérèse Chouteau, who died on August 14, 1814, also is buried in the lot.

CHARLES GRATIOT
(1753–APRIL 20, 1817)

Charles Gratiot was perhaps the most widely known citizen of St. Louis, bringing more attention to the village than even his in-laws, the Chouteaus. He was born and schooled in Lausanne, Switzerland, and at the age of 17 went to stay with his uncle in London before coming to America to reside with another uncle in Montreal, where he worked six years in the family's fur-trading business.

In 1777, Gratiot partnered with two other men in David McCrae & Company, and in December of that year opened a fur-trading store in Cahokia, Illinois. The partnership was dissolved, and Gratiot moved to St. Louis in early 1781, when about 500 settlers called the village home. On June 25, he married Victoria Chouteau, Auguste's half-sister. The marriage brought Gratiot into the most prominent and wealthy family in town. The couple lived in a fine house at Main and Chestnut streets. They had 13 children; four died in infancy. His son, Charles, Jr., was in charge of eliminating Bloody Island.

Gratiot ran his own prosperous trading business by traveling extensively to New Orleans and the East Coast. He had an incredible drive and energy, often pushing himself to his limit. During a trip to New York, he met the wealthiest fur trader in America, John Jacob Astor. The two did business together and became lifelong friends. Gratiot expanded his business to include a distillery and a tannery.

His most prestigious moment may have come in March 1804, when he conducted the official transfer of the Louisiana Purchase territory from France to the United States on his portico in St. Louis. He was appointed the first presiding justice of the court of St. Louis. He had a great knowledge of the law, although he was never formally educated in the practice. In 1809, when St. Louis was incorporated as a town, Gratiot was elected to the board of trustees and served as its president from 1811 to 1813.

Except for the Chouteaus, Gratiot was the wealthiest man in St. Louis when he died of a stroke in 1817. His funeral was held on Monday, April 21, a cool, rainy afternoon. His wife Victoria joined her husband in death in June 1825. They are laid to rest in Section 3.

JOHN MULLANPHY
(? 1758-AUGUST 29, 1833)

John Mullanphy was the first millionaire and the first true philanthropist in St. Louis. He was born in Northern Ireland. At the age of 20, he joined the Irish Brigade of the French Army. He returned to Ireland after the fall of the Bastille and married Elizabeth Browne. The couple had 15 children; seven died in infancy. The family came to America in 1792 and settled in Philadelphia before moving to Baltimore. He moved again, this time to Frankfort, Kentucky, and opened an extremely profitable bookstore.

Mullanphy came to St. Louis in 1804, months after Thomas Jefferson purchased the Louisiana Territory. He began his business career by opening a bookstore close to his home on Second Street. He won over customers by, among other things, speaking French, which he had learned during his time in the French Army. For a time, he served as a justice of the peace, and in that capacity married, among others, Alexander McNair, later the first governor of Missouri. He purchased real estate for small sums in  and around the St. Louis area. Mullanphy established his wealth by selling cotton to England and other European countries while living in New Orleans.

Understanding the importance of a solid education, Mullanphy sent his children to the best schools in New Orleans and Paris. The family left St. Louis and lived for a time in Natchez, Mississippi, and Baltimore before returning in 1819 to make St. Louis their permanent home. His philanthropy included financing the St. Louis Mullanphy Hospital at 4th and Spruce Streets, the first hospital west of the Mississippi. He also gave land in Florissant for St. Ferdinand Church, and in 1827 donated to the Sisters of the Sacred Heart a tract of land at Broadway and Chouteau Avenue. Mother Philippine Duchesne and her order built a church and a convent on the site and educated orphaned girls at Mullanphy's request.

Seven of his daughters and a son lived to adulthood. His daughter Ann married Major Thomas Biddle, the paymaster at Jefferson Barracks. In August 1831, Biddle was killed in a duel on Bloody Island. After the death of her husband, Ann dedicated her life to charitable pursuits with liberal donations of land and money, including the acreage for Kenrick Seminary. The remains of Ann (she died in 1846) and Thomas were moved to a grand mausoleum in the new Calvary Cemetery in 1858. The monument was built at a cost of $40,000.

On August 29, 1833, John Mullanphy passed away in his home "after an illness of some days duration." He was surrounded by his surviving children. Mayor John Darby, a close friend of Mullanphy, eulogized, "Among the distinguished men who were engaged in laying the foundations of St. Louis and building up the city, no one was more prominent than John Mullanphy. He read much and had one of the finest libraries west of the Mississippi. He was most liberal in his gifts for charitable objects and purposes." Mullanphy Street is named in his honor.

Mullanphy's one son, Bryan, was perhaps the most well-known member of the family. He was born in Baltimore in 1809 and studied law in Europe. He practiced in St. Louis and later became an alderman and a circuit court judge; he was mayor of St. Louis from 1847 to 1848. The life-long bachelor was described as an eccentric liberal with an impressive intellect. His philanthropy was as generous as that of the rest of the family. He was the founder of the Traveler's Aid Society and gave vast amounts of his wealth to the less fortunate, even providing housing for some. According to his will, a portion of his estate went to the Mullanphy Emigrant Relief Fund, "to furnish relief to all poor emigrants and travellers coming to St. Louis on their way bonafide to settle in the West."

He was only 42 when he passed away on Saturday night, June 15, 1851, at his boarding house in the Missouri Hotel. Because of his eccentric nature, he was thought to be mentally imbalanced. In trying to explain a reason for his death, the June 16th *National Intelligencer* said of him:

> ...he discharged his duties with remarkable fidelity, firmness, and impartiality; but always with certain eccentricities, which led many to suppose even then, that his mind was partially unsound. Since then, these eccentricities had increased to such a degree, as to produce a very general impression that he was insane.

Mullanphy Community School at Tower Grove Avenue is named for him. He was buried in the Mullanphy family lot with his parents, John and Elizabeth. The tall and very ornate monument stands atop a hill overlooking North Broadway (Section 3). In 1867, the Mullanphy Emigrant Home, a three-story brick building at 14th Street, was established to provide temporary room and board for emigrants and travelers, just as his will requested.

JOHN B. C. LUCAS
(AUGUST 14, 1758-AUGUST 29, 1842)

John Baptiste Charles Lucas was born in the small town of Pont-Audemer in Normandy, France. He graduated from law school at the University of Caen in 1782 and returned to his hometown to practice law. He married Anne Sebin before immigrating to America in April 1784. The couple settled on a farm called "Montpelier" near Pittsburgh, where he dedicated himself to learning the laws and history of his new homeland. Lucas was a man of small stature and a good constitution; he was a tireless worker with a touch of eccentricity.

Lucas was elected a member of the Pennsylvania House of Representatives in 1792 and served for six years. In March 1803, he was elevated to the national political scene when he succeeded his friend, Albert Gallatin, in Congress. He resigned after two years when President Thomas Jefferson appointed him United States judge for the northern district of Louisiana. It was this appointment that brought him to St. Louis. Lucas' name first came to the attention of Jefferson by a letter of recommendation from Benjamin Franklin, who was then minister to France.

The Lucas family seemed beset with tragedy. Their child, Adrian, drowned after falling through the ice on Loutre Lake in 1804. Then, in 1811, Lucas lost his wife. Two years later, during the War of 1812, son Robert was killed in battle, and in September 1817, son Charles was killed by Thomas Hart Benton in a duel on Bloody Island. Lucas wrote of his son's death, "Nothing there remains of my late son, Charles Lucas, but his reputation." His hatred for Benton would virtually consume his life, and he often derided his enemy in public.

After the deaths in his family, Lucas built a new stone house at Seventh and Market Streets, where he lived the remainder of his life. His prominence as a political leader led him to be nominated for the first United States Senate seat from Missouri in 1820. He lost the election to his bitter rival, Thomas Hart Benton. Like many distinguished men of the time, he invested aggressively in real estate, becoming one of the largest landowners in St. Louis besides the Chouteaus. In 1816, in order to help expand the village, Lucas and Auguste Chouteau sold parcels of land they owned west of the village. Within a few years, more than 100 homes were constructed on the land, with hundreds more to come in the next decade.

John Lucas died on August 29, 1842, two weeks after his 84th birthday. The Lucas family lot at Calvary (Section 13) is centered by a tall, granite obelisk, simply engraved "Lucas."

Only son James and daughter Anne survived their parents. James became a well-known banker and capitalist in St. Louis; he died in 1873. Anne donated much of her money to educational and religious institutions – more than $1 million during her lifetime. She and her husband once owned the Grant's Farm property later purchased by Frederick Dent. Anne married Theodore Hunt; and after his death in 1832, she married a wealthy merchant, Wilson Price Hunt -- hence the street name, Lucas and Hunt. Anne died on April 12, 1879; she was 82. She and both husbands are buried in a Gothic mausoleum built into a hillside overlooking the Mississippi River, in Section 3.

ALEXANDER MCNAIR
(MAY 5, 1775-MARCH 18, 1826)

The *National Intelligencer* made its official pronouncement on April 7, 1826:

> *It has become our painful duty to announce the death of our late Governor, Alexander McNair, in doing which we cannot refrain from joining with our fellow citizens and the bereaved family in lamenting his loss.*

The first governor of Missouri was born in Dauphin County, Pennsylvania. He was an infant when his father and brother fought in the Revolutionary War; his father died from wounds received in the Battle of Trenton. McNair fought as a lieutenant during the Whiskey Rebellion in 1794, and 10 years later settled in St. Louis as a U. S. commissary before serving as a colonel during the War of 1812. He held a variety of public offices, including inspector-general of the territorial militia and U. S. Marshal for the territory, and he sat on the board of trustees with the Chouteaus for the incorporation of St. Louis.

John Mullanphy married McNair and his wife in March 1805. In the first election for governor of Missouri on August 28, 1820, McNair received 72 percent of the vote over his friend William Clark. Weeks later, his political triumph was marred by personal tragedy when two of his children died of typhoid fever five days apart. McNair was inaugurated as governor during the first session of the legislature, held on September 18 at the Missouri Hotel at Main and North Streets. The capitol of Missouri was moved from St. Louis to St. Charles in 1821, then to Jefferson City in 1826. When he left the governor's office in 1825, he became an Indian agent.

In early 1826, McNair came down with a severe cold, which developed into an influenza that was at epidemic proportions around the country. He received the last rites of the Catholic Church before dying in his home on the morning of March 18, survived by his wife and eight children. He was buried in the old Military Graveyard in St. Louis and reinterred in Calvary when it opened.

His red granite monument (Section 1) was "erected by the Calvary Cemetery Association, August 10, 1921, the one hundredth anniversary of the admission of Missouri to the Union."

DRED SCOTT
(CIRCA 1799-SEPTEMBER 17, 1858)

Dred Scott was a Virginia-born slave standing a mere four feet, nine inches tall. When Peter Blow and his family moved to St. Louis in 1830, they brought Scott with them. Two years later, when Peter Blow died, Scott became the property of his daughter, who sold him for $500 to Dr. John Emerson, an army surgeon stationed at Jefferson Barracks.

Dr. Emerson was transferred to forts in Illinois and then Minnesota, two states that prohibited slavery. While in Minnesota, Dr. Emerson bought a slave girl named Harriet Robinson. In 1836, Dred and Harriet became husband and wife. A daughter, Eliza, was born in 1838 when the couple was returning to Jefferson Barracks after Dr. Emerson had been transferred back to Missouri. Eliza died in her teens. A second daughter, Lizzie, was born at the Barracks.

When Dr. Emerson died in 1843, his slaves became the property of his widow, Irene. The Scotts decided to sue for their freedom on the advice of Henry and Taylor Blow, sons of Peter Blow and childhood friends of Scott. The case was heard on June 30, 1847, at the Old Courthouse in St. Louis. The lawyers argued that their client was entitled to be free because he had lived in the anti-slave states of Illinois and Minnesota. The decision of the court went against Scott. A second trial was conducted at the Old Courthouse, and this time the decision fell in his favor. Irene Emerson appealed the case to the Missouri Supreme Court, and in March 1852 the court reversed the judgment of the second trial.

Irene Emerson, who had moved to the East coast and married a Massachusetts physician, transferred her ownership of the slaves to her brother, John Sanford. Scott and his attorney, Roswell Field, father of author Eugene Field, sued again in federal court but lost. They attempted to get a new trial, but their case was denied. In a final attempt to gain his freedom, Scott appealed to the United States Supreme Court. Montgomery Blair, a leading Washington lawyer and brother of Francis Blair, represented Scott. The decision on Dred Scott v. John Sanford was reached on March 6, 1857. The highest court in the land ruled that because Scott was born a slave he had no rights as a U. S. citizen; hence, he had no right to sue in a federal court. With the case dismissed, Scott's fight for freedom ended, but it had brought national attention to the question of slavery and ignited the arguments that would lead to the Civil War.

Shortly after the decision, John Sanford gave ownership of Scott to Taylor Blow, son of his original owner, Peter Blow. Taylor freed Scott from bondage on May 26, 1857. Scott enjoyed his freedom only a short time, as he died in St. Louis on September 17, 1858. The *Daily Missouri Democrat* announced the death to the city:

> *This celebrated individual died at his residence in this city, on Friday evening last, after an illness of some weeks.*

Dred Scott was laid to rest at Wesleyan Cemetery at Grand and Laclede. When the cemetery closed, his remains were reinterred in Calvary. His roadside grave in Section 1 is marked with both a standing monument and a flat marker. The monument synopsizes his fight for freedom. The flat marker reads, "In memory of a simple man who wanted to be free."

Researchers recently found the final resting place of Harriett Scott in Greenwood Cemetery, a few miles from her husband in Calvary. The exact location of her unmarked grave is not known. Her date of death is believed to be June 17, 1876.

PETER RICHARD KENRICK
(AUGUST 17, 1806-MARCH 4, 1896)

The future archbishop of St. Louis grew up in Dublin, Ireland. His interest in religion undoubtedly came from the influence of his uncle Richard, who was a parish priest in Dublin, and his older brother Francis, a seminary student. He attended St. Patrick's College in Maynooth, Ireland and was ordained a priest on March 6, 1832. The following year, he came to Philadelphia, where his brother Francis was a bishop.

Kenrick was charming and approachable, and known for his persistence and hard work. His manner was simple and his speech slow, with a faint hint of Ireland still in his voice. Besides his official duties, he wrote three books on religion. He impressed Bishop Joseph Rosati of St. Louis when the two met in Rome, and Rosati offered Kenrick the appointment as coadjutor, or assistant bishop. Kenrick accepted and was consecrated a bishop on November 30, 1841. He came to St. Louis a month later, at a time when the St. Louis diocese had only one Catholic church in town.

When Bishop Rosati died in Rome in 1842, Kenrick became bishop of St. Louis. Later, when the city was elevated to the status of an archdiocese, he became the first archbishop of St. Louis. His brother, Francis, celebrated the official ceremony on September 3, 1848.

Kenrick made tremendous strides in developing the St. Louis archdiocese. He invested in real estate and used money collected from rents to support Catholic charities. In 1853, he purchased a farm north of the city and set aside a portion of the acreage to establish Calvary Cemetery.

The St. Louis Archdiocese celebrated the 50th anniversary of his consecration as bishop in November 1891. Clergy from around the country came to pay tribute. The archbishop's health began to decline soon after the anniversary. In 1893, Kenrick appointed Bishop John Kain as his coadjutor; two years later, with Kenrick's health in question, Kain was appointed archbishop of St. Louis. Kenrick was given the title Archbishop of Marcianapolis.

As the year 1896 began, his health was continuing to fail him. Although he appeared to be recovering well, he was feeling tired and ill, and spent most of his time at his residence on Lindell Boulevard. By early March, he was entering the final stages of life. As had become the custom, Brother Heribert from the Alexian Brothers' Hospital was staying with the archbishop through the evenings. A doctor examined him on Wednesday morning, March 4, and said of the archbishop's condition, "The Archbishop had a little chill and has a severe cold, but there's no immediate danger of death."

About 12:30 a.m., Thomas Franklin, Kenrick's servant, brought a warm drink to the archbishop. Thomas sat by his side as the archbishop slept. An hour later, Kenrick awoke and complained of feeling cold. Thomas suggested turning up the furnace. "Yes, Tom, I could stand a little more warmth," the archbishop feebly answered. These were his last known words. The archbishop was lying still, his arms were crossed on his chest, and he had a smile on his face when the housemaid entered the bedroom. She spoke to him, and when no response came, she collected Thomas and the two quietly stepped back into the room. Thomas took the archbishop's hand and spoke to him, but again no response. Thomas felt a faint pulse, but within a matter of minutes the pulse disappeared. Archbishop Peter Richard Kenrick died at 1:55 p.m.

Although Kenrick had been ill for some time, his death surprised many, including his doctor. Kenrick's body lay in state on a bier in the parlor of the residence. He was dressed in a purple cassock, surplice and cape; on his finger was the Episcopal ring of the Catholic Church. Members of the clergy and friends of the archbishop paid their respects during the afternoon and evening. A priest lifted the silk cloth covering the archbishop's face whenever a mourner approached the casket.

The next day, the body was placed in a wooden coffin covered in black cloth; the inside was lined in purple, denoting Kenrick's position as archbishop. The procession of mourners continued until the archbishop was moved to the black-draped Old Cathedral on Sunday, March 8; mourners filed past the coffin until after midnight.

The funeral was celebrated on Wednesday, March 11, in a cathedral filled beyond capacity. The *Globe-Democrat* devoted an entire page to the funeral. Kenrick was dressed in a yellow robe and purple cassock, with his miter on his head. The Catholic and Protestant communities were well represented, including young seminarians from Kenrick Seminary. Several bishops and archbishops from around the country participated in the Mass. Archbishop Kain and Archbishop Ryan of Philadelphia, a close personal friend of Kenrick, celebrated the ceremony. Archbishop Ryan eulogized his friend, "We saw him, a stately lily in the garden of the Church, and we saw the lily droop, till the powerless stem could no longer keep elevated the golden chalice; and when the lily drooped, the stem and lily feel; and we felt that the flower hath fallen."

The funeral cortege started up Walnut to 12th Street (now Tucker Boulevard) before taking Pine to Grand Avenue and the final stretch up Florissant Avenue. Peter Richard Kenrick was buried in the cemetery he had established 43 years earlier. He was laid to rest in front of a large crucifix in the Priests' Lot, Section 3.

Archbishop John Kain led the archdiocese for the next eight years. He was a man of great executive ability and honesty. In May 1903, Kain went to the St. Agnes Sanitarium in Baltimore, where he died on October 13, 1903; he was 62. Bishop coadjutor John Glennon was appointed administrator. Kain's body was returned to St. Louis for a funeral Mass at the Old Cathedral. He is buried in Calvary beside his predecessor. Thomas Franklin, who served both archbishops, is buried in front of his leaders.

WILLIAM TECUMSEH SHERMAN
(FEBRUARY 8, 1820-FEBRUARY 14, 1891)

William Sherman was the sixth child of 11 born to Charles and Mary Sherman in Lancaster, Ohio. After William's father died when he was nine, Thomas Ewing, a family friend and later a prominent U. S. Senator, took Sherman into his home.

Sherman's foster father arranged for him to go to West Point, where he graduated sixth in his class. It was at West Point that he first met Ulysses S. Grant, a man who would become a close friend, military superior, and future president. Like Grant, Sherman had an unsuccessful career in the years following graduation. In the Mexican War, he never saw action during his assignment with the occupational army in California. During this time, he met frontiersman Kit Carson and investigated the discovery of gold at John Sutter's sawmill, which began the great California Gold Rush of 1849. He was stationed at Jefferson Barracks in 1850 and leased a house on Chouteau Avenue near 12th Street.

He returned east and married Ellen Ewing, the daughter of his foster father, Thomas Ewing, who by this time was Secretary of the Interior under President Zachary Taylor. Among the guests at the wedding were the President and his cabinet and prominent Senators Daniel Webster, Henry Clay, and Thomas Hart Benton. William and Ellen would have eight children.

Sherman worked in several occupations during the next few years. He resigned from the army to become a banker in San Francisco and later in New York City. When the banks failed in the financial panic of 1857, he became a lawyer. Although he never studied law, he was admitted to the bar in Kansas and joined a firm with two of his brothers-in-law. In 1859, he became the superintendent of a new military school in Louisiana.

Differences around the country were becoming more extreme by 1861, with several states on the verge of seceding from the Union. Although Sherman had an affinity for the South, he was a northern man at heart. When Louisiana seceded from the Union in January 1861, Sherman resigned his post at the military school and returned to St. Louis, where he took over the presidency of the Fifth Street Railroad Company. The position would last but a short time.

His future was decided on April 12, 1861, with the Confederate bombing of Fort Sumter. He rejoined the army and was a colonel in the infantry during his first major fight of the war, the Battle of Bull Run. Months later, he was promoted to brigadier general. Shortly thereafter, Sherman asked to be relieved from duty because of physical and mental exhaustion

and a reoccurrence of his lifelong affliction with asthma. He was thought by some of his superiors to be insane. Brigadier General Don Carlos Buell replaced him.

When Sherman returned to active duty, even though his demeanor was intense and his temperament restless, his military judgment was sound. His attitude toward battle was reflected in a letter to his wife, "I begin to regard the death and mangling of a couple thousand men as a small affair, a kind of morning dash -- and it may be well that we become so hardened." By March 1862, he was promoted to major general. He took part in the bloody battle at Shiloh, where he was wounded in the hand and had three horses shot out from under him. His armies went on to capture Vicksburg, Chattanooga, and Knoxville. While Sherman was fighting the battle at Chattanooga in 1863, his nine-year-old son, Willie, fell ill with typhoid fever and died on October 3 in a Memphis hotel. It was a terrific blow to the Sherman family. Sherman wrote a friend on October 4, 1863:

> The child that bore my name, and in whose future I reposed with more confidence than I did in my own plan of life, now floats a mere corpse, seeking a grave in a distant land, with a weeping mother, brother, and sisters, clustered around him. For myself, I ask no sympathy. On, on I must go, to meet a soldier's fate, or live to see our country rise superior to all factions...

In the spring of 1867, Willie's body was disinterred and then buried in Calvary Cemetery.

When Grant became commander of the Union Army, Sherman succeeded him as commander of the military division of the Mississippi. His 100,000-man army took Atlanta in September 1864. His men completely destroyed Atlanta and proceeded to cut a path through Georgia and the Carolinas in his now famous "March to the Sea." During the march, Sherman found out from a New York newspaper that his infant son Charles had died. The general had never seen his six-month-old boy. Charles was buried at Calvary; Willie would later be buried alongside.

Sherman became commander in chief of the U.S. Army when Grant entered the White House in 1869. During the next decade, he wrote his memoirs and gave speeches to veterans' groups. In one speech he said,

"There is many a boy here today who looks on war as all glory, but, boys, it is all hell." Soon afterward, citizens were quoting from Sherman's "war is hell" speech.

In 1883, he retired from the army and returned to St. Louis, living at 912 Garrison Avenue. Officials within the Republican Party urged him to run for the presidency, but he happily declined. He enjoyed his retirement by visiting old acquaintances, including Ulysses S. Grant, who was dying of cancer and attempting to finish his own memoirs when Sherman paid him a visit. Sherman participated in Grant's funeral in New York City after the former president died in July 1885.

Less than a year after the funeral, Sherman and his family moved from St. Louis to New York City. It was in New York that his wife Ellen died of heart disease in November 1888. She was buried at Calvary beside her two sons. Friends and family could hardly communicate with the grieving general. For weeks his own health declined, he lost weight and his asthma worsened. But, as a new year dawned, Sherman was again giving speeches and socializing with friends.

In late 1890 he confided to a friend, "I feel it coming sometimes when I get home from an entertainment or banquet, especially these winter nights. I feel death reaching out for me, as it were. I suppose I'll take cold some night and go to bed, never to get up again." As he predicted, he came down with a severe cold and sore throat on February 6, 1891. His asthma and acute erysipelas, a bacterial infection of the skin, contributed to his illness. His personal physician and a nurse attended to the ailing general.

By Saturday the 14th, he was unconscious, his breathing labored. The erysipelas had caused his neck and hands to swell, and the inflammation was choking off air to his lungs. Although Sherman's condition was severe, he suffered no pain. Two other doctors were consulted and agreed that there was no hope for recovery. His daughters Minnie, Lizzie, Ellie, and Rachel were by his side, as was the general's brother, Senator John Sherman. Members of his adopted family, the Ewings, also were present. West 71st Street, in front of his residence, was filled with onlookers when news spread of Sherman's impending death.

At 1:50 p.m., he breathed a heavy sigh and his body quit. The nurse lifted his head and said in a whisper, "He is dead." The only sign of the erysipelas was slight swelling under the eyes.

President Benjamin Harrison, who served under Sherman during the March to the Sea, sent a message to the family:

I loved and venerated General Sherman, and would stand very near to the more deeply afflicted members of the family in this hour of bereavement. It will be as if there were one dead in every loyal household in the land.

On Tuesday, February 17, the body lay in state amid roses, lilies, and violets in the front parlor of his home. Sherman was dressed in full military uniform. The coffin was draped with an American flag, with the general's sword, scabbard, and hat resting on top. A candelabrum stood at the head of the coffin, a marble bust of Sherman at the foot. Three military guards stood at attention.

At 10:00 a.m., hundreds of citizens began moving through the parlor to view him. Dignitaries, military personnel, and friends paid their respects, including the widows of George Armstrong Custer and Winfield Hancock, who wept upon viewing Sherman. Thousands more passed by the coffin the following day. That evening, a plaster cast of his face was taken.

In tribute to Sherman, government offices were closed and all flags in New York City were set at half-mast during the Thursday funeral. Sherman's son Thomas, a Catholic priest, who was out of the country when his father died, viewed his father for the first time and conducted the funeral service. About 150 people, including cabinet members and numerous generals, attended the private service. Julia Dent, widow of President Grant, was also in attendance. Father Thomas Sherman recited prayers and read from Scripture during the half-hour ceremony. After the service, former presidents Grover Cleveland and Rutherford B. Hayes arrived for the procession. President Benjamin Harrison reached the house a short time later.

At 2:00 p.m., six lieutenants carried the casket on their shoulders to the caisson waiting outside the residence. Among the honorary pallbearers was Sherman's friend, former Confederate General Joseph Johnston, who had fought against Sherman during the Civil War and ultimately surrendered to Sherman at the end of the war. (Ironically, Johnston came down with pneumonia from the cold weather during the funeral march. He died one month later at the age of 84.) Thousands lined the streets of the procession route, and hundreds more watched from windows and rooftops. Sherman's remains were placed on a ferry for transport to New Jersey before the Pennsylvania Railroad brought him back to St. Louis. Rutherford B. Hayes was among those who came to St. Louis with the family.

On February 21, hundreds of St. Louisans, including Governor David Francis, awaited the arrival at Union Depot. The train, entirely draped in mourning, arrived at 8:30 in the morning. Some were lucky to view the casket, which rested on a catafalque in the center of the rail car. At 10:30 a.m., the flag-draped coffin was placed on a caisson for a procession that moved up 11th Street to Pine, then north on Grand Avenue to Florissant Avenue to the gates of Calvary Cemetery. The streets were jammed with people. The two-hour, 50-minute procession was the largest and most impressive the city had ever seen.

Approximately 300 people, including a large contingent of family, military, and dignitaries, surrounded the grave to hear Thomas Sherman conduct a 10-minute service for his father. An honor guard fired three rifle volleys, and a bugler played "Taps."

William Tecumseh Sherman was laid to rest beside his wife Ellen and his two sons in a roadside grave in Section 17.

KATE CHOPIN
(FEBRUARY 8, 1851-AUGUST 22, 1904)

Kate Chopin's writing career lasted a short 14 years, during which she wrote more than 100 works -- short stories, poems, and novels. Her stories appeared in magazines and newspapers nationwide. Readers were gripped by her passionate tales, told through her warm, fluent style and sympathetic yet strong characters. Her personality and charm were as engaging as her stories. She was an individualist who smoked Cuban cigars and wore the most fashionable clothing.

Her father, Thomas O'Flaherty, had come to America from Ireland. He opened a successful boat shop on the St. Louis levee and established himself among the elite in the city. He went on to become one of the founders of the Pacific Railroad. He married into a successful family, but his wife died five years into the marriage. Six months later, he married Eliza Faris. The family settled into a new home on Eighth Street, between Gratiot and Chouteau. Kate arrived in 1851.

Disaster struck the family on November 1, 1855, when Thomas was one of 31 people killed in the Gasconade Bridge collapse. Archbishop Peter Richard Kenrick, a longtime family friend, conducted the funeral service. O'Flaherty is buried at Calvary Cemetery (Section 3) near Kenrick and the Priests' Lot. Kate was only four years old at the time of his death.

She attended the Sacred Heart Academy at Fifth and Market. She quit school for two years after her father died but later returned to her studies, only to stop again during the Civil War. She spent much of the war years writing. During the war, her half-brother George died of typhoid fever while serving as a Confederate soldier. And her brother Tom was killed in 1873 in a carriage accident. Both were buried next to their father in Calvary.

She married New Orleans native Oscar Chopin in 1870 and lived in Cloutierville, Louisiana, raising six children. The Creole culture in Louisiana provided the setting for many of her tales. When Oscar died in 1881, Chopin returned to St. Louis with the children and bought a house at 3317 Morgan Street (now Delmar) between Jefferson and Grand. She remained in the city the rest of her life.

It was during this period that she began her writing career. Her first novel, *At Fault*, was published in 1890, but it was her book of short stories, *Bayou Folk*, that gained her literary fame. Her final book, *The Awakening*, published in 1899, was the story of a young wife and mother who falls in love and has an adulterous affair with another man. At the time, Chopin was condemned for writing about such a subject. Only later did the story win critical acclaim. The American classic is now considered a benchmark in women's writing.

By the turn of the century, she was one of St. Louis' most well-known citizens and was included in the first edition of *Who's Who in America*. She moved to a rented house at 4232 McPherson Avenue at the end of 1902, continuing to raise five of her children. She made a will and during a period of illness told her children, "I hope I will die first so that I will not lose any one of you."

Chopin lived only six blocks from the park grounds of the St. Louis World's Fair and visited the fair almost every day after it opened in April 1904. She returned home tired from the fair on Saturday, August 20, and by midnight was suffering from a terrible headache. She lost consciousness, but revived the next day to the sight of her children, including her son, Dr. George Chopin. She complained about the pain in her head. She improved, but on Sunday night she once again slipped into unconsciousness. At noon, Monday, August 22, Kate Chopin died in her bed. According to the *Post-Dispatch*, the cause of death was "from hemorrhage of the brain, seemingly the result of unaccustomed exercise and exertion."

William Marion Reedy, editor of the *Mirror* and one of Chopin's publishers, wrote of his friend:

> St. Louis lost a woman of rare intellect and noble character when death removed, last Monday, Mrs. Kate Chopin. A host of friends today honor her memory and cherish the boon of her acquaintance. She was a remarkably talented woman, who knew how to be a genius without sacrificing the comradeship of her children. As a mother, wife, and friend she shone resplendent and her contributions to fiction, though few, showed that she possessed true literary genius.

The funeral Mass was conducted on Wednesday, August 24, at the New Cathedral. Chopin was buried beside her daughter-in-law in Calvary Cemetery; her six children are now buried with her in Section 17.

One of the last poems Chopin wrote was entitled *To the Friend of My Youth: To Kitty*. It reflected her views of life and death.

It is not all of life
To cling together while the years glide past.
It is not all of love
To walk with clasped hands from first to last.
That mystic garland which the spring did twine
Of scented lilac and the new-blown rose,
Faster than chains will hold my soul to thine
Thro' joy, and grief, thro' life--unto its close.

ROBERT HANNEGAN
(JUNE 30, 1903-OCTOBER 6, 1949)

Robert Hannegan was a prominent member of the Democratic Party and the man credited with keeping Harry Truman in the White House. It took only 11 years for him to rise from local politics to the national scene.

Hannegan was born in St. Louis and attended St. Louis University, where he gained a reputation as an excellent athlete. He received a law degree from the university in 1925. He established a law practice and entered the local political scene. In 1933, he was the Democratic committeeman in the 21st Ward, where his support of Mayor Bernard Dickmann helped him to win chairmanship of the Democratic City Central Committee. In 1940, he threw his support behind the renomination of Senator Harry S Truman of Independence, Missouri; when Truman won the election by a slight margin, he publicly credited Hannegan with making it possible. Hannegan returned to his law practice until he was persuaded by Truman to accept the vacant position of Commissioner of Internal Revenue. The post offered him the opportunity to become intimate friends with President Franklin D. Roosevelt and other top political leaders. This lead to Hannegan's being appointed Chairman of the Democratic National Committee in January 1944, making him instrumental in Roosevelt's renomination to a fourth term and Truman's nomination as Vice President.

In April 1945, just weeks after the death of President Roosevelt, Hannegan moved to Washington, D. C. He served as Postmaster General in President Truman's new cabinet and was one of the President's chief political advisors. His poor health forced him to step down as Postmaster General and National Democratic Committee chairman in November 1947. Ignoring doctor's orders for complete rest, he returned to St. Louis, where an announcement was made that he and Fred Saigh, Jr., had purchased a majority interest in the St. Louis Baseball Cardinals, with Hannegan becoming president of the club.

High blood pressure was taking its toll by early 1949. In January, he sold his interest in the St. Louis Cardinals for an estimated $1,000,000. To relieve his ill health, he traveled with his family to Europe in 1949. While in Rome, he had a private audience with Pope Pius XII; three years earlier, the Pope had made him a Knight of St. Gregory, Grand Order of the Holy Cross. He also spent time during 1949 as a backer, with Archbishop Joseph Ritter, of the proposed Cardinal Glennon Memorial Hospital.

He now spent much of his time in his home at 5745 Lindell Boulevard. In one of his final public appearances, a week before he died, he hosted President Truman in St. Louis and attended a dinner with him in Kansas City. On the evening of October 5, he suffered a mild heart attack after he and his wife Irma returned home from visiting friends. His personal physician was summoned and stayed until midnight. When the doctor returned to the Hannegan house about 6:00 a.m., he found that his patient's condition had worsened and he administered a sedative to ease the discomfort. Hannegan's wife and three of their four children were at his bedside when he died at 9:30 a.m. His doctor attributed the death to a heart condition caused by high blood pressure. Robert Hannegan was 46. Reverend Gerald McMahon, a family friend and pastor of St. Mary Magdelen Church in Brentwood, arrived shortly after the death and administered the last rites.

President Truman sent a telegram to Irma. It said in part:

> *Despite the handicap of long continued ill health, Bob was a prodigious worker, with executive and administrative ability of the highest order... Mrs. Truman and I are thinking of you and the children in this hour of sorrow and send out with our heartfelt sympathy a prayer that the God of all comfort will sustain you in a loss so overwhelming.*

The body was taken to Arthur Donnelly Mortuary on October 9 for visitation. An estimated 4,000 people, including city, state, and national political leaders, crowded the St. Louis Cathedral for the funeral the next day. President Truman himself was unable to attend, but members of his cabinet were present to pay their respects. Two justices of the Supreme Court, the governor of Missouri, and Texas Senator Lyndon Johnson were at the ceremony. The funeral Mass was celebrated by Reverend McMahon. In his eulogy, the priest related a discussion he had had with Hannegan after a meeting for the proposed Cardinal Glennon Hospital. "He said then that while physicians had talked encouragingly to him, he realized that he might die at any time. 'And I am ready in every way,' he added."

Hannegan is buried just inside the main gate to the right, Section 18. A large cross engraved with flowers stands behind the flat marker of Robert and Irma.

TENNESSEE WILLIAMS
(MARCH 26, 1911-FEBRUARY 25, 1983)

Thomas Lanier Williams was one of the greatest and most admired playwrights of his time. In 1918, at the age of seven, he moved to St. Louis with his family; they rented a tenement apartment at 4633 Westminister Place. He chose the gloomy, dark apartment building as the setting for *The Glass Menagerie*. His two decades in St. Louis were the unhappiest of his life. Years later, he described St. Louisans as "cold, smug, complacent, intolerant, stupid, provincial."

Williams had an overbearing, hard-drinking father; the two were never able to form a close relationship. His mother, Edwina, suffered most of the abuse from her husband's harsh temperament. Williams was dearly devoted to his sister Rose, who spent much of her life in a St. Louis sanitarium suffering from schizophrenia. Rose died in September 1996 and was buried at Calvary.

Williams attended Soldan High School and later graduated from University City High School. He went on to college at the University of Missouri at Columbia, but dropped out during the Depression to take a job at International Shoe Company in St. Louis, where his father was a clothing salesman. After two unhappy years of work, he enrolled at Washington University, but later transferred to the University of Iowa, where he earned a bachelor's degree in 1938. During this time, he spent countless hours at the typewriter, punching out the words that would one day make him famous.

His literary breakthrough came with the success of *The Glass Menagerie* in 1944. The main character of Amanda Wingfield was modeled after his mother. Three years later, *A Streetcar named Desire* won him his first Pulitzer Prize. His second Pulitzer was for *Cat on a Hot Tin Roof*.

Williams' plays were a reflection of his life. In 1979 he wrote, "My greatest affliction... is perhaps the major theme of my writings, the affliction of loneliness that follows me like a shadow, a very ponderous shadow too heavy to drag after me all of my days and nights." He often spoke of death, his favorite obsession. As a child, he suffered from diphtheria, which affected his kidneys and paralyzed both legs for a time. His eyesight was damaged and remained poor the rest of his life. He was terrified at the threat of heart or respiratory problems, real or imagined. As an adult, he was a hypochondriac with an addiction to drugs and alcohol. In 1969, his brother Dakin had him hospitalized for three months in the psychiatric unit at Barnes Hospital for treatment of his addictions. From that point on, Williams was estranged from his brother.

By mid-February 1983, he was back in his Manhattan home, the Elysèe Hotel, after extensive travel around the world. He was in a state of total exhaustion and once again addicted to drugs. He repeatedly told friends that death was closing in on him but ignored the advice of doctors to be hospitalized.

On the morning of February 25, his longtime friend, John Ucker, discovered Williams' body, slumped at the side of his bed. He was officially declared dead at 11:10 a.m. An empty prescription bottle lay near him; other medications and empty wine bottles were on the night table. The coroner ruled his death as accidental. The autopsy showed that Williams had choked to death on a plastic cap from one of the prescription bottles. Friends claimed he had often pried the caps from bottles with his teeth; apparently one had caught in his windpipe on the night of February 24.

By noon, as radio and television announced his death to the nation, a huge crowd gathered outside the Elysèe. The February 25 *St. Louis Post-Dispatch* headline read, "Tennessee Williams Found Dead in Hotel." Williams lay in state at the Campbell Funeral Home in Manhattan before being moved to Lupton Chapel in University City. On March 6, a funeral Mass was held at the St. Louis Cathedral, only a few short blocks from his first home. More than a thousand people attended the hour-and-a-half service, with hundreds more gathered outside. Reverend Jerome Wilkerson, who conducted the service, said of Williams, "The tragedy of Tennessee seems to be that the revelatory sword of suffering that pierced his heart seemed to be so much more therapeutic to others than to himself. He would seem to have remained all his life among the walking wounded."

Reverend Sidney Lanier, a second cousin of Williams, read a passage from the Old Testament.

A light rain fell as the casket was carried from the church. The procession made its way through University City and Clayton, where he had grown up. People stood in their doorways and watched the famous playwright pass before them. At 1:00 p.m., the casket was placed under a canvas tent at the gravesite before burial in the family plot at Calvary Cemetery (Section 15), near his mother Edwina. He had wished to be cremated and "given back to the sea from which life is said to have come." Instead, his brother buried him in the city he most hated.

On March 8, the marquees at 20 Broadway theaters were darkened for one minute in his memory. His raised headstone is engraved with a quote from his story *Camino Real*:

> The violets in the mountains
> have broken the rocks.

TOM DOOLEY
(JANUARY 17, 1927-JANUARY 18, 1961)

Tom Dooley was born in St. Louis and attended St. Louis University High School. In 1941, after one year of pre-med training at the University of Notre Dame, he left college to serve in the Navy as a medical aid. It was during this time that his older brother Earle was killed in action in Germany. After the war, Tom continued his education at the Sorbonne in Paris and at St. Louis University Medical School, from which he graduated in 1953.

Dooley rejoined the Navy, and in 1954 was assigned to a camp at Haiphong, Vietnam, as medical officer. He aided in the "Passage to Freedom," a program to evacuate refugees from Communist North Vietnam to South Vietnam. He was awarded the Legion of Merit in recognition of his work at Haiphong. He lost a significant amount of weight during this time and spent a short stint in a Japanese hospital to recuperate. While in the hospital, he began to write *Deliver Us From Evil*, a book about his medical experiences in Vietnam. It was the first of three bestsellers. Twentieth Century Fox purchased the movie rights to all three books.

When Dooley was discharged from the Navy in 1956, he decided to dedicate his life to aiding the people of Southeast Asia. With permission from the government of Laos and help from former Navy colleagues, he established a small hospital in Nam Tha, near the Chinese border. He

financed the hospital with the royalties from his first book. In 1957, he returned to the U. S. and, with Dr. Peter Comanduras, a Washington D. C., medical professor, founded MEDICO, the Medical International Cooperation Organization. The non-profit business brought aid to areas that lacked medical facilities. He financed the organization with royalties from his second book, *The Edge of Tomorrow*, and funds generated from numerous speaking engagements. Within a year, MEDICO had established 17 programs in 12 countries.

In June 1959, while doing work for MEDICO in Asia, he slipped in the jungle and injured his right side. A few months later, a malignant growth was found on his chest wall. He went to New York's Memorial Hospital for cancer surgery. After recovering, he went back on the lecture circuit to raise more funds for MEDICO and then returned to Laos. In December 1959, while Dooley was in St. Louis for the final stop of his fundraising speaking tour; he told the audience, "We in MEDICO simply go out and take care of sick people in parts of the world where medical care is almost entirely unknown. We take care of them simply and unselfishly. By our deeds, and not by words, we demonstrate what is really in the hearts of the American people."

He entered a Hong Kong hospital in November 1960, suffering from fatigue and exhaustion and a debilitating pain in his spine. He returned to the United States in December and once again entered Memorial Hospital, where examinations showed a recurrence of the cancer. By January, his condition had worsened, and he was in and out of consciousness. The doctors could do nothing but ease his pain. His mother in St. Louis was contacted, and she was by his side when he died at 8:40 p.m. on the 18th. The bachelor doctor succumbed one day after his 34th birthday. Outgoing President Dwight D. Eisenhower said of him, "There are few if any men who have equaled his exhibition of courage, self-sacrifice, faith in his God and his readiness to serve his fellow man." Dooley died two days before John F. Kennedy was inaugurated President of the United States.

The body was returned to St. Louis on Friday, January 20, with visitation at the Arthur Donnelly Funeral Home on Lindell Boulevard. He rested in a flag-draped, bronze coffin, dressed in a dark suit with a Legion of Merit pin on his lapel and a rosary in his hands. On Sunday evening, the body lay in state in All Souls Chapel at the St. Louis Cathedral.

Bishop Leo Byrne celebrated the funeral Mass on Monday. Father George Gottwald gave the eulogy. He said of Dooley, "...he spurned material comfort and, with utter and complete selflessness, went to minister to the sick and needy and underprivileged in a far corner of the world because he was fully conscious that his ability as a physician was given him to serve God." More than 2,000 mourners from all over the world attended the ceremony, including representatives from the Laotian government. Dr. Peter Comanduras, co-founder of MEDICO, and 25 other members of the organization were among those in attendance. The pallbearers were six medical students from St. Louis University.

The medical missionary was buried with full military honors. An honor guard representing the five armed services escorted the cortege to the gravesite. Dooley was laid to rest in Calvary beside his father and his brother Earle in Section 19, near the mausoleum. He was buried with a medal of St. Christopher that was inscribed on the back with a poem by Robert Frost:

The woods are lovely, dark and deep,
But I have promises to keep,
And miles to go before I sleep.

The same words are inscribed on the large, flat stone that marks his grave. His accomplishments and awards also are listed.

OTHER NOTABLES AT CALVARY CEMETERY

JOHN SCULLIN (AUGUST 17, 1836-MAY 28, 1920) was chairman of the board of Scullin Steel Company. The native of St. Lawrence County, New York, started his career selling stoves for $20 month. He then went to work in the railroad business as a brakeman before establishing himself as a railroad contractor. His largest project was the construction of the Missouri, Kansas, and Texas Railroad in 1860. Scullin came to St. Louis in 1875 and constructed several streetcar lines. He later worked as a financier and then founded the steel company.

On Saturday, May 22, 1920, Scullin became ill while attending a function at the Log Cabin Club in Ladue and was taken to his home at

5218 South Broadway. The next day, he was transported to St. Luke's Hospital and was diagnosed with uremic poisoning, a renal condition that progressively deteriorates the body. He died less than a week later. David Francis attended the funeral at St. Mary and St. Joseph Catholic Church on Monday, May 31. Scullin's mausoleum is located near the entrance to the cemetery in Section 18.

JULIUS WALSH (DECEMBER 1, 1842-MARCH 21, 1923) served as president of numerous financial and rail companies in St. Louis. He was born into affluence in the family home at Sixth and Olive. He left the city to attend St. Joseph's College in Kentucky and received his law degree from Columbia University in New York. Upon his father's death, he inherited four railroads and the directorship of the Bank of the State of Missouri.

In 1885, he established the Northern Central Line, which used horse cars, and he went on to become one of the most dominant figures in streetcar development. He was a member of the St. Louis Bridge Company and later its president; it was this company that financed James Eads and his bridge across the Mississippi. In 1870, Walsh married Josephine Dickson, daughter of Charles Dickson, who was president of the bridge company. President Ulysses S. Grant, a family friend, gave a dinner at the White House for Walsh and his wife while they were on their honeymoon.

Among the significant positions he held were president and chairman of the Terminal Railroad, the Union Electric Light and Power Company, and the Mississippi Valley Trust Company. He served as president of numerous companies and sat on the board of other institutions, such as his friend Henry Shaw's Botanical Garden, and was a director of the St. Louis World's Fair in 1904.

Walsh and his wife, Josephine, lived at 4510 Lindell Boulevard with their seven children. Their daughter Mary was killed near Tucson, Arizona, in April 1916, when she and her husband were shot by police who mistook them for wanted bank robbers.

During the early part of March 1923, Walsh was severely ill and bedridden with a diseased heart. He rallied on Monday, March 19, as he received the final sacrament from Archbishop John Glennon. The hope of a full recovery was dashed when he slipped into a coma early Wednesday morning. His six surviving children were at his bedside when he died at 9:00 a.m. at the age of 80. Saturday morning, a short service was conducted at the home before the body was taken to the St. Louis Cathedral. Offices of the Terminal Railroad stopped work for two minutes in honor of their former chairman, and other companies that he had owned showed similar respect. Archbishop Glennon celebrated high Mass at the cathedral. Company officers served as pallbearers. The Walsh family is buried in Section 1, a short distance from the Mullanphys.

JOSEPH C. CABANNE (OCTOBER 16, 1846-MARCH 17, 1922) and his family were direct descendents of Madame Chouteau. Cabanne got into the dairy business at age 21, on the advice of his uncle; he established the Mont Cabanne Dairy in what is now Forest Park. In 1872, he started the St. Louis Dairy Company at 12th and Chestnut. His innovations included the covered milk wagon, the first creamery in  the city, first delivery of milk in bottles, and the inauguration of a milk filtering system. He delivered the first whole milk sold in St. Louis, and at a lesser price than skimmed milk.

Cabanne and his wife, Susan, had seven children. He was an avid sportsman who participated in amateur boxing and played golf every day on the Triple A course in Forest Park. He was the first president of the Civic League and one of the founders of the Missouri Athletic Club.

By 1922, he was living with his daughter and her husband at the Buckingham Hotel. In February, he came down with pneumonia and suffered for six weeks, unable to shake its effects. The normally healthy Cabanne became depressed over his condition. On Thursday afternoon, March 16, 1922, he cut his throat with a razor and was rushed to St. John's Hospital, where he died the next day. The body was taken to a second daughter's home at Westminster Place in preparation for the funeral. The funeral took place at the St. Louis Cathedral on March 20. Cabanne and his wife (she died in March 1910) are buried in a roadside lot in Section 1, just to the right of Alexander McNair.

JAMES CAMPBELL (? 1848- JUNE 12, 1914) was considered one of the wealthiest citizens of St. Louis when he died of pneumonia at Indian Field, his summer home in Greenwich, Connecticut.

The native of Ireland had come to the United States with his family when he was an infant. During the Civil War, the 14-year-old served as a messenger at General John Fremont's headquarters. After the war, Campbell worked as a surveyor for the Atlantic & Pacific Railroad and began buying land ahead of the tracks. His first fortune was made when property values increased dramatically as the construction was coming to an end. He multiplied his wealth in the bond market and invested in the streetcar business. In 1909, he was appointed chairman of the board of the Union Electric Company and of the North American Company, parent to United Railways.

In May 1914, he began feeling the effects of a carbuncle on the back of his neck. Two minor operations were performed during that summer; but, while he was recovering from the second one, Campbell came down with a high fever and was confined to bed. It was later discovered that he had blood poisoning as a result of the operation. His wife and daughter stayed with him as his health declined steadily. He developed pneumonia and died at 9:00 p.m., Friday, June 12, in his Connecticut summer home.

The next morning, his body was placed aboard a train for St. Louis and was taken to his home at 2 Westmoreland Place. The next day, the funeral was celebrated at the St. Louis Cathedral to a capacity crowd. John Scullin, a friend of the family, accompanied the widow and her daughter. At three o'clock, all streetcars run by the United Railway Company stopped for five minutes to mourn its chairman.

Campbell's mausoleum at Calvary was built in 1911; it is located in Section 18 near the main entrance. The inscription above the door reads, "The Family of James Campbell."

WILLIAM MARION REEDY (DECEMBER 11, 1862-JULY 28, 1920) was one of the most notable literary figures of his generation and the well-known editor of his own literary journal, *Reedy's Mirror*. He was born in St. Louis and educated at Christian Brothers Academy and St. Louis University, receiving his degree in 1880. He began his writing career at the *Missouri Republican* and later worked for the *Globe-Democrat*, for which he wrote a weekly column called "Sunday in Forest Park." In 1893, he founded the *St. Louis Mirror*, and three years later changed the name to *Reedy's Mirror*. He was an excellent orator with a wonderful gift for storytelling.

Reedy was highly regarded in his efforts to giving young, unknown writers a voice. He encouraged and often published new literary talent from around the St. Louis area, such as short-story writer Fannie Hurst, playwright Zoe Akins, poet Sara Teasdale, and novelist Kate Chopin.

Reedy was suffering from heart disease in 1920 when he traveled to San Francisco to cover the Democratic National Convention. He died suddenly and unexpectedly of heart disease at 1:00 p.m. on Wednesday, July 28. His body was returned to St. Louis and taken to his home at Berry and Manchester Roads. A week after his death, the funeral was celebrated in the auditorium of the St. Louis University Institute of Law. Frederick Lehmann, a longtime friend of Reedy, gave the eulogy. "It is evident that he lived his life in its utmost fullness to the last. From the day's activity, whether it had been of recreation or of labor, he sought the repose of sleep and while thus at rest the messenger with the inverted torch called him to awake in another world."

Reedy is buried near the top of the hill in Section 17; his red marble marker is strangely tilted back and denotes him as "Editor and Author."

URBAN SHOCKER (AUGUST 22, 1890–SEPTEMBER 9, 1928) was a member of what many people consider to be the greatest baseball team in history, the 1927 Yankees. Also called "Murderer's Row," this team was comprised of future Hall of Famers Babe Ruth, Lou Gehrig, Tony Lazzeri, Earle Combs, and manager Miller Huggins.

Shocker began his career with the Yankees before being traded to the St. Louis Browns in 1918. The spitball pitcher was a 20-game winner for four consecutive seasons from 1920 to 1923, with his best year coming in 1921, when he led the American League with 27 wins. Shocker's greatest single-day achievement came on September 6, 1924, when he pitched two complete game wins in a doubleheader against the Chicago White Sox. He was sent back to the Yankees a few months later and pitched three more seasons. He started Game 2 of the 1926 World Series but lost the game and, in the end, the series, to the Cardinals. The Yankees won the series in 1927 by sweeping the Pittsburgh Pirates. By the time his career ended, he had compiled a record of 187-117, with an ERA of 3.17.

In August 1928, Shocker was in a weakened condition when he arrived at St. Luke's Hospital in Denver, suffering from pneumonia. He was thought to be recovered when he suffered a relapse and died at the age of 38. He was the first of the 1927 Yankees to die. Urban Shocker is buried in front of a square, white marker in Section 24.

RAYMOND TUCKER (DECEMBER 4, 1896-NOVEMBER 23, 1970), the former mayor of St. Louis, died peacefully at 10:06 p.m. in Barnes Hospital of congestive heart failure. His wife, Edythe, and one daughter were at his bedside. In June 1961, while still in the mayor's office, Tucker had had his cancerous right lung removed at Barnes. Another malignancy had developed on his remaining lung at the time of his death.

A native St. Louisan, Tucker received degrees from both St. Louis University (1917) and Washington University (1920). He was a professor of mechanical engineering at Washington University for 13 years before accepting a position as secretary to Mayor Bernard Dickmann in 1934. He continued to serve in the next administration, that of William Dee Becker, before returning to Washington University. In 1953, he won the Democratic primary and, ultimately, the election. He served the city for three terms, until 1965. Tucker was instrumental in the passing of bond issues that led to the building of the Planetarium and the highway system, among other projects.

Tucker's funeral was celebrated on Wednesday, November 27, 1970, at St. Mary and St. Joseph Catholic Church. Nearly 300 mourners, including Governor Warren Hearnes and Mayor Alfonso Cervantes, attended the service. Cervantes said of his predecessor, "The community has suffered a serious loss in the death of Ray Tucker. His contributions to the community were twofold; as an educator, he prepared young men well in the field of engineering; as a public official, he became a strong administrator who started St. Louis on the way back."

Raymond Tucker is buried on the second floor of the mausoleum at Calvary, in the St. Louis Room. His wife Edythe, who died in 1987, is buried with him. Tucker Boulevard, alongside City Hall, is named in his honor.

ROBERT HYLAND (MARCH 25, 1920-MARCH 5, 1992) started at KMOX in 1951. At the time of his death, he was senior vice president of CBS Radio and General Manager of the station. He established the now-familiar format of talk radio with his "At Your Service" call-in programs, making "The Voice of St. Louis" one of the most imitated radio stations in the country. He assembled and developed some of the most talented broadcasters in the business: Jack Carney, Bob Hardy, Jack Buck, Jim White, Bob Costas, Harry Caray, and others.

Hyland's father, Robert, Sr., was a well-known surgeon and a pioneer in sports medicine. He was a surgeon for the St. Louis Cardinals and the St. Louis Browns for more than 30 years. Among his baseball patients were Ty Cobb, Babe Ruth, and Lou Gehrig. Baseball commissioner Kenesaw Mountain Landis called him the "Surgeon General of Baseball." Robert, Sr., died on December 14, 1950, and was buried at Calvary Cemetery.

Robert Hyland attended St. Louis University, where he was captain of the baseball team. Upon graduation, he was offered a contract by Branch Rickey to play for the Cardinals but, with his mother's persuasion, he rejected the offer.

Hyland's philanthropy was widespread and included founding Hyland Center, the drug and alcohol treatment center at St. Anthony's Hospital. He served in a civic capacity for the St. Louis Zoo, the St. Louis Symphony, and Municipal Theatre, among others.

Late on the evening of Thursday, March 5, 1992, Robert Hyland died of cancer in his Creve Coeur home. He was 71. KMOX Radio dedicated the entire next day to memories of their fallen leader. The St. Louis Cathedral was the site of the March 9 funeral. Governor John Ashcroft and Archbishop John May were among the dignitaries present at the ceremony. Monsignor John Ronquest, pastor of the Old Cathedral, where

Hyland attended church every morning before work, celebrated the service with the assistance of 13 priests. Jack Buck and Bob Costas were among the pallbearers.

Hyland's remains were taken to Calvary Cemetery and placed in the cemetery mausoleum, in the Our Lady of Consolation Room on the second floor.

IV

1849:
A Disastrous Year

IMMENSE CONFLAGRATION!

FIFTEEN BLOCKS OF HOUSES INJURED OR DESTROYED BY FIRE.

TWENTY-THREE BOATS BURNED!

LIVES LOST.

THREE MILLIONS OF PROPERTY DESTROYED.

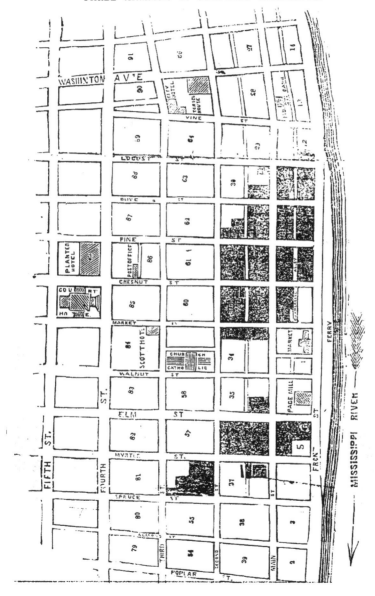

A map from the Missouri Republican in 1849 shows the fire damage in the shaded areas

Medical epidemics were widespread in 19th-century America, with diseases such as smallpox, yellow fever, and typhoid fever killing thousands of people. Moreover, infant mortality was extremely high, with only half the children born living to maturity. The use of vaccines was still in its earliest stages. Many diseases were spread by unsanitary conditions and lack of good medical care. One such disease was cholera, which first appeared in St. Louis in 1832. The highly contagious disease killed hundreds, but quickly faded and finally disappeared, before reoccurring for a short time the next year.

In December 1848, cholera once again appeared in foreign immigrants, mostly Germans, arriving by ship in New Orleans. As the immigrants moved through the Ohio and Mississippi valleys to make their new homes in America, the cholera spread. Several ships arrived in St. Louis during the last week of 1848 and early 1849 with passengers and crew carrying the disease, some dead on arrival. At the time, city officials didn't recognize the disease as a threat. The immigrants stayed in boardinghouses in the city without medical examinations or quarantines. With the disease firmly planted among its citizens, the 70,000 inhabitants of St. Louis were now seriously threatened.

The year 1849 may have been the most tragic in St. Louis history. The first cholera death came on January 5th. Thirty-six people would die of cholera in January; the February toll was 21. In March and April, the numbers jumped to 78 and 126, respectively, with Jefferson Barracks reporting 27 deaths from cholera. Although 261 people were dead, the city still did nothing to curtail the disease, as ships continued to disembark their infected passengers on the St. Louis riverfront from New Orleans. Another 78 people died in the first week of May. After the second week, about 26 people per day were dying. St. Louis Hospital was filled beyond its capacity. Patients often were given heavy doses of medicines containing mercury and laxatives, probably hurting them more than helping.

Many St. Louisans were afraid to leave their homes. Elizabeth Wyman, a housewife with children at home, wrote to her sister:

> We live very plain, eat no vegetable, not even potatoes, no pies, no fruit, no rich cake, we do not go anywhere, for I am afraid to go from home, and we have no company, for visiting is out of the question.

Some people blamed God for taking out His vengeance on a helpless city. Others blamed the poor, as reports spread that cholera was confined to districts where sanitary measures were neglected, where alleys and streets were accumulating refuse and garbage.

The temperature was warm and the wind blew a steady breeze on May 17, 1849. It was another busy day on the riverfront, with dock workers moving goods to stock St. Louis merchants' shelves and riverboats cruising out with products manufactured in the city. At about 10:00 p.m., the steamship *White Cloud* arrived at the foot of Franklin Avenue, joining 24 other steamships. Shortly after tying off, the ship burst into flames, and the fire quickly spread to the ships on either side, the *Eudora* and the *Edward Bates*. In all, 23 burning ships lit up the night sky. Two managed to steam away from the flames.

A stiff wind spread the flames to the levee, igniting crates awaiting shipment and those unloaded but not yet distributed. Volunteer fire departments were all that existed in the city at the time, and one of the first to respond was Missouri Fire Company No. 5, at Third and Olive. The fire raged out of control on the levee before spreading to warehouses between Locust and Vine, and then south to a 10-block area of densely packed stores and warehouses in the central business district. The blaze consumed structures on Olive, Pine, Chestnut, and Market Streets as far west as Second Street. The fire burned through the wooden buildings with alarming speed; some newer brick buildings were able to survive. The volunteer fire department blew up buildings along Market Street with gunpowder in order to create a firebreak and halt the flames. Captain Thomas Targee had already blown up several buildings when he ran into a building at Second and Market Streets carrying a powder keg. Moments later the building was leveled when a premature explosion collapsed the walls. The detonation killed Targee, one of three firefighters killed that day.

A few blocks south, at Elm and Front Streets, a burning, floating steamship ignited a house, and fire spread another four blocks to Third Street. By the time the Great St. Louis Fire was brought under control, nine barges, 23 steamers, and more than 400 buildings in a 15-block area were destroyed. Citizens had their first look at the devastation at sunrise the next morning. Stores, warehouses, and residences were in ruins, some still hot and smoldering. The store of Campbell & Sublette burned to the ground, as did the house of Henry Blow. The estimated loss in property was $6.1 million. The Tuesday, May 22, headline of *Missouri Republican* told the city what it already knew:

IMMENSE CONFLAGRATION!

TWENTY-THREE BOATS BURNED!

LIVES LOST.

It took two years to rebuild the city. Stricter building codes were put into place, requiring the use of brick, cast iron, and other non-flammable materials. The fire resulted in the establishment of a full-time municipal fire department in 1856.

The death rate from the cholera epidemic declined slightly in the weeks after the fire but later ballooned to a high of more than 86 deaths per day. On a single day alone, Monday, June 25, Catholic cemeteries buried 126 people, 99 of them dead from cholera. One St. Louisan wrote, "The streets are the almost constant scenes of funeral trains." A total of more than 1,250 people died before the end of June. The June 19 issue of the *Missouri Republican* described the epidemic:

The cholera is still sweeping off its scores of victims every day, and this at a time when the atmosphere is pure and elastic, and there appears to be no good reason for the prevalence of the mortality… Even while the purification is going on, many unfortunate persons must die, but still the effort to save others should be made.

An ordinance was passed to establish the Committee of Public Health, which set guidelines to improve conditions. The guidelines included designating schools as hospitals, thoroughly cleaning streets and alleys, draining ponds around the city, boiling drinking water, including meat in the diet, and avoiding vegetables unless they were cooked properly. The sale of most produce was forbidden in the city. One factor in the spread of the disease was the infected drinking water from the Mississippi River. Also, although St. Louis did have a few drains connecting to the river, the city lacked an efficient sewer system, so pools of rainwater and human waste often formed. (Construction began on a public sewer system in March 1850.)

A particularly dangerous area of the city, the blocks between Market and Clark Streets from Ninth to 11th, was nicknamed "Shepherd's Graveyard." This area, the former location of Chouteau's Pond, had the highest death rate in the city because of its low ground level; its residents often were flooded out. Edward Bates pointed out in his diary that, after a heavy rain, the area was awash in garbage, manure, and carcasses. Although many of the cabins were built on posts, the water sometimes rose as high as the floors, and the stench rose even higher.

On July 1, Dr. Barnard Farrar, one of many physicians, nurses, and nuns who contracted cholera from their patients, died of the disease. Eight days later, Pierre Chouteau, one of the final links to the origins of St. Louis, also succumbed to cholera. His passing, which at any other time would be significant news, attracted only a small gathering of family and friends.

The Committee of Public Health established a quarantine station on Arsenal Island, just south of the city, where steamships were required to dock so that doctors could make full examinations of each immigrant aboard. By July 10, there were more than 300 immigrants quarantined on the island; 1,700 by August 1. Immigrants carrying the disease were forced to remain on the island until they recovered or died, most dying at the island hospital. Unfortunately, none of the steps taken by the Committee had any apparent effect on slowing or stopping the disease. The July 11 *Missouri Republican* reported that the population of the city was greatly reduced by the thousands of deaths, the quarantine of immigrants, and abandonment of the city by citizens trying to escape the epidemic. That same day, Edward Bates confirmed it in his diary:

Vast numbers had fled, fearful for their own safety or sick of the sight of the place where so many of their friends and loved ones had recently perished.

In July, the Committee of Public Health forbade hogs within the city limits, and taverns were notified to close on Sundays until the epidemic was over. Breweries also were instructed to shut down operations until further notice, because of a theory advanced by chemists that malt liquors caused cholera.

July was the peak month for fatalities, with more than 2,200 people dead. July 1 through 9 accounted for nearly 1,300 deaths, and July 10 was the single worst day, with 145 deaths. Finally, the death rate began to decline, and rapidly, with only 54 people dying in August, 13 more in September. October, November, and December had fewer than five deaths per month.

The final toll of about 4,280 cholera-related deaths was six percent of the population, with nearly one-third children under the age of six. Most of the victims were the poor, who lived unhealthy lives in unsanitary conditions that promoted the disease. It could be said that every family in St. Louis had at least one member die of the disease. Cholera, however, didn't completely disappear from St. Louis. In 1850, 883 people died, and another 845 the following year. It wasn't until 1883, when a water-born bacterium was discovered, that a scientific answer could explain how the disease was transmitted through poor sanitary conditions and polluted water.

V

Other Prominent
St. Louis Cemeteries

Jefferson Barracks

JEFFERSON BARRACKS NATIONAL CEMETERY
2900 SHERIDAN ROAD
ST. LOUIS, MO 63125

Jefferson Barracks National Cemetery stands on a bluff overlooking the Mississippi River, next to the military post of the same name. The cemetery's beautiful, green, rolling hills offset the stark white headstones standing like small soldiers in perfect alignment. Deer often can be seen roaming amid the stones, usually during the early morning hours. The memorial chapel was dedicated in 1978. Every Memorial Day weekend, local Boy Scout troops place small flags at every gravesite to honor the men and women who have served our country.

The cemetery was established by a bill, enacted in July 1862, that authorized President Abraham Lincoln to purchase grounds around the country to be set aside for national cemeteries. Fourteen cemeteries were created before the year ended, including Jefferson Barracks, which was officially named a national cemetery in 1866. The number of gravesites increased dramatically when the remains of more than 10,000 soldiers were moved to the cemetery in 1869 from other Missouri burial grounds.

The 331 acres contain more than 150,000 graves, ranging from veterans of the Revolutionary war to the war in Iraq. One Continental Army soldier is Private **Richard Gentry** (1763–1843) who, at the age of 17, was present at the Battle of Yorktown in October 1781 during the capture of Lord Cornwallis. His white monument in Section OPS2 acknowledges his service. More than 13,000 Civil War veterans, including 1,100 Confederates, rest at Jefferson Barracks, as do thousands of veterans of the two World Wars.

Although the cemetery was not officially established until the 1860's, the first known burial on the barracks grounds took place August 5, 1827, a year after the post was established, when **Elizabeth Ann Lash**, the 18-month-old daughter of a barracks officer, was laid to rest. She is now in Section OPS1. Several Medal of Honor winners rest at Jefferson Barracks, as do more than 3,200 unknown soldiers.

The saddest story of the cemetery's interments may be the six Confederate soldiers executed during the Civil War. On the afternoon of October 29, 1864, six rebel prisoners were marched out of the Gratiot Street Prison at Eighth and Gratiot Streets under heavy guard and taken to a Union army fort near present-day Lafayette Square, where they were to be executed in retaliation for the killing of Major James Wilson and six of his men by rebel guerillas. The six prisoners selected by random were **James Gates, John Nichols, Charles Minniken, Asa Ladd, George Bunch,** and **Harvey Blackburn**. Three thousand people, mostly soldiers, watched the 36-man firing squad stand a mere 10 paces from the condemned. The six innocent Confederates are now buried in consecutive graves in Section 20 at Jefferson Barracks. One of the prisoners, 21-year-old Asa Ladd, wrote his wife:

I take my pen with trembling hand to inform you that I have to be shot between 2 & 4 o'clock this evening. I have but few hours to remain in this unfriendly world... My dear wife, don't grieve after me. I want you to meet me in Heaven. I want you to teach the children piety, so that they may meet me at the right hand of God... I send you my best love and respect in the hour of death. Kiss all the children for me. You need have no uneasiness about my future state, for my faith is well founded and I fear no evil. God is my refuge and hiding place. Good-by Amy.

Some of the notable people buried at Jefferson Barracks include Cardinals Baseball broadcaster **Jack Buck** (1924-2002) and Air Force 1st Lt. **Michael Blassie** (1948-1972), who originally had been interred in the Tomb of the Unknowns at Arlington Cemetery. Blassie was shot down over South Vietnam on May 11, 1972, and remained unknown for 26 years until DNA testing identified him in 1998. Hundreds of people attended his July 1998 funeral at Jefferson Barracks, including U.S. Secretary of Defense William Cohen and St. Louis Archbishop Justin Rigali.

John Francis "Jack" Buck, a World War II veteran, was given the Purple Heart after receiving a shrapnel wound in Germany. He first start-ed broadcasting Cardinals baseball when he joined Harry Caray in 1954. He was the original host of KMOX's "At Your Service" pro-gram when it premiered in 1960. For many years, Buck was the radio voice for the CBS network, call-ing games for Monday Night Foot-ball, Super Bowls, and World Series games. He was elected to the broad-

casting wing of the Baseball Hall of Fame in 1987.

He spent more than five months in Barnes-Jewish Hospital before his death in June 2002. (Five days later, Cardinals pitcher Darryl Kile died in his Chicago hotel room at the age of 33.) Following his funeral at Twin Oaks Presbyterian Church, Buck was buried with military honors. Buck and Blassie are buried near one another in Section 85.

Johnnie Johnson (1924—2005), called by some "The Founding Father of Rock and Roll", first came to St. Louis in the early 1950's. He worked by day and played piano in his own R & B band in the evenings. It was during this time that Johnson asked Chuck Berry to sit in with his band. The self-taught pianist displayed his talent on most of Berry's songs, including "Maybelline", "Roll over Beethoven", and "Johnny B. Goode," Berry's tribute to Johnson. The Marine Corps veteran was in poor health in his final years, which included bouts of pneumonia, and died in his sleep on April 13, 2005 at the age of 80. Johnnie Johnson was inducted into the Rock and Roll Hall of Fame in 2001. He is buried in the first row along the road in section 1J.

Jefferson Barracks National Cemetery was added to the National Register of Historic Places in 1998. The cemetery is open every day; office hours are Monday through Friday 8:00 a.m. to 4:30 p.m. A computerized grave locator is behind the office/administrative building to assist visitors in finding a burial site.

OLD CATHEDRAL
209 WALNUT STREET
ST. LOUIS, MO 63102

CATHEDRAL BASILICA OF ST. LOUIS
LINDELL BOULEVARD AT NEWSTEAD AVENUE
ST. LOUIS, MO 63108

The Old Cathedral in downtown St. Louis was consecrated in October 1834, making it the first cathedral west of the Mississippi River. The Greek Revival church was commissioned by Bishop Joseph Rosati and designed by St. Louisans George Morton and Joseph Laveille. The cost of the cathedral was more than $63,000 and put the diocese into debt. The cathedral survived the 1849 Great St. Louis Fire while other buildings surrounding it were reduced to ashes. Pope John XXIII designated the Old Cathedral a basilica in 1961.

The Cathedral Basilica of St. Louis, or New Cathedral, on Lindell Boulevard was the original dream of Archbishop John Kain, who purchased the land in 1895 but died before launching his plans. His successor, Archbishop John Glennon, took over the project and selected Barnett, Haynes & Barnett as the architects for the cathedral. Designed in the Romanesque style, its granite walls, duel towers, and central dome started taking shape when construction began in 1907. On October 18, 1908, the cornerstone was laid for the new cathedral, which was dedicated exactly six years later to the day. The inside is covered with 83,000 square feet of mosaic art.

The men who have led local Catholics over more than 170 years are included below in the order in which they served St. Louis:

While in Rome as a seminary student, **Joseph Rosati** (1789–1843), a native of Sora, Italy, met Bishop DuBourg of New Orleans and accepted the bishop's invitation to come to America. He arrived in Baltimore in July 1816, and from there spent time in Louisville, Kentucky, before landing in St. Louis on October 17, 1817.

He served as an administrator of the diocese of New Orleans; in 1824, he was appointed coadjutor to Bishop DuBourg. Three years later, he became the first bishop of the St. Louis diocese. As bishop, he supervised construction of the Old Cathedral and consecrated the holy building upon its completion in 1834. He lent assistance to Father Peter De Smet and the Jesuits in founding St. Louis University and did work with Philippine Duchesne and the Sisters of the Sacred Heart. He also founded St. Louis Hospital and opened the first orphanage in the city.

In September 1843, while traveling from Rome to St. Louis by way of France, he became ill in Paris. The bishop returned to Rome to recover from his illness but died on September 25 at 59 years of age. He was buried in the chapel of the Vincentian House in Rome. The St. Louis diocese received a letter from Rome that read, in part, "Here died Joseph Rosati, citizen of Sora (a town in Italy), a Vincentian, a man of unusual virtue, the highest fervor and of singular modesty. He was a zealous propagator of the holy name throughout America."

On August 26, 1954, 111 years after Bishop Rosati's death, he was returned to St. Louis for burial in the crypt at the St. Louis Cathedral in the Central West End. Clergy from around St. Louis attended a Mass celebrated by Archbishop Joseph Ritter. The archbishop said in his eulogy, "We may hope that through our prayers it may please God to raise the saintly Bishop Rosati along with his equally holy confreres and contemporary founders of the Catholic faith in this area, the Rev. Felix Andrels, C.M., and Blessed Philippina Duchesne, to honors of the altar." Following the service, Rosati's remains were blessed and then entombed in the crypt under the Chapel of All Souls. His body was placed beneath that of Cardinal Glennon. On May 23, 1971, Rosati's remains were moved once again, this time to the crypt beneath his Old Cathedral.

Following the death of Archbishop John Kain in October 1903, the leadership of the Catholic Church went to **John Cardinal Glennon** (1862–1946). Like the first archbishop of St. Louis, Peter Richard Kenrick, John Joseph Glennon emigrated from Ireland. He came to America to serve at the diocese of Kansas City, where he was ordained a priest in 1884. Less than two years later, he was elevated to bishop and became the coadjutor of Kansas City before coming to St. Louis. He was archbishop of St. Louis for 42 years.

Archbishop Glennon was known for his simple, friendly manner and good humor, and he had great oratory skills that made him a frequent guest at speaking engagements. His greatest accomplishments were the building of the Cathedral Basilica and Kenrick Seminary, which moved to its current location near Webster Groves in 1915.

In February 1946, Archbishop Glennon left St. Louis to be elevated to the Sacred College of Cardinals by Pope Pius XII. On February 15, feeling weary from a cold, he had a private audience with the Pope. He spent 18 days in the Italian capital, where he took part in a number of ceremonies over a five-day period. On February 18, he and 32 others were elevated to the status of cardinal. He said of the occasion, "It is a wonderful thing to be thus remembered at a time of life when I really should be forgotten, to be given this great honor before I die." Glennon was the first Cardinal of St. Louis.

Cardinal Glennon left Rome on March 4 and returned to Dublin, where he was bedridden in a stateroom at the president's residence, suffering from bronchitis and pneumonia before slipping into a semi-comatose state. When the Sister of Charity who was nursing him asked where he wanted to be buried, he smiled and responded, "Not in Ireland, not even in Kinnegad, but in St. Louis among the people I love so well and where I have spent my life and labors. In fact, sister, I have marked a little crypt for myself in the Chapel of Holy Souls in the St. Louis Cathedral. It is there I wish to go."

On the evening of March 8, with his sisters, nephews, and nieces by his side, Cardinal Glennon was anointed and given the last sacraments. During the evening, he spoke what would be his last words, "I belong to St. Louis." The next morning, his breathing became irregular and labored; he died peacefully at 8:51 a.m. (1:51 p.m. St. Louis time.)

Cardinal Glennon lay in state at the presidential residence before the body was moved to All Hallows College, where he had been a seminary student, to allow the townspeople to view his remains. A metal plate on his casket was inscribed in Latin:

Cardinal of the Holy Roman Church, priest, title of St. Clement. By the grace of God and of the Apostolic See, the Archbishop of St. Louis. Died March 9, 1946.

St. Louis Mayor Aloys Kaufmann and Auxiliary Bishop George Donnelly met the plane when it arrived at Lambert Field on March 14. A two-mile procession took the cardinal's body to his residence on Lindell Boulevard. He was then returned to his cathedral, where thousands of St. Louisans filed past his open casket. At one point, the line of mourners extended for three blocks. Glennon was dressed in a purple cassock and his white miter; a crucifix was in his hands. His red cardinal hat rested at the foot of the bier.

Thousands came to the funeral on March 16, 1946, and many more listened to the ceremony on loudspeakers outside the cathedral. Among the special guests attending were Governor Phil Donnelly and Postmaster General Robert Hannegan. Three cardinals who had been newly appointed with Glennon in Rome also were in attendance, as were more than 70 bishops. At 2:30 p.m., after the service had concluded, the casket was taken to the crypt beneath All Souls' Chapel for final burial.

In April 1967, **Joseph Cardinal Ritter** (1892–1967) celebrated the 50th anniversary of his ordination into the priesthood. In less than two months, he was dead of a heart attack.

Joseph Ritter was ordained a priest in 1917, and later became one of the youngest bishops in the United States when he was appointed auxiliary bishop of Indianapolis. One year later, in 1934, he became bishop of Indianapolis, and a decade later was the first archbishop when the city was elevated to an archdiocese.

The archbishop arrived in St. Louis and was enthroned as the Catholic leader on October 8, 1946, succeeding the late John Cardinal Glennon. He was soft spoken and approachable, never seeking attention or publicity. He fought for racial justice by integrating Catholic schools in 1947. He was responsible for the fund drive sponsoring the construction of Cardinal Glennon Memorial Hospital and established the Archdiocesan Expansion Fund for the building of new churches and schools. In December 1960, he was ordained to the College of Cardinals in Rome by Pope John XXIII. He was a liberal member of Vatican Council II and wanted to expand church philosophies.

On Monday, June 5, 1967, the 74-year-old cardinal suffered a heart attack and was given the last sacraments of the church. He was taken to DePaul Hospital, where he rested comfortably until he suffered another attack two days later. His sister, a nun with the Sisters of Charity of Nazareth, was by his side when he died on Saturday at 5:47 a.m.

His body was taken to Arthur Donnelly Funeral Home before removal on Monday, June 12 to the St. Louis Cathedral, where it lay in state for two days. Thousands of St. Louisans viewed the Catholic leader, clad in his violet vestments. His cardinal hat rested beside the coffin and would later hang in the cathedral.

The cathedral was draped in black when mourners arrived for the funeral, which was broadcast on KMOX Radio. Four cardinals and more than 100 bishops from around the country attended. Cardinal Cody of Chicago celebrated the Mass, while Bishop Helmsing of Kansas City, a former St. Louisan and friend of Ritter, delivered the sermon. He said of his friend, "He habitually radiated the joy of the Resurrection, while he knew that he would have to suffer persecution for justice's sake, as we well remember his pioneering efforts for racial and social justice." The pallbearers were eight of Cardinal Ritter's close friends.

The cardinal chose to be buried in the Priests' Lot at Calvary Cemetery rather than the crypt in the cathedral. A large stone cross monument with the inscription, "Thou Art a Priest Forever" marked his final resting place.

On May 2, 1994, Archbishop Justin Rigali had Ritter's remains moved to the St. Louis Cathedral for burial in the crypt.

John Cardinal Carberry (1904–1998) began to study for the priesthood at the age of 15. He was ordained in Rome in 1929, and he became archbishop of St. Louis eight months after the death of Cardinal Ritter. He served as archbishop from 1968 to 1980 and was named a cardinal one year later. Cardinal Carberry participated in the Second Vatican Council and helped to elect two popes, including John Paul II. The warm and jovial Carberry improved the financial health of the St. Louis archdiocese during his term. He built the St. Patrick's parish downtown and five new parishes in St. Louis County.

Church law required him to retire at age 75. Carberry spent his retirement years at St. Agnes Home in Kirkwood, playing the harmonica and spending long hours of prayer in the chapel. He suffered a stroke in the late 1980's and several more in the next decade. On his final day, Wednesday, June 17, 1998, he took a short walk and soon after developed a cough. At 2:50 p.m., 20 minutes after being put to bed, the cardinal died.

The Sunday before his funeral, mourners were allowed to file past his casket at the Cathedral Basilica after the afternoon service. Seven cardinals and 22 bishops attended his June 22 funeral.

On Wednesday, March 30, 1994, the St. Louis cathedral was filled to capacity for the funeral Mass of Archbishop **John May** (1922–1994). The sound of trumpets preceded a procession of cardinals, bishops, priests, and other members of the clergy. Archbishop Justin Rigali, who had been installed as archbishop two weeks earlier, celebrated the Mass.

John May was ordained a priest in May 1947. He worked as a parish priest and a hospital chaplain before taking over an administrative position with the archdiocese of Chicago. He became a bishop in August 1967, and by Vatican decree was installed archbishop of St. Louis on March 25, 1980, replacing the retiring prelate, John Cardinal Carberry. He was well read on many topics and enjoyed classical music. His diplomatic talents contributed to his appointment to the presidency of the National Conference of Catholic Bishops.

The archbishop was originally diagnosed with cancer in the summer of 1992. On March 13, 1994, he slipped into a coma while residing at the Mary, Queen and Mother Center, a nursing facility in Shrewsbury. He died Thursday, March 24, at 11:50 p.m., of brain cancer. On March 29, his body was taken to the Cathedral Basilica where about 800 people waited to pay their respects, including wheelchair-bound Cardinal Carberry. Mourners filed past the archbishop, who was dressed in a white robe with a bishop's miter, throughout the day and night. A single candle burned next to the catafalque.

The funeral Mass was conducted the following day. After the service, the coffin was taken to the eastern side of the cathedral and placed in the crypt.

NEW MT. SINAI CEMETERY
8430 GRAVOIS ROAD
ST. LOUIS, MO 63123

New Mt. Sinai Cemetery is very reminiscent of Bellefontaine and Calvary cemeteries, with its touch of history, rich monumental architecture, and equally impressive list of prominent citizens buried there. Its lush, rolling hills contain more than 10,600 graves, with many names notable to the St. Louis community. More than 500 military veterans also are interred at New Mt. Sinai.

In 1852, two Jewish congregations, the B'nai Brith Society and Emanu El, joined to form the B'nai El Congregation. Prior to the merger, the B'nai Brith Society had purchased one acre of land on Gravois Road that would become the foundation for the cemetery. The Mt. Sinai Cemetery Association was incorporated in 1869 after the

merger of the B'nai El Congregation and Shaare Emeth, at which time five more acres were authorized for purchase next to the single acre already owned. When Temple Israel joined the Cemetery Association in 1888, the association reincorporated under the name "New Mt. Sinai Cemetery Association." They continued to purchase acreage through the years and now have more than 52 acres, with 40 private mausoleums dotting the landscape.

New Mt. Sinai may have one of the best web sites of any St. Louis cemetery, with plenty of concise historical information, a death registry, and a map with a walking tour profiling its prominent citizens. The address is www.newmtsinaicemetery.org. The cemetery is open dawn to dusk; the office hours are Monday through Friday, 9:00 a.m. to 4:00 p.m. The cemetery office, once known as the "House of Comfort," was built in 1917 as a place of rest for visitors who had made the day-long trek by horse-drawn carriages from the city of St. Louis.

Among the notable people buried on its grounds is **Rabbi Solomon Sonneschein** (1839–1908), who was the first rabbi of Shaare Emeth and later became the first rabbi of Temple Israel. His roadside grave, which reads "A Pioneer of Western Judaism," is behind the office. Succeeding Sonnes-

chein was **Rabbi Samuel Sale** (1854–1937), who served as leader of Shaare Emeth for 32 years and was the first native St. Louis rabbi. He also was adjunct professor of Hebrew at Washington University. Rabbi Sale died in Jewish Hospital, which he had helped to establish. His roadside, corner grave holds a place of prominence as one of the first headstones visible to visitors entering the cemetery. Another rabbi, **Moritz Spitz** (1848–1920) was leader of B'nai El Temple for 42 years, beginning in 1878, and was editor of the Jewish community newspaper, *The Voice*.

Among the retailing giants buried at Mt. Sinai are **Moses Shoenberg** (1852-1925), president of May Department Stores Company (which owned Famous-Barr), who died after suffering a stroke, his second in four years. He had gone into business with his brother-in-law, **David May** (1848–1927), when both men moved to St. Louis from Denver. Two years after Shoenberg died, May passed away in his sleep from a heart attack while at his summer home in Charlevoix, Michigan. He was chairman of May Department Stores at the time of his death and employed more than 14,000 people. His funeral at Temple Israel was officiated by Rabbi Samuel Sale, who called May, "A merchant prince indeed." Famous-Barr was closed on the day of the funeral. The Shoenberg and May mausoleums are next to each other.

Stix, Baer, & Fuller also are all buried at New Mt. Sinai. German-born **Julius Baer** (1860-1940) and his brother **Sigmund** (1861-1929) opened a prosperous dry goods store in Fort Smith, Arkansas, in 1879 before being joined by their brother-in-law **Aaron Fuller** (1858-1936). In an attempt to expand the business, the men came to St. Louis and joined forces with **Charles Stix** (1861–1916), who had come to St. Louis in 1886 and soon gained prominence as a retailer and civic leader. In 1892, the firm of Stix, Baer, and Fuller opened its first store under the name "Grand Leader." The business grew quickly and eventually expanded into an eight-story building on Washington Avenue. Charles Stix, in charge of customer relations, personally greeted shoppers and handed out candy to children. Aaron Fuller supervised employee relations, and the Baer brothers handled merchandising and finance. Dillard's Department Stores later purchased the company and eliminated the Stix, Baer, and Fuller name. All four men gave generously to St. Louis cultural and charitable institutions.

In 1916, Charles Stix was the first of the group to die. He passed away at his Portland Place home; his funeral at Temple Israel drew a huge crowd, including Grand Leader employees. His burial place is directly across the street from the Shoenberg and May mausoleums. Aaron Fuller died at his Park Plaza apartment in July 1936 from complications of a heart attack he had suffered a year earlier. Julius Baer, the last surviving founder, died of a heart attack at his Chase Hotel apartment in December 1940. The Baer and Fuller families are buried in similar mausoleums near each other.

The Edison brothers (Mark, Simon, Samuel, Henry, and Irving) started their women's shoe business in Atlanta before coming to St. Louis in 1929 and establishing one of the largest shoe merchandising companies in America. The names of some of their stores such as Chandler's, Baker's, Leed's, and Bert's, were selected by picking names out of a telephone book. Edison Brothers Stores later added such retail outlets as Jeans West, J. Riggings, and The Wild Pair to their roster. However, the business collapsed and went into bankruptcy in the 1990's.

Mark was the first of the brothers to die, in 1951, while Irving was the last surviving brother, dying in 1989. All five brothers are buried in the cemetery.

David Wohl (1886–1960) founded Wohl Shoe Company in 1916. He retired in 1951 after merging his company with Brown Shoe Company. His charitable trust, the Wohl Foundation, gave more than $8 million to area institutions, including Washington University and the St. Louis University School of Medicine. Wohl died of cancer in his Forsyth Blvd. home at the age of 73.

Among the other notables is **Moses Fraley** (1843–1917), perhaps the most well- known Jewish resident in St. Louis when he died in his Portland Place home at the age of 74. He was in the merchandise business before becoming a banker and broker, and later worked in the insurance business. He was one of the founders of Temple Israel and later served as president of the congregation. His small, modest headstone at the front of the cemetery near Gravois simply shows his name.

Nathan Frank (1852–1931) served two terms in the U. S. House of Representatives and was founder of the *St. Louis Star* newspaper. He owned a significant amount of real estate downtown. In 1925 he donated the funds for a new bandstand in Forest Park, saying "All that I have, all that I have acquired, I owe to St. Louis." Frank and his unique monument are across the street from Charles Stix.

Founder of the Central Institute for the Deaf, **Dr. Max Goldstein** (1870–1941) established his school in 1914 and was a leader in the field of child care. He died at his summer home in Frankfort, Michigan, at the age of 71. His funeral was attended by numerous physicians, educators, and civic leaders. His gravesite, a large gated tomb, is between the office and the cemetery mausoleum.

Investment broker **Mark Steinberg** (1881–1951) may be best known for the skating rink in Forest Park that is named for him. He was president, director, or board chairman for several St. Louis companies, and was a minority stockholder in the Baseball Cardinals under the ownership of Sam Breadon. He died in Jewish Hospital after suffering a heart attack a few weeks earlier.

Fannie Hurst (1885–1968) was a widely published author of short stories. She began her career by submitting her work to William Reedy, editor of the *Mirror*. Finally interested in one of her stories, he wrote back, "Dear Miss Hurst: So you are a college girl. Hello, college girl. I am going to print our story, 'Episode.' It is as wobbly as a new calf but there is talent in it." She also wrote novels, including *Imitation of Life* and *Humoresque*; both of which were made into movies. Her autobiography, *Anatomy of Me*, was published in 1958.

Sam Koplar (1888–1961) began the road to success by buying theaters and building apartments and flats in the city. He went on to design, build, and own the Chase-Park Plaza Hotel, where he lived until he died of a heart attack at Jewish Hospital at the age of 73. The Koplar family also owned KPLR Channel 11. Other members of the Koplar family buried in the family mausoleum are his son **Harold**, who died in 1985, and his daughter **Lillian**, a well-known lawyer and civic leader. She was married to **Morris Shenker**, a controversial criminal defense attorney who represented organized crime figures and once defended Teamsters Union leader  Jimmy Hoffa. Morris and Lillian owned a controlling interest in numerous businesses, including the Dunes Hotel and Casino in Las Vegas. Shenker, who died in 1989, seven months after Lillian, also is buried in the mausoleum. The modern stone and glass mausoleum dwarfs every monument on the grounds.

Hockey and basketball are represented at New Mt. Sinai in the persons of **Sidney Salomon** (1910–1986), who established and owned the St. Louis Blues franchise, and **Ben Kerner** (1913–2000), owner of the St. Louis Hawks basketball team.

Sid Salomon was asked about the team name at the launch of his hockey franchise. He said, "The name of the team has to be the 'Blues.' It's part of the city where W. C. Handy composed his famed song while thinking of his girl one morning." His Blues made their National Hockey

League debut at the Arena in October 1967 and ended the season by appearing in the Stanley Cup finals, where they lost to the powerful Montreal Canadiens.

Ben Kerner was one of those colorful characters who both celebrated and suffered with his team from his courtside seat. He brought the Hawks to St. Louis in 1955, and during his 13-year run collected five consecutive Western Division titles and the NBA title in 1958. In 1968, he sold the team to an Atlanta group and the Hawks headed south to Georgia. Kerner was a member of the group that later brought the St. Louis Steamers indoor soccer team to prominence. He died at Barnes-Jewish Hospital of a heart attack.

ST. PETER'S CEMETERY
2101 LUCAS AND HUNT ROAD
ST. LOUIS, MO 63121

The St. Peter's German Evangelical Congregation established St. Peter's Cemetery in 1855 by purchasing 50 acres of the old Lindell estate along Lucas and Hunt Road. The first burials took place a year later, after the grounds had been arranged with roads, planted with trees, and enclosed with a fence. Another 50 acres to the south were purchased from the Lindell estate in 1897, doubling the size of the cemetery. St. Peter's employed civil engineer and architect Julius Pitzman, a Civil War veteran who did engineering work for the Union army, to draft a new design for the cemetery. An entrance gate and office were built during this time.

Additions were made to the grounds with the purchase of 18.5 acres in 1907, and another 16 acres in 1911. A new entrance gate with two towers and a new administrative building were constructed in 1926. The undulating, limestone wall that runs along Lucas and Hunt Road was started during the Depression by the Works Progress Administration (WPA), one of President Franklin Roosevelt's "New Deal" programs.

Today, St. Peter's is a handsome cemetery, easy to explore in an afternoon. It encompasses more than 100 acres and more than 70,000 graves. It is bordered by Glen Echo Country Club on the north and the Metrolink line on the west. The grounds of St. Peter's Cemetery are always open. The office hours are Monday through Friday, 8:00 a.m. to 4:00 p.m.

The biggest early supporter of classical ragtime may have been **John Stark** (1841-1927), a piano and organ dealer who became a sheet music publisher and tireless promoter of ragtime. In 1899, Stark published Scott Joplin's "The Maple Leaf Rag," which sold 75,000 copies of sheet music in the first six months and another 500,000 copies over the next decade. That rag established the reputations of both men and Stark began to devote his entire business to publishing music. Reprints of "The Maple Leaf Rag" provided Stark with an income for the rest of his life.

Stark published many of Joplin's compositions, including "The Entertainer," a tune written at Joplin's St. Louis home on Delmar Boulevard and made popular more than a half-century later in the 1970's movie, *The Sting*. Stark moved to St. Louis and then lived in New York for a while before returning to St. Louis in 1910. His final publication was in 1923. His catalogue of more than 120 pieces is considered one of the best collections of ragtime music. John Stark is buried in Section 24.

Another pioneer of ragtime music was **Tom Turpin** (1871–1922). Born in Savannah, Georgia, Turpin came with his family to St. Louis, where his father opened the Silver Dollar Saloon. Turpin played the piano at the saloon and at other taverns before opening his own Market Street establishment in 1900, the Rosebud Café. The café became a hangout for ragtime musicians like Scott Joplin and others traveling through St. Louis. Joplin's "Rosebud March" was named for the café.

Turpin became the first black composer to get an instrumental rag published when his "Harlem Rag" debuted in 1897, predating Joplin's "Maple Leaf Rag" by two years. Six of his rags were published between 1897 and 1904. Although Turpin was not as prominent as Joplin and others, his influence and that of his café helped ragtime music develop into the institution it became.

Because Turpin weighed more than 300 pounds, he had his piano put up on blocks to make it easier for him to play standing up. Complications caused by his weight contributed to his death in August 1922, at the age of 51. He is buried in Section 29 near Albert Burgess and Homer G. Phillips. His monument recognizes him as "The Father of St. Louis Ragtime."

Albert Burgess (1856–1932) arrived in St. Louis in 1877 from Michigan. When he passed the law exam given by the Court of Appeals, Burgess became the first black lawyer admitted to the bar in St. Louis. He was the first treasurer of the Mound City Bar Association and founded the Emigration Aid Society in 1879.

Burgess was appointed Assistant City Attorney by Mayor Cyrus Walbridge in 1894 and served in that position for eight years. His greatest asset, however, was paving the way for other black lawyers in St. Louis, such as Homer G. Phillips.

Burgess died in his home on Cook Street. His funeral was conducted at All Saints Episcopal Church. Today, Albert Burgess and Homer G. Phillips rest a few feet from one another at the top of the hill in Section 29. A fence separates them from Glen Echo Country Club.

At 7:45 a.m., Thursday, June 18, 1931, **Homer G. Phillips** (1880–

1931), a 51-year-old attorney, left his home at 1121 Aubert Avenue. and walked to Delmar Boulevard to catch his daily streetcar for his office on North Jefferson. Witnesses later told police that two black men approached Phillips shortly before 8:00 a.m. and conversed with him for a few moments before one of the men struck Phillips in the face, pulled a pistol, and fired three times at close range. Phillips died instantly. His body was taken to City Hospital No. 2, where an examination showed two bullet wounds to the head and one to the abdomen.

Later that morning, police arrested Augustus Brooks and George McFarland for the Phillips murder. Eyewitnesses saw the two men running from the homicide and identified them as the shooters. McFarland's father, John, also was arrested but later released. In April 1930, Phillips had represented an estate for John and Stella McFarland. When the estate was settled, Phillips placed the $2,200 check in escrow until his $1,000 legal fee was paid. The McFarlands thought the fee was too high and vowed to take whatever action necessary. The police had found a motive for the shooting.

Homer Gilliam Phillips, born in Sedalia, Missouri, was the son of a Methodist minister. Shortly after the St. Louis World's Fair, he graduated from Howard University Law School in Washington D. C., and came to St. Louis to practice. At the time of his death, he was an established attorney known for his persuasive oratory skills in the courtroom. He ran unsuccessfully for mayor against Victor Miller and placed third as a candidate in the 1926 Republican primary for Congress. During Henry Kiel's administration, Phillips negotiated with the mayor for a health care facility on the city's north side. In 1932, a year after Phillips' murder, construction began on a new hospital. On February 22, 1937, Homer G. Phillips Hospital celebrated its grand opening. City officials closed the hospital in 1979.

The funeral of Homer G. Phillips was conducted at St. Paul's Methodist Church at Leffingwell and Lawton Avenues on Monday, June 22. The five-foot marble headstone for Phillips and his wife Ida (she died in 1934) reads:

> *Two American Patriots: Your lives exemplify a*
> *commitment to equality, justice and peace.*
> *Your legacy lives on among us.*

In February 1932, George McFarland was tried for Phillips' murder. Individuals testifying on his behalf placed him somewhere else at the time of the shooting. A jury agreed and found him innocent of the murder. When Augustus Brooks was tried in August of the same year, he too was found not guilty.

Eighteen-year-old **Allen Britt** (1881–1899) was popular among the women at Blachelor's and the Lonestar, his two favorite nightclubs. He often was seen in the company of his live-in girlfriend, Frankie Baker. The two were known to have heated arguments at their Targee Street flat about Britt's paying too much attention to other women.

On Sunday, October 15, 1899, Britt returned home from a dalliance and was stabbed to death by Baker. The incident was said to have erupted after Baker caught Britt at a downtown hotel with another woman. When questioned, Baker claimed self-defense. When the trial got underway, witnesses testified that Britt had in fact tried to kill her. Baker was acquitted when a judgment of justifiable homicide was rendered.

Baker left St. Louis for Nebraska, and later went to Oregon, before dying in a mental institution in 1950. Bill Dooley, a pianist and songwriter at the time of the Britt killing, composed a song about the two, originally titled "Frankie and Albert." The title later was changed to "Frankie and Johnny." Today, Allen Britt rests in Section 5 in an unmarked grave at the top of the hill, fronted by an area set aside for babies.

James Bell (1903–1991) was born in the Deep South and came to St. Louis with his family when he was 16. He played semi-pro ball for the Compton Hill Cubs before starting his career in the Negro Leagues in 1922 with the St. Louis Stars. He went on to play with the Pittsburgh Crawfords, Homestead Grays, and the Kansas City Monarchs. Bell was a quiet man who gained the nickname "Cool Papa" because of his calm demeanor under pressure. His best quality as a player was his speed; he stole 175 bases in 1933. His roommate, Satchel Paige, once said that Bell was so fast that he could turn out the light and be in bed before the room got dark.

Bell started his career as a pitcher and later moved to center field. He hit over .400 several times during his 29-year career. His color prohibited him and hundreds of other talented black players from ever playing in the major leagues. He once commented, "So many people say I was born too early, but that's not true. They opened the doors too late."

Bell retired from baseball in 1950. He worked as a janitor and later was a security guard for the city of St. Louis until he retired in 1973. The following year, "Cool Papa" became the fifth Negro League player to be elected to Baseball's Hall of Fame. In 1983, Dickson Street was renamed for James "Cool Papa" Bell.

In January 1991, Bell's wife of 62 years, Clara, died following a brief illness. By this time Bell was blind in one eye and his health was declining. On February 27, he suffered a heart attack and was hospitalized at St. Louis University. At 5:00 p.m., Thursday, March 7, "Cool Papa" Bell died at the age of 87.

About 200 people attended the Saturday funeral at Central Baptist Church. Pallbearers included baseball great Lou Brock and one-time Cardinals third baseman Ken Reitz. Lester Lockett, a former Negro League player, gave the eulogy. "You were put to bed way too soon," said Lockett. "But the light, especially for those who knew you, will never go out." Not until 1994 did a headstone mark his grave in Section 16, near the entrance to the cemetery. The monolithic granite stone now in place acknowledges his baseball exploits.

Sumner high school graduate **Wendell Pruitt** (1920–1945) was a World War II flyer and proud member of the Tuskegee Airmen. These first black combat fighter pilots were trained after the War Department agreed to establish a flight school at the Tuskegee Air Base in Alabama in 1941.

Pruitt, a member of the 302nd Mustang Fighter Squadron, is credited with shooting down three Nazi planes, destroying eight others on the ground, and assisting with the sinking of a Nazi destroyer. He flew 70 missions during the war before returning stateside. He received the Distinguished Flying Cross for his efforts in the war. The flyer was honored when he returned to St. Louis, and December 12, 1944, was declared "Captain Wendell O. Pruitt Day."

On April 15, 1945, Pruitt was at Tuskegee again, this time training fighter pilots, when he was killed in a plane crash at the air base. He was only 24 years old at the time of his death. His funeral took place at St. Elizabeth's Catholic Church on Pine Street. He is buried in Section 29, near Albert Burgess and Tom Turpin, directly down the hill from Homer G. Phillips. The Pruitt-Igoe housing project was named in his honor.

Lemuel Steeples (1956–1980) was an up-and-coming boxer who in 1979 won a Golden Gloves title, a Pan American Games gold medal, and the National AAU title by racking up an impressive 61-7 record. He was inspired by the success of the Spinks brothers, Leon and Michael, who lived in the same housing projects.

Steeples trained at the South Side gym owned by a relative, John Radison. In 1980, wanting to prepare himself for the Olympic trials, Steeples joined the U. S. boxing team on a trek to Poland. The team's jet left Montreal on March 13 and crashed the following morning just south of its destination, the Warsaw airport, killing all aboard. The U. S. boxing team, consisting of 14 fighters and eight officials, were among the 87 passengers and crew killed. John Radison also was on board as a referee-judge for the Polish matches. Steeples is buried in Section 28.

RESURRECTION CEMETERY
6901 MACKENZIE ROAD
ST. LOUIS, MO 63123

In 1928, when St. Peter and Paul Cemetery on Gravois was full and could no longer take interments, Archbishop John Glennon established New St. Peter and Paul Cemetery. One year earlier, he had purchased land on Watson Road to establish Catholic institutions such as the Kenrick Theological Seminary. The cemetery, which was laid out on both sides of Watson Road, was intended for the use of parishes that didn't have their own burial grounds. The first burial took place in November 1929. The name was later changed to Resurrection Cemetery. The two small chapels

resting atop the highest point in the cemetery were constructed in 1974. As of 2002, more than 54,000 people were buried at Resurrection.

The 280-acre cemetery is open every day from 8:00 a.m. to 5:00 p.m. The office is open Monday through Friday, 8:30 a.m. to 4:30 p.m.; and 8:30 a.m. to 12:30 p.m. on Saturdays. More information on Resurrection Cemetery can be found on the Catholic Cemeteries web site at www.stl-cathcem.com.

No fewer than a dozen major league baseball players are buried in Resurrection Cemetery, including former Cardinals pitcher **Joe Hoerner** (1936–1996). The left-handed reliever appeared in nearly 500 games during his career, compiling a 39–34 record with 99 saves and a 2.99 ERA. Debuting in 1966, he played four seasons with the Cardinals, including the World Series teams of 1967 and 1968. He is buried in Section 40. His red granite monument features a cardinal bird on each side.

The St. Louis Blues are represented by Bob Gassoff, Doug Wickenheiser, coach and general manager Lynn Patrick, and legendary broadcaster Dan Kelly.

Bob Gassoff (1953–1977) was a tough and aggressive defenseman for four seasons, starting in 1973. Although he was improving his skills as a player at the time of his death, in the more than 250 games he played with the Blues, Gassoff compiled nearly 900 penalty minutes to go with his 11 goals. On Memorial Day weekend 1977, Gassoff was attending a post-season party at a farm owned by teammate Garry Unger near Gray Summit when his motorcycle collided with another vehicle. He died a short time later; he was 24 years old. The Blues have retired his No. 3. Gassoff is buried in Section 40.

Another Blues player who died too young was **Doug Wickenheiser** (1961–1999). He was drafted first overall in 1980 by the Montreal Canadiens and traded to the Blues in 1983. He missed the entire 1984 season because of a serious injury to his knee; he had been hit by a car during a team outing. The biggest goal of his career was in a game dubbed the "Monday Night Miracle," when Wickenheiser scored in overtime during Game 6 of the 1986 playoffs against the Calgary Flames. In 1994, after retiring from hockey, he had surgery on his wrist to have a cancerous cyst removed. The cancer returned three years later, but this time in his lung, and it was inoperable. He died in January 1999 at 37 years of age. The Blues established a charitable trust called the "Fourteen Fund" in honor of Doug Wickenheiser. He is buried in Section 43 near the small St. Vincent De-Paul Chapel.

Another gravesite in Resurrection Cemetery with ties to the St. Louis Blues is that of **Lynn Patrick** (1912–1980). Patrick was born in Victoriaville, British Columbia, Canada, in 1912. He played 10 seasons with the New York Rangers before retiring to coach the Rangers and the Boston Bruins. He came to St. Louis in 1967 to become the first coach and general manager of the Blues when they entered the league as an expansion team. Patrick suffered a heart attack while driving home from a Blues game on January 26, 1980. His car hit a fire hydrant at Oakland Avenue near the Arena and he was rushed to nearby Deaconess Hospital, where he was pronounced dead. Patrick is buried in Section 48.

"He shoots... he scores!" was **Dan Kelly's** (1936–1989) trademark call. He had picked up that phrase as a kid listening to Toronto Maple Leafs broadcaster Foster Hewitt. His older brother Hal was a broadcaster for both the Leafs and Minnesota North Stars. Like many children in Canada, Kelly lived and breathed hockey. His dream job came in 1968 when he hosted Hockey Night in Canada. He became a national figure in his homeland.

In 1967, when the St. Louis Blues entered the National Hockey League, Jack Buck and Jay Randolph handled the broadcasting duties. But Blues owner Sidney Salomon, Jr., heard Kelly and wanted him as the voice of the Blues. Dan Kelly worked for the Blues for more than 20 years. Most of those years he shared the broadcast booth with Walter "Gus" Kyle. (Gus Kyle died in November 1996 after a long battle with heart disease. He donated his body to medical science.) Besides his hockey duties, Kelly did play-by-play for the St. Louis Baseball Cardinals and the University of Missouri football games.

In the summer of 1988, a large, malignant tumor was discovered in his back; it quickly spread to the lungs. Kelly broadcast his final Blues game on November 19 and then was hospitalized at St. Luke's, where he died on February 10, 1989, almost exactly one year after the death of another Blues icon, Barclay Plager. He was 52. Robert Hyland said of Kelly, "In

my opinion, he was the greatest, or at least one of the two greatest, hockey broadcasters ever. But he could also do football, and there weren't many better than him. He prided himself in that. He was just one of the greats of all time." A month before his death, Kelly was given the Lester Patrick Award for his service to hockey and named to the broadcasters wing of the Hockey Hall of Fame. He received the award in St. Luke's Hospital.

More than 500 mourners from across the country and Canada attended the funeral at Ascension Church in Chesterfield. Gus Kyle was among those in attendance. The pallbearers were Mike Shanahan, Jack Quinn, Joe Micheletti, Jack Buck, and former Blues coaches Red Berenson, Al Arbour, and Scotty Bowman. After the service, the Blues players led the procession out of the church and lined the path for the other mourners. Kelly, like Doug Wickenheiser, is buried near the St. Vincent De-Paul Chapel in Section 43. His upright monument reads, "Voice of the Blues."

Frank "Pee Wee" Wallace (1922—1979) is not a name many St. Louisans will recognize, but his sporting achievement may be the most impressive. Wallace was one of the five St. Louisans on the 1950 World Cup Soccer team that beat England 1 - 0 in one of the biggest upsets in World Cup history. The team's exploits were the subject of the 2005 movie, *The Game of Their Lives*. Wallace was a World War II veteran who spent 15 months in a German prison camp. After the war, he won U.S. Open Cup medals in 1948 and 1950 and went on to have three international goals to his credit in seven matches. He was inducted into the U.S. Soccer Hall of Fame in 1976 with the rest of his 1950 World Cup teammates. Wallace is buried in Section 48. (His World Cup teammate, Charles "Gloves" Colombo, died in 1986 and is buried at St. Peter & Paul Cemetery.)

The "Benchwarmer," as **Bob Burnes** (1914–1995) and his sports column were called, appeared in the *Globe-Democrat* from 1945 to 1986. He first joined the paper in 1935, two months after graduating from college. He covered the St. Louis Browns and went on to become sports editor eight years later. During his 51 years at the *Globe*, it is estimated that he wrote more than 15,000 articles. He premiered on KMOX radio in 1953 and was the first host of "Sports Open Line."

Burnes was educated at CBC High School and St. Louis University. He married Adele Daut in the early 1940's; they had four daughters, including Cathie, a sportswriter at the *Post-Dispatch*, who died of a brain aneurysm in 1993.

On Tuesday, July 11, 1995, three days before his 81st birthday, he died in his home after suffering a heart attack. Reverend William Drennan said of Burnes, "He was a giant of a man. He did countless little things for so many unknown people that made them feel like a million dollars." He is buried in the northern portion of Section 42.

In his 1984 farewell column, Burnes wrote:

It had been fun; it had been the greatest experience of my life. If in some small way it has brightened a day, added a word of explanation, espoused a cause or exposed a fraud, I have had ample reward.

Another person buried in Section 42 is the "first lady of St. Louis television." **Charlotte Peters** (1912-1988) started out by winning an amateur talent contest sponsored by KSD-TV, singing "Won't You Come Home, Bill Bailey?" She then auditioned for and became a regular cast member of the show *To The Ladies*, the first local daytime show. In the early 1950's, she appeared in stage plays; her success there led to an offer to host her own locally produced television show on KSD.

She became one of St. Louis' most popular entertainers with her noonday variety show, *The Charlotte Peters Show*, first at KSD, from 1956 to 1964, then later at KTVI. During her often spontaneous and unrehearsed shows, she sang and acted out skits in front of live audiences. She also interviewed Hollywood's top entertainers when they came to town, including Bob Hope, Frank Sinatra, and Jerry Lewis.

Charlotte Peters died at the age of 75 at the Mother of Good Counsel nursing home, where she had been living after suffering several strokes during her last eight years. Her tall, black monument features an embossed portrait of her and her husband and the words "Let's Wing It." Her son, Mike Peters, is a Pulitzer Prize-winning editorial cartoonist and creator of the comic strip, "Mother Goose and Grimm."

Beginning in 1953, **Albert "Red" Villa** (1909–1990) served 37 years as a city alderman, the longest term in St. Louis history. The aldermanic chambers at City Hall are named in his honor. He died of cancer at the age of 81. Among the more than 500 people who attended his funeral Mass at Sts. Mary and Joseph Catholic Church were Mayor Vince Schoemehl and newly elected St. Louis County Executive George "Buzz" Westfall. He was buried with one of his trademark cigars in his coat pocket. Today, he rests in Section 13.

VI

Other Notables Buried in St. Louis

Busch Family

John Sappington
(? 1750–September 10, 1815)

In the winter of 1777, George Washington and his troops encamped at Valley Forge. Many soldiers succumbed to the harsh realities of that winter in Pennsylvania: cold temperatures, insufficient food, and lack of proper clothing. Among the Continentals at Valley Forge were John Sappington and his two brothers. Sappington also was present at Yorktown in 1781, at the close of the war.

John Sappington was born in Maryland in 1750. A few years after Cornwallis surrendered to Washington, Sgt. Sappington moved to Kentucky with his wife, Jemima. Besides farming, he was active in state politics, serving in the Kentucky House and Senate. The Sappingtons spent 20 years tilling the land and raising their large family of 18 children, one dying in infancy.

Sappington first arrived in St. Louis in the spring of 1805, and in May purchased 1,920 acres along Gravois Creek for $800. The acreage was located in the area of what is today Crestwood Plaza. He built a log cabin on the property before returning to Kentucky to collect his family. Sappington spent the rest of his life on his Missouri farm. His son Thomas constructed Sappington House in Crestwood. John Sappington died on September 10, 1815, and is buried with his family in Sappington Cemetery in Crestwood.

The first burial in the cemetery, the third-oldest burial ground in the St. Louis area, was Sappington's 17-year-old daughter, who died in 1811. Sappington and his wife are buried beside their daughter. The Daughters of the American Revolution placed a bronze marker at the grave in 1928. The City of Crestwood now maintains the cemetery.

Sr. Rose Philippine Duchesne
(August 29, 1769-November 18, 1852)

Mother Duchesne was canonized a saint on July 4, 1988, at a Mass celebrated by Pope John Paul II at St. Peter's Basilica in Rome. She was born to wealthy parents in Grenoble, France and, ironically, was baptized in the Church of St. Louis in France. She attended school at a French monastery, where she was influenced by the religious order. At the age of 18, she decided to become a nun.

At the advent of the French Revolution, religion became increasingly unacceptable and finally was outlawed. During this turbulent period, in which her aunt and uncle were killed, Duchesne risked her life to help others. After the Revolution, she joined the order in which she would remain for the rest of her life, the Society of the Sacred Heart.

For years, she longed to come to America and work with the Indians; and, when Bishop Louis DuBourg of New Orleans asked the Society for help with his missions, Mother Barat, founder of Sacred Heart, gave permission for Duchesne and four other nuns to come to America. The holy sisters reached New Orleans after a 73-day voyage, which included being attacked by a pirate ship, before sailing up the Mississippi to St. Louis, arriving August 21, 1818. The nuns proceeded west to their new home in the village of St. Charles, living in nothing more than a small log cabin. In September, they opened the first free school west of the Mississippi; a tuition-based academy opened weeks later. Among the first students were the relatives of Auguste Chouteau and Manuel Lisa. The income from the academy helped to fund missionary work with the Indians.

After one year in St. Charles, Bishop DuBourg transferred the nuns to Florissant. They built new schools and a novitiate where girls could study to be nuns. Wishing to be close to the chapel and not disturb others as she often prayed through the night, Mother Duchesne chose as her convent bedroom a small closet under the stairs. She had simple needs, owned few possessions, and lived the life of an impoverished soul, the life of a saint. She would ultimately supervise six schools in Missouri and Louisiana. In 1827, she opened the Academy of the Sacred Heart in St. Louis and the city's first orphanage for girls. The academy merged with Villa Duchesne in 1968.

She cherished the few relationships she had. Father Peter De Smet and the Jesuits, who came to St. Louis three years after the nuns, were benefactors of the Sacred Heart. Archbishop Peter Kenrick and Bishop Joseph Rosati also were fond acquaintances. In 1841, when Mother Duchesne was 72, she lived with the Potawatomi Indians in Sugar Creek, Kansas, in what became one of the most pleasant aspects of her missionary work.

Mother Duchesne's eyesight began to fail in her 81st year. Her body was weakening at an increasing rate, and her mind was wracked with forgetfulness. She wrote to her sister, "I have stopped calculating when I shall meet death. It will be when God wills. Old age has many sacrifices to make, and it can be a period of great value as one's purgatory. It will certainly be a less rigorous one than that of the next life."

Although Mother Duchesne was bedridden by August 16, 1852, she continued to attend Mass in the chapel every morning. She wrote to Father De Smet, "Your kindness toward me in the past gives me the assurance that I shall see that kindness continue to the end of my life. Yesterday I received the last sacraments, and I hope you will not forget me in your prayers. If you do me the favor of asking prayers for me that will be a great charity." Her doctor prescribed medications, but nothing improved her condition.

She was much too weak to leave bed on the morning of November 16, missing church services for the first time. The next day, she developed a cough. Father Verhaegen, a Jesuit priest she had known for many years, came to hear her last confession and anoint her. In response to the invocation, she said, in a barely audible tone, "I give you my heart, my soul, and my life -- oh, yes -- my life, generously." Mother Rose Philippine Duchesne died shortly after noon. She was 83.

Her body was placed in a wooden coffin and moved to the chapel. Father Verhaegen celebrated the funeral Mass at St. Charles Borromeo Church, followed by burial in a cemetery near the church. Her original grave marker was a piece of wood inscribed with the words, "Very severe to herself and very kind to others."

Father Verhaegen recorded her burial:

> On the 20th of November, 1852, I, the undersigned, buried the mortal remains of Madame Philippine Duchesne, professed religious of the Society of the Sacred Heart, aged 83 years.
>
> [signed] P.J. Verhaegen, S.J.

Mother Duchesne now rests in the chapel at the Academy of the Sacred Heart in St. Charles. A small, pink monument with the inscription, "Mother Duchesne," marks her final resting place.

HENRY SHAW
(JULY 24, 1800-AUGUST 25, 1889)

Henry Shaw worked for two years in the hardware business when, at age 19, he left Europe to settle in St. Louis. He arrived on May 4, 1819, rented a house on Main Street, and started a small hardware store on the levee that he operated alone for several years. By 40 years of age, after only 21 years in America, he had amassed a fortune.

Shaw sold the business and traveled in Europe for the next 10 years. During this period, he was struck by the beauty of the botanical gardens throughout the continent. Upon returning to the United States, he set aside a portion of his property in the southwest part of the city for the cultivation of plants and flowers. He built a house in the middle of his garden and a second residence downtown, at what is now Seventh and Locust Streets.

Shaw dedicated the remainder of his life to his botanical garden and philanthropic activities. He established Tower Grove Park on his property near the garden, and he donated the park to the city in 1868. He was simple and sensitive in his nature, always acting as a benefactor for those who had no voice by giving financial support to orphanages, churches, and hospitals.

As illness consumed him, he delegated his duties with the garden. In 1889, he spent the summer on Mackinac Island, Michigan, to rest his feverish body and regain his strength. The trip was a great benefit to his spirit, but he declined again soon after his return to St. Louis. He spent his last weeks in his garden home, reading Dickens and other favorite authors. His personal physician attributed the fever to malaria, which affected the brain and heart. At times, Shaw would fall into a stupor, become inattentive, and have difficulty speaking.

Shaw's family and friends were called to his side on August 25, 1889. His sister Caroline wept uncontrollably at his bedside, while Mrs. Rebecca Edom, his housekeeper of 30 years, held his hand and stroked his forehead. Three of Shaw's trusted employees were by his side: superintendent of the garden, James Gurney, associate David MacAdam, and supervisor of collections, D. F. Kaime. They all watched as Shaw's breathing became more labored. As the night went on, there were irregular gasps of breath. Then the great man whispered, "Seventy-nine." Those around him were surprised by the words. "No, eighty-nine," Mrs. Edom responded, referring to his age. Shaw looked at her but was unable to speak. A few moments later his doctor pronounced, "He is gone."

The gates to the garden were wreathed in mourning, and the flags in Tower Grove Park were set at half-mast. Governor David Francis sent the following telegram:

Please express my sincere condolence to the relatives and devoted friends of Henry Shaw. In his taking off St. Louis loses a magnificent benefactor, Missouri a distinguished citizen. May the memory of his life full of good acts and noble sentiments incite his fellow men to higher aims and better deeds.

Henry Shaw's estimated worth at the time of his death was $2,500,000. The body lay in state at the garden museum in a cedar coffin covered with black velvet. The room was decorated with 15-foot palms. The pallbearers included his doctor and employees MacAdam and Kaime. There were more than 50 honorary pallbearers, including Adolphus Busch, William Lemp, and James Yeatman.

Christ Church Cathedral was the setting for the funeral on Saturday, August 31. Offices around the city closed early, and hundreds of spectators crowded the streets and sidewalks around the cathedral long before the service began. Afterward, a procession led the body back to the botanical gardens, where Shaw was placed in the previously built mausoleum in front of his garden home. The mausoleum, an octagonal structure with eight pillars of red granite supporting a double dome topped with a Latin cross, is an impressive mixture of Byzantine and Renaissance architecture. The Italian marble sarcophagus is topped with a likeness of Henry Shaw, asleep with his left hand on his chest, clutching a rose.

According to his will, much of his estate was donated to several charitable and business institutions in St. Louis, among them Washington University, the Missouri Historical Society, Good Samaritan Hospital, Little Sisters of the Poor, and his own botanical garden. Shaw Boulevard and Shaw Elementary School were named for him.

Today, the 79-acre Missouri Botanical Garden is a leading research center for botanists. It boasts the world's first geodesic dome greenhouse and the largest Japanese garden in North America.

FATHER PETER DE SMET
(JANUARY 30, 1801-MAY 23, 1873)

Father De Smet immigrated to the United States at the age of 20 from his native Belgium. He left behind his father, stepmother, and 16 brothers and sisters. He was in a Jesuit novitiate in Baltimore when he was transferred to Florissant, Missouri, a village of about 400 people. He and his fellow Jesuits cleared the land and built what became the Jesuit Province of Missouri. Mother Duchesne and the Ladies of the Sacred Heart helped the Jesuits get settled in their new home. It was during this time that Mother Duchesne and Father De Smet came to know and respect each other.

On September 23, 1827, Peter John De Smet was ordained into the priesthood by Bishop Joseph Rosati. He celebrated his first Mass the following day. The next year, at the request of the bishop, he and his Jesuits began the work of establishing a college in St. Louis. Father De Smet himself helped with the construction by cutting stones and carrying bricks. The college, located at Ninth and Washington, opened in November 1829 with 40 students, but quickly expanded and soon became a university: St. Louis University. Father De Smet was the treasurer and a professor of English. He spent the next decade in pursuit of expanding Jesuit activities in both America and Europe.

His most fulfilling work was as a missionary to the Indians, who affectionately referred to the holy man as "Blackrobe;" others called him the "apostle of the Rocky Mountains." He traveled extensively through the unexplored regions of the west and established missions for both the white man and the Indians. His closeness with the Indians led to his becoming a mediator in conflicts between the Indians and the white settlers who were coming West. In 1849, the honor of assistant vice-province of Missouri was bestowed on Father De Smet. Later, he was named procurator general of Missouri.

Father De Smet was back home in Belgium in February 1872 when he suffered an attack of nephritis, an acute inflammation of the kidney. He wrote a friend, "I am so weak that even a short conversation tires me." His condition improved enough for him to sail back to America in April. Forced to retire because of his illness, he occupied his time by writing a history of the Jesuit Province in the Midwest. He had hardly begun the project when his kidney problem returned. On June 21 he wrote:

As regards my health, the machine is completely out of order. For two months I have been confined to my room by order of the doctor, and I have to follow a very strict and, for me, quite new regime. My mantelpiece looks like a drug-shop and the very sight of it takes away my appetite. I am extremely feeble. Nevertheless, I am not without hope, for I am convalescing. May God's will be done.

His condition steadily worsened, and by May he lost sight in his left eye. Days later, after saying Mass, he told a server, "This is the end. I shall never again ascend the altar." Father De Smet requested the Last Sacraments on May 20, 1873; and, on his final day, May 23, 1873, he was calm and accepting of his fate. Father Peter De Smet ascended to his God at 2:15 a.m.

St. Louisans were deeply taken aback upon the news his death. The *Missouri Republican* wrote of him:

> In him the world loses one of the most intrepid pioneers of Christian civilization. If he did not accomplish all that he believed possible, he at least gave an example of what a profound conviction can do in the struggle against insurmountable obstacles.

The May 24th funeral took place at St. Francis Xavier Church. His coffin, draped in black and covered with flowers, rested on a catafalque near the front of the church. A wreath of white roses was placed over his head. Mourners proceeded by the coffin for their final look at the missionary who had meant so much to so many. The archbishop of St. Louis, Richard Peter Kenrick, conducted the service. After the ceremony, Father De Smet was taken back to Florissant for burial.

He rests on the grounds of the Museum of Western Jesuit Missions, 700 Howdershell, formerly St. Stanislaus Seminary. The cemetery can be seen from the road; a large stone cross centers the small burial ground.

THE BUSCH FAMILY

After the death of Adolphus Busch in 1913, August Busch, Sr., took over the beer empire. While the Lemps' company and other breweries collapsed during Prohibition, Anheuser-Busch produced yeast, corn, and syrups for the baking industry. When Prohibition ended in 1933, Anheuser-Busch sent its first case of beer to President Franklin D. Roosevelt.

August Busch, Sr., was born December 29, 1865. He attended the Morgan Park Military Institute in Chicago, and later the Kemper Military Academy in Boonville, Missouri. After studying brewing in Europe, he worked for Anheuser-Busch as a brewer's apprentice. During his reign as president of the brewery, he built Bevo Mill and an extravagant French Renaissance chateau, dubbed the "Castle" on the Grant's Farm property. He was quiet and retiring, seldom seen at society functions. He and his wife, Alice, had three daughters and two sons; Adolphus III and August, Jr., each in turn would later run the brewery.

Adolphus III was born at his parents' home, Two Busch Place, on February 10, 1891. He bore a strong resemblance to his father and, like him, was shy and preferred the home life. In June 1913, when he was 21, he married Florence Parker Lambert at Grant's Farm. They had a daughter in 1914. The couple divorced in July 1930; and two months later Adolphus married Catherine Bowen, a member of a wealthy political family in Texas.

August Busch, Jr., was born in St. Louis on March 28, 1899. His first job was with the Manufacturers Railway Company, a subsidiary of Anheuser-Busch. He served as a sergeant in World War I before becoming general superintendent with the brewery on January 1, 1924. August, or "Gussie," as he was affectionately known, quickly moved up the ranks during the Prohibition era. It was after the repeal of Prohibition that Gussie first used the horse-drawn beer wagon for brewery promotions. The famous Clydesdale hitch was born.

By September 1933, August Busch, Sr.'s physical condition was deteriorating: he was suffering from gout, chest pains, and dropsy. He rarely visited the brewery. On Sunday evening, February 10, 1934, he awoke several times during the night from intense pain and had trouble breathing. His cousin, John Busch, who slept in his room and served as a part-time nurse, called the doctor, who gave Busch a shot of morphine to relieve the pain. On Monday morning, Busch picked up a pamphlet entitled *An Open Letter to Rev. Charles E. Coughlin* and on the back cover wrote simply, "Goodbye precious mama and adorable children."

At 8:00 a.m. his chauffeur, Tony Feichtinger, came to the room, as was his daily practice. Feichtinger asked Busch if he wanted to listen to some music on the radio. Busch nodded his approval; as Feichtinger moved to the console, Busch pulled a .32-caliber revolver from the nightstand and shot himself in the left side of the chest, below the heart. Family members rushed to the bedroom. His wife screamed as she held her husband in her arms. He died 15 minutes later.

Busch lay in state in the living room of the Castle. He was dressed in a dark blue suit and white shirt, his casket surrounded by violets and lilies. More than 10,000 mourners viewed the body and paid respects to the family. The funeral took place at the mansion on Friday, February 15, with members of the St. Louis Symphony playing, just as they had for Adolphus' funeral 20 years earlier. His body was removed from his home and taken by hearse the short distance up Gravois Road to Sunset Memorial Park. He was buried on a hilltop facing Grant's Farm, where he could forever view his chateau in the distance. A simple grave marker denotes his final resting place.

Adolphus III took over the brewery, with Gussie as first vice president. When the United States entered World War II, Gussie joined the army and was given the rank of colonel. His rise to the top of the brewery was complete in 1946, when his brother Adolphus died of cardiac failure on

August 29, having spent eight days at Barnes Hospital. He had suffered from stomach cancer and other ailments for some time. He was buried beside his father in Sunset Memorial Park. Adolphus III had run the brewery for 12 years, the shortest run of a Busch family member.

When Gussie was named President and Chief Executive Officer, he was only the fourth Busch to head the company. The red brick schoolhouse where his father had attended classes became his office. He began a program of major company expansion by constructing new breweries in Tampa and Jacksonville, Florida. In 1953, he purchased the St. Louis Baseball Cardinals from Fred Saigh for less than $4 million, and later was instrumental in the development of the Busch Gardens theme parks. He was one of the most popular and well-respected citizens in St. Louis. He was married four times between 1918 and 1988, marrying for the last time at age 82. He had 11 children, including his successor, August Busch III.

Gussie resigned his position as Chief Executive Officer of Anheuser-Busch in May 1975, and his chairmanship two years later. He was given the title of Honorary Chairman of Anheuser-Busch, and remained as Chairman and President of the Baseball Cardinals. In 1988, *Forbes* magazine ranked him No. 36 among the richest Americans. His philanthropy included gifts to Washington University and the Busch Memorial Student Center at St. Louis University. In 1950, he hosted President Harry S Truman at Grant's Farm, and the two became close friends.

He suffered from arthritis for many years, and walked with a cane near the end of his life. In August 1989, he spent three weeks in St. Luke's Hospital, suffering from pneumonia. When he insisted on going home to Grant's Farm, medical equipment and nurses were dispatched to care for him in his final days. He slipped into unconsciousness and died on Friday, September 29, at 12:25 p.m., with his 10 surviving children at his bedside, in the same room where his father had committed suicide. The cause of death was pneumonia and congestive heart failure. The Busch Stadium flag was set at half-mast, and a moment of silence was observed before the Cardinals-Cubs game that evening; the Cardinals players wore black armbands in mourning. President George H. W. Bush said of him, "He had been a legendary figure in American life for almost a century as a successful businessman, community leader and philanthropist."

A private funeral service was conducted in the Castle on Sunday, October 1. Only family and close friends, numbering about 120, were in attendance. Gussie's longtime friend, Reverend Paul Reinert, chancellor of St. Louis University, officiated at the service. Among the pallbearers were five of his sons, including August Busch III. At noon, a team of Clydesdales pulling a beer wagon escorted the funeral procession to the gates of Grant's Farm before a police escort led his flag-draped coffin the short distance to Sunset Memorial Park. Gussie was laid to rest beside his daughter Christina, who had died in an automobile accident in 1974.

On October 3, the Cathedral Basilica was filled for a memorial Mass. Governor John Ashcroft and television announcer Ed McMahon attended, as did many baseball dignitaries, including Red Schoendienst, former Yankee Joe DiMaggio, and several baseball owners. Hundreds of brewery employees were shuttled to the service. Archbishop John May and Reverend Reinert were among several clergy conducting the service.

The members of the Busch family are buried in a semi-circle facing a monument depicting a boy feeding a fawn. The base of the sculpture is a piece of red granite engraved with the name "Busch." A row of hedges and shade trees conceal the area.

Buried along the cemetery road near the Busch family plot is Hall of Fame sportswriter Bob Broeg (1918-2005). He spent nearly 60 years writing for the *St. Louis Post Dispatch*. Broeg joined the newspaper in 1945 and went on to author 20 books. A Who's Who of Cardinal baseball history attended his funeral: Musial, Brock, and Herzog, among others.

HENRY KIEL
(FEBRUARY 21, 1871-NOVEMBER 26, 1942)

In November 1942, Archbishop John Glennon said of Henry Kiel, "I knew Henry Kiel very well. I admired his work as a mayor and his character as a man. He did a great deal for the city of St. Louis and I regret very much to learn of his death." Kiel was the first man to serve in the mayor's office for three four-year terms. He was regarded as the "father of the Municipal Opera," which opened during his administration; he was serving as its president at the time of his death.

A native of St. Louis, Henry Kiel attended Smith Academy and then worked as a bricklayer for his father's construction company. He took over the business upon his father's death and was responsible for the construction of Soldan High School, the *Post-Dispatch* Building, and the Ambassador Theater, among others.

He entered politics as a ward committeeman and was appointed chairman of the Republican City Central Committee. He was elected mayor of St. Louis in 1913. During his administration, the city charter and zoning laws were revised, the MacArthur Bridge was completed, construction on the Municipal Auditorium (Kiel Auditorium) and the Civil Courts Building was started, and the St. Louis Zoo and the Municipal Opera were established. He was described as friendly and politically social, and was a man who would listen to all concerns before making a decision. His dedication to the less fortunate earned him the Distinguished Service Cross from the Salvation Army, only the seventh person in the United States to receive the award. In 1931, after retiring from office, he was appointed president of the St. Louis Police Board.

During the summer of 1941, Kiel suffered a paralyzing stroke. Eighteen months later, still confined to bed at his home, 1625 Missouri Avenue, he became seriously ill. He slipped into a coma at 8:00 p.m. on November 26, 1942, and died less than an hour later, his family at his side. The cause of death was a blood clot.

Kiel's funeral was held at the Scottish Rite Cathedral on Lindell Boulevard. His body rested in a bronze casket covered with a blanket of chrysanthemums. Governor Forrest Donnell gave the eulogy, and Mayor William Dee Becker served as a pallbearer. (Less than a year later, Becker died in the glider crash at Lambert Field.) Afterward, a private service for the family was held at St. Mark's English Lutheran Church on Clayton Road.

Henry Kiel is buried in the mausoleum at Oak Grove Cemetery, 7800 St. Charles Rock Road. His crypt is on the second floor, in the first hallway to the right. The inscription denotes his service as mayor of St. Louis.

GEORGE SISLER
(MARCH 24, 1893-MARCH 26, 1973)

Baseball Hall of Famer George Sisler was the best player in St. Louis Browns history. Ty Cobb said of him, "Sisler could do everything. He could hit, run, and throw and he wasn't a bad pitcher, either."

Sisler was born in Manchester, Ohio. He studied engineering and played baseball at the University of Michigan for coach Branch Rickey. When Rickey became manager of the St. Louis Browns, he signed Sisler to a contract upon his graduation from Michigan in 1915. The young college kid was mild mannered and likeable, and quickly became a fan favorite. He began his career on June 28, 1915, pitching in a 4-2 loss to Chicago. He continued to pitch, and played first base between starts before permanently moving to first base in a few years. In his second season, he twice secured victory for the Browns by outpitching the great Walter Johnson.

Sisler and his wife Kathleen had three sons and a daughter. His sons all played in the majors like their father: George, Jr., played one year with the St. Louis Browns, Dick played outfield for the Cardinals and Philadelphia Phillies before managing the Cincinnati Reds, and Dave pitched for the Boston Red Sox, Detroit Tigers, and Washington Senators.

Sisler was a lieutenant in World War I and fought in the same unit as Ty Cobb and Christy Mathewson. (Mathewson died in October 1925 from tuberculosis, which he acquired after inhaling poison gas during the war.) Sisler became the best hitter for the Browns, finishing his career with 2,812 hits and a lifetime average of .340, batting over .400 in 1920 and 1922. In the 1922 season, he had a 41-game hitting streak, which remained a record until Joe DiMaggio hit in 56 games in 1941. He won his second batting title that season with a .420 average and was named the American League's Most Valuable Player for the season.

During the off season in 1922, Sisler came down with influenza, which impaired his vision and forced him to miss the entire 1923 season. He had successful surgery and returned in 1924 as the Browns player-manager. His team was never able to win the pennant, and Sisler resigned as manager in 1927, although he played for the Browns one more year. The next season, with his talents declining, he was sent to the Washington Senators, then to the Boston Braves. He officially retired in September 1930, having spent 13 of his 16 seasons with the Browns.

In June 1939, Sisler was among those inducted when baseball officially opened the Hall of Fame in Cooperstown, New York. The 13 others inducted with him included Babe Ruth, Ty Cobb, and Cy Young. Once his playing days were over, he became a scout for Branch Rickey and the Brooklyn Dodgers and later scouted for the Pittsburgh Pirates.

In March 1973, he celebrated his 80th birthday in St. Mary's Health Center. He spent eight days at the hospital in a weak, rundown condition before dying of kidney failure on March 26, two days after his birthday, with his wife Kathleen and two of his children by his side. On March 29, a service was conducted at Lupton Funeral Home on Delmar, followed by burial at Oak Grove Cemetery. In 1993, his cremated remains were moved to the churchyard behind the Old Stone Meeting House of Des Peres Presbyterian Church. The church, founded in 1833, is one of the oldest west of the Mississippi and is now a National Historic Site. The cemetery and Old Stone Meeting House are located on Geyer Road between Clayton and Manchester.

In 2005, George Sisler was honored with a star on the St. Louis Walk of Fame.

JOE MEDWICK
(NOVEMBER 24, 1911-MARCH 21, 1975)

In March 1975, Joe Medwick was in St. Petersburg, Florida, for spring training, serving as hitting instructor for the Cardinals' minor league teams. At about 10:00 p.m., March 20, Medwick walked into the Bayfront Medical Center, complaining of chest pains. The Cardinals team physician, Dr. Stan London, was notified, and diagnosed Medwick with a massive heart seizure. Within a few hours, one of the most legendary members of the Gashouse Gang was dead.

Medwick was born and raised in Carteret, New Jersey. In high school, he was all-state in football, baseball, and basketball, and he received numerous scholarships, including an offer to play football at Notre Dame. His first professional tryout was with a farm team of the New York Yankees, but they felt he was too young and inexperienced and released him. Medwick came to the Cardinals organization in 1930 and played for their minor league team in Scottsdale, Pennsylvania. He was a powerful, right-handed hitter with a compact and muscular build who played under the name "Mickey King" to protect his eligibility in case he decided to play football at Notre Dame. He was moved up to play in the Texas League, where he picked up the nickname "Ducky" from a female fan.

Medwick came into the major leagues in August 1932 at the age of 20. He was given the number 7 and played left field. He was a tough, fiery competitor, and his outbursts often were directed toward his own teammates. Within a few seasons, he became the hitting star of the Cardinals. General Manager Branch Rickey and Player-Manager Frankie Frisch collected a group of tough, hardnosed individualists, such as pitching ace Dizzy Dean, shortshop Leo Durocher, third baseman Pepper Martin – and outfielder Joe Medwick. Dubbed "the Gashouse Gang," these unique characters excited baseball fans and took the Cardinals to the top. "They wouldn't let us play in the American League," Durocher is supposed to have said. "They'd just say we were a bunch of gas house players." In 1934, the Cardinals and their Gashouse Gang defeated the Detroit Tigers to win the World Series. Medwick was the center of controversy during the seventh game when he made a hard slide into Tigers third baseman Marv Owen. The two started fighting until umpires separated them. Fans pelted him with fruit when he went to his left field position in the bottom of the inning. Baseball commissioner Kenesaw Mountain Landis, who watched from his field box, removed Medwick from the game for his own protection.

The next three seasons were Medwick's most prolific, concluding with the 1937 Triple Crown. He led the league in home runs, RBI's, batting average, and nine other categories. He was named Most Valuable Player for the season. By 1940, his talents had diminished, along with his popularity among fans. In June, one week after he was traded to the Brooklyn Dodgers, the Cardinals faced the Dodgers in Ebbets Field. When Medwick came to bat in the first inning, Cardinals pitcher Bob Bowman hit him in the head with the first pitch. Medwick spent time at a Brooklyn hospital with a concussion and blurred vision, but within a week he returned to the lineup. He played with various teams over the next seven seasons with little success, including a stint in 1947 as a pinch-hitter for the Cardinals. He played 16 years in the major leagues and accumulated 2,471 hits and more than 200 home runs.

In retirement, Medwick coached in the minor leagues before opening an insurance business. He returned to coaching in 1966 as hitting instructor in the Cardinals minor league system. On January 23, 1968, he was elected to the Baseball Hall of Fame.

In March 1975, the evening before his heart attack, he attended a dinner given by the Florida governor for baseball's Hall of Famers. At about 3:00 a.m., Friday, March 21, Joe Medwick died of a heart attack at Bayfront Medical Center. He was survived by his wife Isabelle, whom he married in 1936, and his two children. The funeral took place at Michael Fitzgerald Mortuary on South Lindbergh.

Joe Medwick is buried in the churchyard of St. Lucas United Church of Christ, 11735 Denny Road. His headstone is engraved with the Cardinals insignia. A flat marker in front of his headstone is a testament to his baseball exploits:

Member of 1934 World Champion St. Louis Cardinals.
National League's Most Valuable Player and Triple
Crown Winner in 1937. Lifetime Batting Average .324.
He was elected to Baseball's Hall of Fame.
Cooperstown, New York, in 1968.

VII

Notable St. Louisans Buried Elsewhere

Eugene Field

EUGENE FIELD
(SEPTEMBER 2, 1850-NOVEMBER 4, 1895)

Poet and journalist Eugene Field was feeling ill during the fall of 1895. On Sunday, November 3, he canceled a speaking engagement in Kansas City and stayed at his Chicago home in the hope of improving his condition. He went to sleep late, his 14-year-old son staying in the same room to watch over him. Early in the morning, Field turned in his bed and groaned. His son was unable to awaken him, and the doctor was summoned. Field was pronounced dead of heart failure caused by a blood clot.

Eugene Field was born in St. Louis to Roswell and Frances Field. His father had been an attorney for Dred Scott. (Roswell is buried at Bellefontaine.) The family lived at 634 South Broadway, which is now the Eugene Field House and St. Louis Toy Museum. After his mother passed away when he was seven, Field was sent to Amherst, Massachusetts, to live with his aunt, who became his foster mother. His first job was with the *St. Louis Evening Journal* in 1872. He worked at several newspapers before arriving in Chicago in August 1883 to work on the editorial staff at the *Chicago Morning News*, where he stayed until his death. His national daily column, called "Sharps and Flats," was a straightforward, humorous look at society.

In October 1873, Field married Julia Comstock, whom he met at the University of Missouri. The couple had seven children. Two of his children preceded him in death, including his son Melvin in October 1890. "While our boy still lived, I battled constantly in spirit and I think that another week would have killed me," Field wrote his wife. "Now that all is over, I am content, wholly reconciled. I believe our boy is happy now. It is selfish to wish him back."

Dubbed "the children's poet," Eugene Field's reputation was built from his stories and poetry; his most famous poems include *Little Boy Blue; Wynken, Blynken and Nod; and Dutch Lullaby*. His great popularity and warm, engaging personality helped him to gain friends easily. His last visit to St. Louis was a year before he died, when he gave a lecture at the First Congregational Church on Delmar. Upon his passing in November 1895, the *Globe-Democrat* wrote, "He could entertain a crowd of twenty for hours at a time, and his wit was as spontaneous as his good humor was contagious."

Thousands mourned Field's sudden and unexpected death. On Wednesday, November 6, his funeral Mass was celebrated at Fourth Presbyterian Church in Chicago. Six of his former newspaper associates served as pallbearers. He was buried with a private service at Graceland Cemetery on the near north side of Chicago.

On December 30, 1925, his remains were moved approximately 10 miles north to the Church of the Holy Comforter in Kenilworth, Illinois, 222 Kenilworth Avenue.

T. S. ELIOT
(SEPTEMBER 26, 1888-JANUARY 4, 1965)

April is the cruelest month, breeding
Lilacs out of the dead land, mixing
Memory and desire, stirring
Dull roots with spring rain.
Winter kept us warm, covering
Earth in forgetful snow, feeding
A little life with dried tubers.

Excerpt from *The Waste Land, 1922*

Thomas Stearns Eliot was born in St. Louis, the seventh son of Henry and Charlotte Eliot. His father was president of the St. Louis Hydraulic Press Brick Company, and his grandfather was William Greenleaf Eliot, founder of Washington University. Eliot completed his undergraduate studies at Harvard in three years and obtained a Masters degree in his fourth year. He also studied in Paris at the Sorbonne.

Eliot became established with the publication of his poem, *The Love Song of J. Alfred Prufrock*. Five years later, *The Waste Land* won him literary fame; the poem was edited by his friend and fellow poet, Ezra Pound. His writings also included several plays and essays. He moved to London at the beginning of World War I and became a teacher at the Highgate School. A year later, he was employed by Lloyd's Bank before working as an editor and director for the publishing house, Faber and Faber. He became a British citizen in 1927. In 1948, he was awarded the Nobel Prize for literature. A year later, King George VI conferred upon him the Order of Merit. Andrew Lloyd Webber based his production of *Cats* on Eliot's *Old Possum's Book of Practical Cats* (1939).

Eliot was quiet in his demeanor, lacking the flamboyance and eccentricity of many others in his field. He spent much of his leisure time reading books on philosophy and languages. He often suffered bouts of bronchitis, and his emphysema was exacerbated by his heavy smoking. He married Vivienne Wood in 1915, but she was sickly during much of the marriage and died unexpectedly in 1922. Eliot was shattered by her death.

In 1957, he surprised everyone by marrying his secretary, Valerie Fletcher, a woman 38 years his junior.

Eliot came back to St. Louis in 1953 to speak at Washington University and again in 1959 to talk at Mary Institute. He also was awarded a Medal of Freedom by President Lyndon Johnson, but did not go to Washington to receive it.

During the early 1960's, the bronchitis and emphysema were taking their toll on his body. In December 1962, he collapsed in his home and was rushed to the hospital in a comatose state. Although his condition was critical, he pulled through and went home in five weeks. In October 1964, he again collapsed, this time falling into a coma. He surprised his doctors, who didn't expect him to live the night, by regaining consciousness the next morning.

Thomas Stearns Eliot relapsed into a coma at the end of December and died on January 5, 1965, in his London apartment. He was 76. Ezra Pound said of his friend's death, "I am deeply saddened and profoundly moved by the death of T. S. Eliot, a grand poet and my dear and brotherly friend." St. Stephen's Church in East Coker, England, was the site of the funeral two days later. East Coker was the town from which his ancestors had emigrated in the 17th century. Eliot had memorialized the village in the second of his *Four Quarters* poems, entitled *East Coker*. Only his family and a few close friends attended the 10-minute service. His body was cremated, as he had requested; and on April 17, his ashes were returned to St. Stephen's for burial in the church. On that same day, it was announced that the first college of the newly established University of Kent would be named Eliot College in the poet's honor. His memorial in the church reads:

'In my beginning is my end.'
of your charity
pray for the repose
of the soul of
Thomas Sterns Eliot
Poet
26th September 1888 - 4th January 1965
'In my end is my beginning.'

A memorial service was held at Westminster Abbey on February 4. Ezra Pound, who had not been seen in public for many years, came to express his sympathy. A statement was received from the White House: "The President wishes to pay tribute to a poet and playwright who had a profound impact on his times and who achieved distinction on both sides of the Atlantic." Stage actor Alec Guinness read from Eliot's poems.

JOSEPHINE BAKER
(JUNE 3, 1906-APRIL 12, 1975)

Josephine Baker was born Freda McDonald in the Female Hospital in St. Louis to an impoverished, 20-year-old laundress. The family was so poor that Baker and her three siblings had to sleep together on a single mattress.

Baker often played hooky from school, preferring to spend much of her time dancing and watching musicals, movies, and vaudeville acts at the Booker T. Washington Theatre at 23rd and Market. What little education she did have ended in December 1919, when at the age of 13 she married Willie Wells; of course, the marriage was illegal because of her age. She married legally four times in all, taking her stage name from her second marriage to Billy Baker.

When Baker was 16, she joined a traveling dance troupe based in Philadelphia, and the following year made it to Broadway as a member of the chorus line of *Shuffle Along*. She also appeared at the Cotton Club in Harlem. In 1925, she went to Paris to appear in *La Revue Negre* at the Théâtre des Champs-Elysées, where she appeared nude except for a flamingo feather. She later appeared in the *Folies Bergere* wearing nothing but a skirt of bananas. The new "queen of the music halls" then opened her own club, where she danced into the hearts of Parisians. She added singing to her dance routines and appeared in several French motion pictures before returning to America in 1936 to appear in the *Ziegfeld Follies* on Broadway.

In 1940, while the war raged in Europe, Baker, by this time a French citizen, lived in a château called "Les Milandes" in southwestern France. During World War II, she served as a volunteer for the Red Cross and was a member of the Resistance movement. She was awarded the Legion of Honor for her work.

After the war, she attempted to build a resort on her 300 acres, but fell into debt and was forced to sell the estate at auction in 1969. After Les Milandes was auctioned off, she purchased a villa at Roquebrune-Cap-Martin in the French Riviera with help from Princess Grace of Monaco and income from her return to the stage.

Baker had begun adopting children of varied origins beginning in 1954. In all, she adopted 12 children, whom she nicknamed the "Rainbow

Tribe" because of their different nationalities. Baker faced discrimination much of her life and had bitter feelings toward the United States for the injustices heaped upon blacks. She came to Washington D. C., in 1963 to take part in Martin Luther King's March on Washington. She once told a radio interviewer, "I was born in America and grew up in St. Louis. I was very young when I first went to Europe. I was 18 years old. But I had to go. I wanted to find freedom. I couldn't find it in St. Louis, of course. It was one of the worst cities in America for racial discrimination. I hear it has changed, but I have never been there since. I have very bad memories of that time."

In early April 1975, Baker attended an opening-night party celebrating her 50th anniversary as a French entertainer. She had a habit of calling her friend Marie Spiers every morning; so on Thursday morning, April 10, when Spiers didn't hear from the dancer, she called, to find Baker still sleeping. When Baker's maid was unable to wake her, Spiers called a doctor and rushed over to Baker's Paris apartment, where the entertainer was found lying on her side with a hand to her head. Newspapers with reviews of her show lay about the room. She was taken to Salpietre Hospital in Paris, where she was diagnosed with a cerebral hemorrhage. The press was told that she was suffering from exhaustion.

Marie and Margaret, Baker's sisters, stayed with the entertainer, who never regained consciousness. Princess Grace was present when a priest gave Baker the last rites. Baker passed away at 5:30 a.m., Saturday, April 12.

The nationally televised funeral took place on April 15 at Church of the Madeleine, the Paris cathedral where Napoleon had been crowded Emperor. Josephine Baker was dressed in the gown she had worn to the opening-night party and rested in a coffin lined in pink. Twenty thousand people crowded the streets outside the cathedral. French dignitaries from around the country attended the ceremonies. Princess Grace and actress Sophia Loren paid their respects to the entertainer. But only two of Baker's 12 children were present.

Her body was taken to Monaco for a second funeral arranged by Princess Grace. Mourners viewed the body at the Athanée, a Monte Carlo funeral home, before the April 19 funeral. Two thousand people attended the funeral at St. Charles Church. Her coffin was taken to a Monaco cemetery overlooking the Mediterranean and placed on an altar supported by four columns. It then was placed in the cemetery storage shed until a stone was selected for her tomb. Josephine Baker finally was laid to rest on October 2, 1975.

VINCENT PRICE
(MAY 27, 1911-OCTOBER 25, 1993)

The actor known for his ghoulish portrayals in horror movies was born the youngest of four children in his family's home at 3748 Washington Avenue. Price's family tree can be traced back to Peregrine White, who was born on the Mayflower in Plymouth harbor shortly before the first Thanksgiving. Vincent's grandfather was a chemist who made his fortune by inventing baking powder and later producing flavor extracts for bakers. His father, also named Vincent, ran the Pan Candy Company. His company merged with another manufacturer in 1902 to establish the National Candy Company at 4320 Gravois. The elder Price was named president of the enterprise, which made a fortune during the 1904 World's Fair.

His family's wealth allowed Price to attend the best schools. He went to St. Louis Country Day and then Yale, where he received a Bachelor of Fine Arts degree in 1933. He immediately went to New York and tried to get work in the theatre. When his attempt failed, he took a position as an apprentice teacher. A year later, he enrolled at London University's graduate program.

In 1935, his dream of a career on the stage was finally realized when he played a role in *Chicago* at the Gate Theatre in London. His next role, as Prince Albert in *Victoria Regina*, landed him on Broadway playing opposite Helen Hayes. His first motion picture appearance was in *Service de Luxe*. After a decade of "straight" roles, he joined the ranks of actors such as Bela Lugosi and Boris Karloff when he began appearing in low-budget horror films, such as *House of Wax* in 1953. He once said of his ghoulish portrayals, "The best parts in movies are the heavies. The hero is usually someone who has really nothing to do. He comes out on top, but it's the heavy who has all the fun." He first appeared at the St. Louis Muny Opera in 1940 in *The American Way*.

Besides acting, Price was a gifted storyteller and an avid art collector who had his own gallery. He gave art lectures on college campuses and wrote several books on fine art, the most popular of which was *The Vincent Price Treasury of American Art*. He also served as president of the art council for the University of California at Los Angeles.

He was an accomplished cook who wrote best-selling cookbooks with his second wife, Mary. Price wed actress Edith Barrett in 1938. They had one son, Vincent, but divorced after 10 years of marriage. He wed again, this time to Mary Grant, but this marriage also ended in divorce; their daughter, Mary Victoria, was named after his first Broadway show. In 1974, he was married a third time, to actress Coral Browne, who died in 1991.

By 1993, his 80-plus years were taking a toll. He used a motorized scooter at home and a wheelchair for outings. By October of that year, he was suffering from emphysema and arthritis. He had his daughter and a tight circle of friends to keep him company. He once told his daughter, "Being elderly is a miserable period of life – from the physical standpoint, I mean. Mentally, there are great rewards. You have an entire lifetime during which, if you have spent your time on Earth profitably, you have accumulated enormous amounts of knowledge." He died of lung cancer on Monday, October 25, at his home in Los Angeles, three days before the A&E cable network was to air his story on their program, *Biography* – and, perhaps appropriately, one week before Halloween.

The world made note of his passing. Film critic Leonard Maltin said, "Other actors may have made better movies, but few lived better lives, or touched so many people with their warmth and gentility."

After his remains were cremated, a small service for family and friends was held at Hollywood Cemetery. A private boat was chartered and, as Price had requested, his ashes were scattered at sea. Long-stem red roses and Price's old straw hat also were tossed into the waves.

Harry Caray
(March 14, 1914–February 18, 1998)

Holy Cow! St. Louis native Harry Carabina was foremost a baseball fan. For more than five decades, he delivered the game in one of the most unique and unconventional styles in sports broadcasting. His unmistakable voice and unbridled enthusiasm were endearing to fans, as was his rendition of *Take Me Out to the Ballgame* during the 7th-inning stretch.

He petitioned for the job when the Cardinals broadcasting position became available for the 1945 season. Caray made his first Cardinals broadcast on April 17 of that year, and he spent the next 25 years announcing Cardinals baseball.

When Caray was fired by the Cardinals in October 1969, he was hired by Charles Finley to announce for the Oakland Athletics. From there, he spent 11 seasons with the Chicago White Sox before moving across town to begin a new career as the Cubs announcer on WGN. In 1989, Caray was elected to the Baseball Hall of Fame.

He collapsed on Valentine's Day 1998, while dining with his wife in a Rancho Mirage, California, restaurant; he never regained consciousness. His family, including his son, Atlanta Braves announcer Skip Caray, was by his side when he died four days later at Eisenhower Medical Center.

On February 26, people lined up for more than five hours to view his casket at Holy Name cathedral in downtown Chicago. More than 1,000 family and friends attended the funeral the following day.

Harry Caray is buried at All Saints Cemetery in Des Plaines, Illinois, a suburb of Chicago. Baseball Hall of Famer and Cubs catcher Charles "Gabby" Hartnett also is buried at All Saints.

BETTY GRABLE
(DECEMBER 18, 1916 -JULY 2, 1973)

Betty Grable said of her life, "I had the best of both worlds. A family and a career. And millions of friends all over the world." Ruth Elizabeth Grable appeared in more than 40 films. Her $300,000 a year salary was the highest paid to any actress in the mid-1940's. During World War II, her famous bathing suit pose was the favorite pin-up for G.I.'s fighting around the world.

The blue-eyed blonde was born in South St. Louis to Conn and Lillian Grable. Lillian enrolled her four-year-old daughter in dancing classes and saxophone lessons. Within a few years, Grable was appearing in vaudeville shows at the West End Lyric Theatre and singing on radio shows.

In the summer of 1929, her mother took her to Hollywood, where she was cast in small parts on the Sam Goldwyn lot. Four years later, she danced in *The Gay Divorcee*. In 1941, producer Daryl Zanuck signed her to a contract, and she appeared in the musical, *Down Argentine Way*. It was her first starring role -- and it launched her career.

Grable married actor Jackie Coogan in November 1937, but the marriage ended in divorce two years later. She had a relationship with actor George Raft before marrying band leader and trumpeter Harry James in 1943. They were married for 22 years. The couple had two daughters and lived on an estate raising horses.

Grable retired from the movies after her last picture, *How to Be Very Very Popular*, in 1955. She later attempted a comeback without much success. She seldom visited St. Louis. Her final appearance came in 1971 in the Muny Opera production of *This Is Show Business*, co-starring Don Ameche.

In the early 1970's, she moved to Las Vegas and lived with Bob Remick. The two had met while appearing in a show together. In April 1972, Betty was a presenter at the Academy Awards. After the show, she had difficulty breathing and felt pain in her chest. Tests run at St. John's Hospital in Santa Monica revealed inoperable lung cancer; Grable had been a heavy smoker all her life. She was hospitalized for four months and underwent chemotherapy and cobalt treatments. She wrote to a friend about her condition, "I finally decided after all these years it might be a good idea to get a physical.... Well, it's a good thing I did, 'cause my chest x-ray came back abnormal. Lucky me, just in time. Here I was with a big malignancy."

Grable recovered enough to appear in the stage show *Born Yesterday* in 1973. After the show closed, she began to suffer severe stomach pains and nausea. When abdominal surgery was performed at St. John's, a large tumor was removed, but by this time the cancer had spread throughout her body. She left the hospital and returned to Las Vegas, where her health continued to fail. By early July, she was back in St. John's for her final stay. Actor George Raft wept when he heard Grable was dying. He claimed never to have loved anyone else.

Grable's daughters and her older sister spent a great amount of time with the dying entertainer, who often was heavily sedated. She faded in and out of consciousness before dying at 5:15 p.m., July 2. She was 56. Headlines all over the world told the sad news about the popular actress.

Eight hundred mourners, including her two ex-husbands, Jackie Coogan and Harry James, attended the funeral at All Saints Episcopal Church in Beverly Hills. Actors Cesar Romero, Fred MacMurray and Dorothy Lamour also were on hand to say goodbye to their friend. The reverend eulogized: "We have come here today to offer our prayers and thanksgiving to God for a life. This life we remember here is one who was precious to all of us – for I know I speak for all of us and millions who are not here that we loved Betty Grable. Betty was one of those who shined even in the darkness."

Betty Grable is buried at Inglewood Cemetery in Inglewood, California. Other notables in Inglewood include musician Ray Charles, singer Ella Fitzgerald, actor Cesar Romero, ventriloquist Edgar Bergen, and former Cardinals Baseball player Curt Flood.

Appendix

Six Degrees of Historical Separation

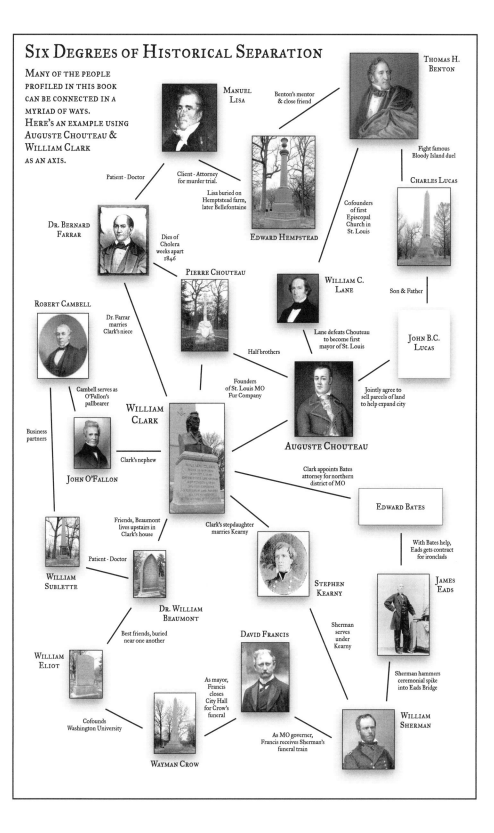

Many of the people profiled in this book can be connected in a myriad of ways. Here's an example using Auguste Chouteau & William Clark as an axis.

Manuel Lisa

Thomas H. Benton

Benton's mentor & close friend

Fight famous Bloody Island duel

Charles Lucas

Patient - Doctor

Client - Attorney for murder trial.

Lisa buried on Hemptstead farm, later Bellefontaine

Cofounders of first Episcopal Church in St. Louis

Dr. Bernard Farrar

Dies of Cholera weeks apart 1846

Edward Hempstead

Pierre Chouteau

William C. Lane

Son & Father

Robert Cambell

Dr. Farrar marries Clark's niece

Lane defeats Chouteau to become first mayor of St. Louis

John B.C. Lucas

Cambell serves as O'Fallon's pallbearer

Half brothers

Founders of St. Louis MO Fur Company

Jointly agree to sell parcels of land to help expand city

William Clark

Business partners

Clark's nephew

Auguste Chouteau

Clark appoints Bates attorney for northern district of MO

John O'Fallon

Edward Bates

Friends, Beaumont lives upstairs in Clark's house

Clark's stepdaughter marries Kearny

With Bates help, Eads gets contract for ironclads

Patient - Doctor

James Eads

William Sublette

Stephen Kearny

Dr. William Beaumont

Sherman serves under Kearny

David Francis

William Eliot

Best friends, buried near one another

As mayor, Francis closes City Hall for Crow's funeral

Sherman hammers ceremonial spike into Eads Bridge

William Sherman

Cofounds Washington University

As MO governer, Francis receives Sherman's funeral train

Wayman Crow

Bibliography

BOOKS

Ackroyd, Peter. *T.S. Eliot*. London: Hamish Hamilton, 1984.

Auble, John. *The History of St. Louis Gangsters*. St. Louis: The National Criminal Research Society, 2000.

Baker, Jean-Claude and Chris Chase. *Josephine: The Hungry Heart*. New York: Random House, 1993.

Baldwin, Helen. *Heritage of St. Louis*. St. Louis: St. Louis Public Schools, 1964.

Barnes, Harper. *Standing on a Volcano: The Life and Times of David Rowland Francis*. St. Louis: Missouri Historical Society, 2001.

Bartley, Mary. *St. Louis Lost*. St. Louis: Virginia Publishing Company, 1994.

Borst, Bill. *Baseball Through a Knothole: A St. Louis History*. St. Louis: Krank Press, 1980.

Burnett, Betty. *St. Louis at War*. St. Louis: The Patrice Press, 1987.

Cain, Marvin R. *Lincoln's Attorney General: Edward Bates of Missouri*. Columbia, MO: University of Missouri Press, 1965.

Callan, Louise. *Philippine Duchesne: Frontier Missionary of the Sacred Heart 1769-1852*. Westminster, MD: The Newman Press, 1957.

Chambers, William Nisbet. *Old Bullion Benton: Senator From The New West*. Boston & Toronto: Little, Brown, & Company, 1956.

Christian, Shirley. *Before Lewis & Clark: The Story of the Chouteaus, the French Dynasty that Ruled America's Frontier*. New York: Farrar, Straus and Giroux, 2004.

Clarke, Dwight L. *Stephen Watts Kearny: Soldier of the West*. Norman: University of Oklahoma Press, 1961.

Corbett, Katherine T. *In Her Place: A Guide to St. Louis Women's History*. St. Louis: Missouri Historical Press , 1999.

Cuoco, Lorin & William H. Gass, editors. *Literary St. Louis: A Guide*. St. Louis: Missouri Historical Society, 2000.

Darby, John F. *Personal Recollections*. St. Louis: G. I. Jones and Company, 1880.

Dennis, Charles H. *Eugene Field's Creative Years*. Garden City, New York: Doubleday, Page & Company, 1924.

Drake, William. *Sara Teasdale: Woman and Poet*. New York: Harper & Row Publishers, 1979.
Faherty, William Barnaby, S.J. *Henry Shaw: His Life and Legacies*. St. Louis: University of Missouri Press, 1987.

Foley, William E., and C. David Rice. *The First Chouteaus: River Barons of Early St. Louis*. Urbana & Chicago: University of Illinois Press, 1983.

Freeman, Douglas Southall. *R.E. Lee*. New York: Charles Scribner's Sons, 1961.

Gill, McCune B. *The St. Louis Story*. Hopkinsville, KY & St. Louis: Historical Record Association, 1952.

Gould, E. W. *Fifty Years of the Mississippi: Gould's History of River Navigation*. St. Louis: Nixon-Jones Printing Company, 1889.

Hannon, Robert E. *St. Louis: Its Neighborhoods and Neighbors, Landmarks, and Milestones*. St. Louis: St. Louis Commerce and Growth Association, 1986.

Hasse, John Edward. *Ragtime: Its History, Composers, and Music*. New York: Schirmer Books, 1985.

Hernon, Peter and Terry Ganey. *Under the Influence: The Unauthorized Story of the Anheuser-Busch Dynasty*. New York: Simon & Schuster, 1991.

Hetrick, J. Thomas. *Chris Von der Ahe and the St. Louis Browns*. Lanham, MD & London: The Scarecow Press, Inc., 1999.

Hood, Robert E. *The Gashouse Gang*. New York: William Morrow and Company, 1976.

Horsman, Reginald. *Frontier Doctor: William Beaumont, America's First Great Medical Scientist*. Columbia & London: University of Missouri Press, 1996.

How, Louis. *James B. Eads*. Freeport, NY: Books for Libraries Press, 1900.

Huhn, Rick. *The Sizzler: George Sisler, Baseball's Forgotten Great*. Columbia: University of Missouri Press, 2004.

Hyde, William and Howard L. Conard. *Encyclopedia of The History of St. Louis*. New York: The Southern History Company, 1899.

Kaser, David. *Joseph Charless: Printer in the Western Country*. Philadelphia: University of Pennsylvania Press, 1963.

Kirschten, Ernest. *Catfish and Crystal*. Garden City, New York: Doubleday & Company, Inc., 1960.

Kollbaum, Marc E. *Gateway to the West: The History of Jefferson Barracks from 1826 – 1894*. St. Louis: Friends of Jefferson Barracks.
Koykka, Arthur S. *Project Remember*. Algonac, MI: Reference Publications, Inc., 1986.

Laveille, B., S.J. *The Life of Father DeSmet, S.J.* Chicago: Loyola University Press, 1981.

Leverich, Lyle. *Tom: The Unknown Tennessee Williams*. New York: Crown Publishers, 1995.
Lipsitz, George. *The Sidewalks of St. Louis: Places, People, and Politics in an American City*. Columbia & London: University of Missouri Press, 1991.

Loughlin, Caroline, and Catherine Anderson. *Forest Park*. Columbia, MO: University of Missouri Press, and The Junior League of St. Louis, 1986.

Magnan, William B. and Marcella C. *The Streets of St. Louis*. St. Louis: Virginia Publishing Company, 1994.

McCall, Edith. *Conquering the Rivers*. Baton Rouge: Louisiana State University Press, 1984.

McGee, Tom. *Betty Grable: The Girl with the Million Dollar Legs*. New York: The Vestal Press, 1995.

Mead, William B. *Even the Browns*. Chicago: Contemporary Books, Inc., 1978.

Morris, Ann. *Sacred Green Space: A Survey of Cemeteries in St. Louis County*. St. Louis, 2000.

Nester, William R. *From Mountain Man to Millionaire: The "Bold and Dashing Life" of Robert Campbell*. Columbia and London: University of Missouri Press, 1999.

Oglesby, Richard Edward. *Manuel Lisa and the Opening of the Missouri Fur Trade*. Norman: University of Oklahoma Press, 1963.

Parrish, William E. *Frank Blair: Lincoln's Conservative*. Columbia: University of Missouri Press, 1998.

Price, Victoria. *Vincent Price: A Daughter's Biography*. New York: St. Martin's Press, 1999.

Primm, James Neal. *Lion of the Valley: St. Louis, Missouri*. Boulder, CO: Pruett Publishing Company, 1981.

Reavis, L.V. *St. Louis: The Future Great City of the World*. St. Louis: Gray, Baker, and Company, 1875.

Rose, Phyllis. *Jazz Cleopatra: Josephine Baker in Her Time*. New York: Doubleday & Company, Inc., 1989.
Ross, Ishbel. *The General's Wife: The Life of Mrs. Ulysses S. Grant*. New York: Dodd, Mead and Company, 1959.
Rothensteiner, Reverend John. *History of The Archdiscese of St. Louis*. St. Louis: Blackwell Wielandy Company, 1928.

Scharf, J. Thomas. *History of St. Louis City and County*. Philadephia: Louis H. Everts & Company, 1883.

Scott, Quinta, and Howard S. Miller *The Eads Bridge*. Columbia & London: University of Missouri Press, 1979.

Shalhope, Robert E. *Sterling Price: Portrait of a Southerner*. Columbia, MO: University of Missouri Press, 1971.
Sherman, William Tecumseh. *Memoirs of General W.T. Sherman*. New York: The Library of America, 1990.

Stadler, Frances Hurd. *St. Louis: Day by Day*. St. Louis: The Patrice Press, 1989.

Steffen, Jerome O. *William Clark: Jeffersonian Man on the Frontier*. Norman: University of Oklahoma Press, 1977.

Stevens, Walter B. *St. Louis: The Fourth City 1764-1909*. St. Louis & Chicago: S.J. Clarke Publishing Company, 1909.

Steward, Dick. *Duels and the Roots of Violence in Missouri*. Columbia & London: University of Missouri Press, 2000.

Stiritz, Mary. *St. Louis: Historic Churches and Synagogues*. St. Louis: St. Louis Public Library & Landmarks Association of St. Louis, Inc., 1995.

Sunder, John E. *Bill Sublette: Mountain Man*. Norman: University of Oklahoma Press, 1959.

Toth, Emily. *Kate Chopin*. New York: William Morrow & Company, 1990.

Van Ravenswaay, Charles. *St. Louis: An Informal History of The City and Its People, 1764-1865*. St. Louis: Missouri History Society Press, 1991.

Waldo, Terry. *This is Ragtime*. New York: Hawthorn Books, 1976.

Walker, Stephen P. *Lemp: The Haunting History*. St. Louis: The Lemp Preservation Society, Inc., 1988.

Ward, Geoffrey C. and Ken Burns. *Baseball: An Illustrated History*. New York: Alfred Knopf, 1994.

Warren, Doug. *Betty Grable: The Reluctant Movie Queen*. New York: St. Martin's Press, 1981.

Wheeler, Richard. *We Knew William Tecumseh Sherman*. New York: Thomas Y. Crowell Company, 1977.

Williams, Tennessee. *Tennessee Williams: Memoirs*. New York: Doubleday & Company, Inc., 1972.
Winter, William C. *The Civil War in St. Louis: A Guided Tour*. St. Louis: Missouri Historical Society Press, 1994.

DICTIONARIES/ENCYCLOPEDIAS

Baseball: The Biographical Encyclopedia. New York: Total Sports Publishing, 2000.

Dictionary of Missouri Biography. Columbia & London: University of Missouri Press, 1999.

Missouri Biographical Dictionary. New York: Somerset Publishing, Co., 1995.

Webster's American Biography. Springfield, Massachusetts: G & C Merriam Company Publishing, 1974.

PERIODICALS

Kaiser, Max Jr. "Historical Markers." *St. Louis*. October 1992: 14-19.

The St. Louis Catholic Historical Review. "Alexander McNair." Volume 1, July-October 1919, No. 4-5.

Van Ravenswaay, Charles. "Bloody Island: Honor and Violence in 19th Century St. Louis." *Gateway Heritage*. Spring 1990: 4-21.

ARCHIVES

Bassford Scrapbook, Missouri Historical Society, St. Louis.

Bellefontaine Cemetery Burial Records.

Charless, Joseph, Vertical File, Missouri Historical Society, St. Louis.

Lucas, John B.C., Vertical File, Missouri Historical Society, St. Louis.

Mullanphy, John, Vertical File, Missouri Historical Society, St. Louis.

Phillips, Homer G., Vertical File, Missouri Historical Society, St. Louis.

Stevens, W.B. Scrapbook #100, Missouri Historical Society, St. Louis.

SPECIAL COLLECTIONS

Godwin, Betty. *The Saint Louis Cholera Epidemic of 1849 As It Appeared in the Newspapers.* St. Louis University Graduate School thesis, 1951.

Wotawa, Shirley. *History of St. Peter's Cemetery.*

NEWSPAPERS

Daily Missouri Democrat

The Missouri Gazette

The Missouri Republican

The National Intelligencer

New York Times

St. Louis Globe-Democrat

St. Louis Post-Dispatch

The Sporting News

Index

ADAMS, JOHN QUINCY,14, 18
ANHEUSER, EBERHARD, 44-45, 47
ANTHONY, SUSAN B., 77
ARNOT, JESSE, 33
ASHCROFT, (GOV.) JOHN, 126, 171
ASTOR, JOHN JACOB, 100
BAER, SIGMUND   , 147
BAKER, JOSEPHINE, 181-182
BARNES, ROBERT   , 5
BARRETT, ARTHUR, 94
BARRY, JAMES, 94
BARTON, JOSHUA   , 84, 85, 88
BATES, EDWARD, 24-26, 35, 40, 42, 84, 134, 135
BEAUMONT, DR. WILLIAM, 19-21, 26, 89
BECKER, (MAYOR) WILLIAM DEE, 61-64, 73, 125, 172
BELL, JAMES ("COOL PAPA"), 154
BELLEFONTAINE CEMETERY, 1-7
BENOIST, LOUIS, 95
BENTON, THOMAS HART, 7, 13-16, 22, 26, 82, 84, 86, 109
        DUEL WITH CHARLES LUCAS, 9, 14, 87-88
BERRY, CHUCK, 140
BIDDLE, ANN MULLANPHY, 85, 86
BIDDLE, THOMAS, 85, 86, 87
BISSELL, (GEN.) DANIEL, 5
BIXBY, WILLIAM, 78
BLAIR, FRANCIS, 15, 35, 41-43
BLAIR, MONTGOMERY, 105
BLASSIE, (LT.) MICHAEL, 139
BLOODY ISLAND, 81-89
BLOW, CHARLOTTE, 10
BLOW, HENRY, 34-36
BLOW, PETER, 10
BLOW, SUSAN, 34-36
Bragg, (Gen.) Braxton, 37
Britt, Allen, 153
Brock, Lou, 154
Broeg, Bob, 171
Brookings, Robert, 49-50
Brown, Alanson David
        and George Warren Brown, 56-58
Buchanan, James, 15, 40
Buck, Jack, 126, 127, 139, 157
Buell, Don Carlos, 36-38, 110
Burgess, Albert, 152
Burnes, Bob, 158-159
Burr, Aaron
Duel with Alexander Hamilton, 86, 87
Burroughs, William (1) and (2), 58-59
Busch, Adolphus, 44-47
Busch Family,168-171
Cabanne, Joseph C., 123
Calvary Cemetery, 91-127
Campbell, James, 123-124
Campbell, John, 83
Campbell, Robert, 28-30

Capone, Al, 95
Caray, Harry, 126, 139, 184-185
Carberry, (Cardinal) John,144-145
Carney, Jack, 126
Carson, Kit, 28, 76, 109
Cathedral Basilica of St. Louis, 140-145
Cervantes, (Mayor) A. J., 94, 126
Charless, Joseph, 8-10, 34, 89
Charless, Joseph, Jr., 10, 34
Cholera epidemic, 132, 133-135
Chopin, Kate, 113-115
Chouteau Family, 95-99
Chouteau, Pierre, 134
Clark, William   , 6-8, 14, 16, 22, 26, 89, 104
Clay, Henry, 94, 109
Clemson, Eli, 82, 88
Cleveland, Grover, 37, 43, 52, 53, 112
Cobb, Ty, 126, 172, 173
Cody, Buffalo Bill, 76
Cohen, William, 139
Colbeck, William "Dinky", 95
Colman, Norman, 43-44
Combs, Earle, 125
Comiskey, Charles, 53, 56, 73
Confederate Dead, 138-139
Cooke, William, 94
Costas, Bob, 126, 127
Couzins, Adaline, 6
Couzins, Phoebe, 6
Crow, Wayman, 30-31
Darby, (Mayor) John, 4, 8, 22-24, 86
de Lafayette, Marquis, 98

Dent, Frederick, 75, 103
Dent, Julia, 112
De Smet, (Fr.) Peter, 25, 141, 163, 166-168
Dickens, Charles, 85
Di Maggio, Joe, 170, 173
Dickmann, (Mayor) Bernard, 115, 125
Donnelly, (Gov.) Phil, 143
Dooley, Dr. Tom, 119-121
Doyne, Max, 64
DuBourg, Bishop Louis, 141, 163
Duchesne, (Sr.) Rose Philippine, 101, 141,162-164
Dueling (see Bloody Island)
Duncan's Island, 82, 83, 89
Dysart, Thomas, 64
Eads, James, 36, 39-41
Edison Brothers, 147-148
Edwards, Albert, 5
1849: Disastrous Year, 129-135
Eisenhower, Dwight D., 120
Eliot, T. S., 179-181
Eliot, William Greenleaf, 20, 21, 31, 33-34
Ewing, Thomas, 109

Farrar, Dr.Bernard, 9, 11, 16-17, 82, 83-84, 88, 134
Faust, Anthony, 5
Feheen, George "Sonny", 95
Field, Eugene, 105, 178-179
Field, Roswell, 105, 178
Fletcher, (Gov.) Thomas, 5
Fordyce, Samuel, 47-48
Fraley, Moses,148
Francis, David   , 52-54
Frank, Nathan, 148
Frankie & Johnny, 153
Franklin, Benjamin, 103
Fremont, John, 14, 123
Fuller, Aaron, 147
Gamble, (Gov.) Hamilton, 5
Gardner, (Gov.) Frederick, 5
"Gashouse Gang", 174
Gassoff, Bob, 156
Gehrig, Lou,125, 126
Gellhorn, Edna, 5
Gellhorn, Martha, 5-6
Gentry, Richard, 138
Ginsburg, Allen, 58

Glennon, (Cardinal) John, 63, 108, 122, 141,142-143
Goldstein, Dr. Max, 148
Grable, Betty,185-186
Grace, Princess of Monaco, 181, 182
Graham, James, 83-84
Grant, Ulysses S., 26, 28, 35, 37, 42, 47, 75, 109, 110, 111, 122
Gratiot, (Gen.) Charles, Jr., 89, 99-100
Great Fire, 133-134
Gregg, John, 5
Griesedieck, Joseph, 71, 78-79
Hannegan, Robert, 115-117
Hardy, Bob, 126
Harrison, Benjamin, 111
Harrison, William Henry,12
Hawken, Samuel, 75
Hayes, Rutherford B.,   112
Hazalton, Paul   , 64
Hearnes, (Gov.) Warren, 126
Hempstead, Edward, 11-13, 87
Hempstead, Stephen, 12
Hempstead, Thomas, 84
Hoerner, Joe, 156
Hoffa, Jimmy   149
Hotchkiss, Almerin, 4
Houston, Sam, 15
Higgins, Miller, 125
Hunt, Anne Lucas, 103
Hurst, Fannie, 124, 149
Hyland, Robert, 126-127
Irving, Washington, 28
Jackson, Andrew, 13, 14, 18, 85

Jefferson Barracks Cemetery, 138-140
Jefferson, Thomas, 7, 14, 102, 103
Johnson, Andrew, 25
Johnson, Ban, 73, 74
Johnson, Johnnie, 140
Johnston, (Gen.) Joe, 112
Joplin, Scott, 151
Kain, (Archbishop) John, 108, 141
Kaufmann, (Mayor) Aloys P., 60, 62, 143
Kearny, Stephen Watts, 14, 26-28, 38
Kelly, Dan, 157-158
Kenrick, (Archbishop) Peter Richard, 94, 106-108
Kerner, Ben, 149-150
Kerouac, Jack, 58
Kiel, (Mayor) Henry, 171-172
Kile, Darryl, 140
Klugh, Milton, 64
Koplar, Harold, 149
Koplar, Sam, 149
Krueger, Harold, 64
Kyle, Walter "Gus", 157, 158
Laclede, Pierre, 95-98
Lambert, Albert Bond, 60-61
Landis, Kenesaw Mountain, 73, 126, 174
Lane, William Carr, 21-22, 98
Lash, Elizabeth Ann, 138
Lawless, Luke, 82, 88
Lazzeri, Tony, 125
Lee, Robert E., 20, 89
Lemp, Charles, 44
Lemp Family, 68-72
Lincoln, Abraham, 25, 37, 42, 84, 138
Lindbergh, Charles A., 61, 64
Lindell, Peter, 75
Link, Theodore, 51-52
Lisa, Manuel, 7, 10-11. 75, 163
Lockett, Lester, 154
Longstreet, James, 75
Lucas, Charles   , 82
          Duel with Thomas Hart Benton, 14, 87-88, 103
Lucas, James, 103
Lucas, John B. C., 11, 14, 102-103
Luyties, Herman, 5
Madison, James, 98
Mallinckrodt, Edward, 48-49
Mason, (Gen.) Richard, 37-38
Mathewson, Christy, 173
May, David, 147
May, (Archbishop) John, 126,145
McDonnell, James, Jr.   , 66-68
McDowell, Dr. Joseph, 5
McMahon, Ed, 171
McNair, (Gov.) Alexander, 7, 22, 101, 104
McPherson, William, 4
Medwick, Joe, 174-175

Michaels, James, Sr., 95
Miegs, Montgomery, 89
Miller, (Gov.) John, 5
Minor, Virginia, 76-77
Monroe, James, 85

Mueller, Henry, 64
Mullanphy, John, 85, 96, 100-102, 104
New Mt. Sinai Cemetery, 145-150
Nugent, Byron   , 77
O'Fallon, Benjamin, 18, 19, 86
Old Cathedral, 140-145
Pabst, Frederick, 69-70
Paige, Satchel, 154
Page, (Mayor) Daniel, 5
Patrick, Lynn, 157
Peters, Charlotte, 159
Peters, Mike, 159
Pettis (var. Pettus), Spencer, 85-86
Phillips, Homer G., 152-153
Pickering, Loren, 42
Plager, Barclay, 157
Polk, James K., 19, 27
Polk, (Gov.) Trusten, 5
Pound, Ezra, 179, 180
Price, Sterling, 31-33, 42
Price, Vincent, 183-184
Pruitt, Wendell, 154-155
Quarles, Pryor, 82, 88
Queeny, John, 59-60
Raft, George, 185, 186
Rector, (Gen.) William, 84
Reedy, William Marion, 65, 114, 124-125, 149
Reitz, Ken, 154
Resurrection Cemetery, 155-159
Reynolds, Thomas, 94
Rickey, Branch, 126, 172, 173, 174
Rigali, (Archbishop) Justin, 139, 144, 145
Ritter, (Cardinal) Joseph, 143
Robertson, William, 64
Rombauer, Irma, 5
Roosevelt, Theodore, 53, 60
Rosati, (Bishop) Joseph, 106, 140, 141-142, 163
Ruth, Babe, 125, 126
St. Peter's Cemetery, 150-155
Sale, (Rabbi) Samuel, 146
Salomon, Sidney, 149-150, 157
Sappington, John, 162
Schoendienst, Red, 171
Scott, Dred, 10, 15, 41, 105-106
Scullin, John, 121-122

Sellers, Isaiah, 5
Shaw, Henry, 31, 164-166
Shenker, Lillian Koplar
          and Morris Shenker, 149

Sherman, (Gen.) William Tecumseh, 26, 28, 31, 40, 43, 109-113
Shields, James, 84
Shocker, Urban, 125
Shoenberg, Moses, 147
Shreve, Henry Miller, 17-19
Sisleer, George, 172-173
Sonneschein, (Rabbi) Solomon, 146
Soulard, Antoine, 95
Spink, Al, 54, 56
Spink Family, 72-74
Spitz, (Rabbi) Morris, 147
Stark, John, 151
Steinberg, Mark, 148
Stix, Charles, 77, 147
Sublette, William, 28-30
Sullivan, Louis, 6
Switzer, Frederick, Sr., 95
Taft, William Howard   , 53
Taylor, Zachary, 36, 109
Teasdale, Sara, 64-66, 124
Thomas, (Capt.) Martin, 85-86
Truman, Harry S, 115, 116, 170
Tucker, (Mayor) Raymond, 125-126
Turpin, Tom, 151-152
Villa, Albert ("Red"), 159
Vitale, John, 95
Von der Ahe, Chris, 54-56
Von Puhl, Henry, 95
Wainwright, Ellis, 6
Wallace, Frank ("Pee Wee"), 158
Walsh, Julius, 122
Webster, Daniel, 109
White, Jim, 126
Wickenheiser, Doug, 156-157
Williams, Tennessee, 117-119
Wilson, (Mayor) James, 139
Wilson, Woodrow, 50, 53
Wimer, (Mayor) John, 5
Wohl, David, 148
Wright, Orville, 60
Yeatman, James, 31, 34, 36, 38-39

ABOUT THE AUTHOR

Besides seeing dead people, Kevin Amsler has been writing a column entitled "This Month in St. Louis History" for the *West End Word* since 1997. He has also written a novel and several screenplays, two of which have won honorable mentions in national screenwriting contests. He has just completed a book of humor about his most recent European adventure. Kevin has an associate's degree in architecture from Meramec Community College and a bachelor's degree in business administration from the University of Missouri – St. Louis.